ISLAM Without Illusions

Contemporary Issues in the Middle East

Other titles in Contemporary Issues in the Middle East

The Adam of Two Edens: Selected Poems. Mahmoud Darwish; Munir Akash, ed.

The Arab-Israeli Dilemma, 3d ed. Fred J. Khouri

Extremist Shiites: The Ghulat Sects. Matti Moosa

The Iranian Revolution and the Islamic Republic, 2d ed. Nikki R. Keddie and Eric Hooglund, eds.

Islam: Continuity and Change in the Modern World, 2d ed. John Obert Voll

Islam and Politics, 4th ed. John L. Esposito

Islam in Revolution: Fundamentalism in the Arab World, 2d ed. R. Hrair Dekmejian

The Islamic Impact. Yvonne Yazbeck Haddad, Byron Haines, and Ellison Findly, eds.

Painting the Middle East. Ann Zwicker Kerr

Sandcastles: The Arabs in Search of the Modern World. Milton Viorst

The Second Message of Islam. Mahmoud Mohamed Taha; Abdullahi Ahmed An-Na'im, trans.

The State, Religion, and Ethnic Politics: Afghanistan, Iran, and Pakistan
      Ali Banuazizi and Myron Weiner, eds.

Toward an Islamic Reformation: Civil Liberties, Human Rights, and International Law
      Abdullahi Ahmed An-Na'im

Twenty Years of Islamic Revolution: Political and Social Transition in Iran Since 1979
      Eric Hooglund, ed.

Women in Muslim Family Law, 2d ed. John L. Esposito

Women, the Family, and Divorce Laws in Islamic History. Amira El Azhary Sonbol, ed.

Writing Off the Beaten Track: Reflections on the Meaning of Travel and Culture in the Middle East.
      Judith Caesar

Ed Hotaling

ISLAM
Without
Illusions

*Its Past, Its Present, and
Its Challenge for the Future*

Syracuse University Press

First Edition 2003
03 04 05 06 07 08   6 5 4 3 2 1

Title page: Mosque of Mahmoud II at Tophana, by Thomas Allom. *Courtesy of the author.*

The paper used in this publication meets the minimum requirements of
American National Standard for Information Sciences—Permanence of
Paper for Printed Library Materials, ANSI Z39.48–1984.∞™

Library of Congress Cataloging-in-Publication Data
Hotaling, Edward.
Islam without illusions : its past, its present, and its challenge for
the future / Ed Hotaling.— 1st ed.
p. cm.—(Contemporary issues in the Middle East)
Includes bibliographical references and index.
ISBN 0–8156–0766–0 (cl. : alk. paper)
1. Islam. 2. Islam—Essence, genius, nature. 3. Islam—History. I.
Title. II. Series.
BP161.3.H67 2003
297'.09—dc21
2003009143

Manufactured in the United States of America

A Luc, Greg, et Marthe

Ed Hotaling is an author and broadcaster based in Washington, D.C. He has served as Middle East bureau chief of both CBS News, based in Beirut, and *Business Week*/McGraw-Hill World News, based in the Persian Gulf. He also reported for ABC News from the Middle East. His assignments have taken him to Saudi Arabia, Egypt, Syria, Lebanon, Israel, Iran, Turkey, Bahrain, Cyprus, and beyond, covering war, terrorism, diplomacy, and business. In Washington, he has reported for NBC Radio and for NBC-4 television. He is the winner of six Washington Emmy Awards.

Contents

Preface

Islam Without Illusions is an entirely new introduction to Islam. Its chief goal is to dispel the illusions and myths about Islam that prevail among Westerners and their leaders—and to do so without bias, to the degree possible by an American historian and veteran journalist. *Islam Without Illusions* addresses the so-called politically incorrect subjects that have been left out of earlier studies of Islam and of the Koran, such as war, terrorism, and Paradise. And the book brings the role of women in Islam into the sharp focus of an American reporter with no axes to grind, no illusions to perpetuate.

This is also the first book on Islam to combine scholarly research with field reports, in war and peace, from a correspondent for several major American news organizations. Its theme is the dramatic story of Islam past, present, and future, but along the way it shares personal experiences of combat reporting, kidnapping, and hostage-taking, which have so marked the recent history of Islam, and more pleasant interludes.

There is no way I could thank individually the countless friends from my assignments in the Middle East and Europe as Middle East bureau chief for both CBS News and McGraw-Hill World News; reporter for ABC News, *Business Week,* the illustrious old Paris edition of the *New York Herald-Tribune,* and the *Village Voice;* teacher at the University of Tehran; and editor at the *Tehran Journal.*

Three distinguished American scholars read the manuscript and provided valuable insights: Fred M. Donner, author of *Narratives of Islamic Origins: Beginnings of Islamic Historical Writing* and professor of Near Eastern Languages and Civilizations at the University of Chicago; Bruce B. Lawrence, author of *Shattering the Myth: Islam Beyond Violence* and Nancy and Jeffrey Marcus Hu-

manities Professor and professor of Islamic studies at Duke University; and Sam
B. Girgus, author of *America on Film: Modernism, Documentary, and a Changing America* and professor of English at Vanderbilt University. Of course, only
the author is responsible for the contents.

Helpful tips over the years have come from Monique and Jean Vincent, who
shared field observations from France, Spain, North Africa, and Kazakhstan;
Lydie and Iannis Stefanopoulos and their international Arlington salon; Jensen
Barber; Eve Dubrow and former Middle East peacekeeper Michael Boston; Mur-
ray Zinoman; Charles Osgood; Dan Rather; Peter Jennings; John Palmer; Hamdi
Aljallad; Sandra and David Sonderegger, survivors of unusual times with me in
Persia; Erica and Douglas Rosenthal; television photographer Wayne Wood; Lois
and old Iran hand Ed Berkowitz; Edith and the much decorated combat veteran
Carl Bernard; Dr. Jon Wiseman; and superagents Jenny Bent and Betsy Lerner.

At Syracuse University Press, thanks to executive editor Mary Selden
Evans, who did not stint on her charisma, charm, and valued expertise on the
Middle East; press director Peter Webber; and freelance copy editor Annette
Wenda. A boon in the most recent research were my assistants, Edan Lichten-
stein, a Middle East Institute scholar and Cornell graduate, and Yannis Stefanopoulos, a George Mason University graduate with an anthropology
concentration. As always, Greg and Luc were happily unforgiving editors and
rescuers.

And here is a final, much appreciated comment from the University of
Chicago's Fred Donner: "Hotaling debunks in both directions, correcting the
hostile stereotypes of many Christians and Westerners about Islam (for example,
that it is a 'religion of violence') while also popping the bubbles put forth by some
apologists for Islam (for example, that the Koran offers no support for those Muslims who engage in violence). His main objective, perhaps, may be to contrast
those terrorist fanatics who claim to be acting in the name of 'Islam' with the millions of peaceable and tolerant Muslims who populate the world. . . . Hotaling's
outlook, then, is fair-minded and humane and refuses to 'dehumanize' millions of
people in the service of either an idealized or a demonized image of Muslims."

Washington, D.C.   Ed Hotaling
May 2003

ISLAM Without Illusions

Arabia's northern Red Sea Coast. *Courtesy of the author.*

1

What Would Muhammad Do?

It is the seventh century. The subject is war. God is speaking to the Muslims through their prophet, Muhammad:

> I will instill terror
> Into the hearts of the Unbelievers:
> Smite ye above the necks
> And smite all their
> Finger-tips off them.
> (Koran, Sura 8, verse 12)[1]

Fourteen centuries later, one of the deranged September 11 hijackers told his cohorts what to do on the airliner: "God said, 'Strike above the neck, and strike at all of their extremities.' "

What other orders did God issue to seventh-century Muslim warriors through Muhammad? These:

> . . . fight and slay
> The Pagans wherever ye find them,
> And seize them, beleaguer them,
> And lie in wait for them
> In every stratagem (of war).   (9:5)

At another point Muhammad relays God's policy since Noah and the Flood, namely, to destroy those who are wicked even though they are given, to use God's surprisingly modern seventh-century phrase, "the good things of this life." First

1

God sends a messenger to warn them, such as Moses, or Jesus, or Muhammad himself, but if that is to no avail, he visits them with his wrath. How might a terrorist leader equipped with nuclear or biological weapons read God's warning?

> When We decide to destroy
> A population, We (first) send
> A definite order to those
> Among them who are given
> The good things of this life
> And yet transgress; so that
> The word is proved true
> Against them: then (it is)
> We destroy them utterly.
> How many generations
> Have We destroyed after Noah?
>   (17:16–17)

It's a good thing the terrorists have been not reading the Bible, where in the Old Testament God gave even more graphic warnings twelve centuries earlier, telling Babylon:

> Everyone who is caught shall be run through; to a man they shall fall by the sword. Their infants shall be dashed to pieces in their sight. (Isa. 13:15–16)

But to what extent have terrorists in our time acted on the divine advice Muhammad handed out as embattled Islam's first commander, the equivalent of a modern-day general? Would Muhammad actually have approved of their actions, as they claim? To borrow the title of a Christian radio show, *What Would Jesus Do?*—if he were alive today, what would Muhammad do? Before addressing that question, however, we must answer another. Who was Muhammad?

Astonished, Islam's first wartime enemies began asking that question, or rather answering without bothering to ask, after the Prophet overwhelmed the pagans in Arabia and his followers rushed on to seize Christian strongholds from Jerusalem to Spain, not to mention the entire Persian Empire in the East. He was a sorcerer, they said; a fake who controlled Muslims by advocating sexual license and promising martyrs a paradise of sexual pleasures; not the founder of a new religion at all, but a false prophet, a mere heretic who learned, then stole, from Judaism and Christianity.

Another popular question these days, "Why do they hate us?" was an issue—at least to those followers of Muhammad who cared—centuries before Americans began to agonize over it. One can see why. The historian Francis Robinson has been especially good on the hatred that early Europeans, notably Dante, reserved for Muhammad. After the Muslims mauled the other holy warriors in the Crusades, Dante dumped Muhammad among the Christian heretics, the "sowers of scandals and schism," in one of the worst holes of his *Inferno*, the ninth of ten horrible ditches, where the Prophet was condemned to being continually sliced in two.

Not that Hell or its horrors were uniquely Christian; Islam's descriptions of the place were just as graphic, and the Muslim Shah Ismail of Persia used a sword celebrated for the same vertical slicing capability. For that matter, one Muslim scholar, Miguel Asin of the University of Madrid, has marshaled evidence that Dante even stole the idea for *La divina commedia* from Muhammad's miraculous trip to Heaven, to be described in chapter 3. No wonder Dante tried to get rid of him.[2]

But much less was heard of Muhammad as the evil impostor from the late 1700s onward. The reason was the decline of Islam as a world political and military power, along with the retreat of medieval Christian revelation with its own visions of Satan and his allies. The rise of Western colonialism in the Middle East fostered a paternalistic, romantic, in sum quite insincere and shallow interest in Islam and its heartland—until the discovery of oil rendered Westerners a lot more sincere, though hardly less shallow. In the past quarter century Westerners were forced to change their attitudes once again as the Iranian Revolution ushered in an angry Islamic revival, accompanied by increasingly deadly terrorism against a new "Great Satan."

Finally, in the wake of September 11, 2001, Americans and Europeans began responding to seventh-century hatred by reviving those questions asked by the Christians of the Middle Ages but never really answered. Again, who was Muhammad? Why would a prophet of peace be fighting wars? How could the same man be quoted with devotion by the vast majority of peaceful Muslims around the world and by terrorists and their supporters from the Middle to the Far East? How, as many Christians wonder, could "General" Muhammad be compared with Gentle Jesus?

There have been few answers to date. Much that was written before that September morning ignored or glossed over not only Muhammad's military career, though that career spanned a third of his ministry as the Prophet, but also God's

own military counsel, though it rings loud and clear in two important chapters
and other verses of Islam's holy book, the Koran. This politically correct censor-
ship has been disastrous for the obvious, important reason that these passages
shed much light on terrorism and the much bruited "clash of civilizations" between Islam and the West, and whether there really is one. It is also too bad because Muhammad's true story, wars and all, is a fascinating read. Among its
many surprises for many Americans and Europeans is the fact that they will find
him easy to know because, before he became the Prophet and a general, he was
an ambitious, accomplished businessman, in the employ of another notable business talent, his wife, Khadija.

The first source of information about his life and teachings is the Koran, the
book of God's revelations to Muhammad as the last of the prophets. It is accepted
as the Word of God and recited during daily prayers by hundreds of millions of
Muslims. Each time they pray, they speak both the name of God and that of the
Prophet so little known to their hyperbusy non-Muslims neighbors. "There is no
god but God! And Muhammad is His Messenger." Indeed, like most traditional
poetry, the Koran is meant to be spoken (*koran,* or *qur'an,* means "recitation, lecture, discourse, reading").

I have relied on the Koran published in Arabic and English by the Islamic
Center of Washington, D.C., which was visited by President Bush six days after
the September 11, 2001, attacks. Frequent reference will be made as well to the
Saudi Arabian government's Arabic-English Koran, which will help us understand some of the teachings that have nourished the Saudis, the peaceful majority as well as Osama bin Laden and fifteen of the nineteen terrorists who attacked
New York and Washington.[3]

Other than the Koran the only source from Muhammad's day are the hadiths
(traditions), which purport to be the sayings of the Prophet himself as recalled
by his surviving relatives, friends, and followers. As for early biographies, the
first appeared in Baghdad one hundred years after his death, brocaded with
detail to explain how a single man could have filled his fighters with the flame to
conquer an empire reaching to the shores of the Atlantic Ocean in the west and the
mountains of China in the east. Over the past quarter century Western and other
scholars have been revising and fighting furiously about the original story of
Islam, but that has certainly not troubled the many millions who are followers
of Muhammad.[4]

Was he only a man to Muslims? The answer is yes. He was not divine, was not
and is not worshiped by Muslims as Jesus is worshiped by Christians. The Koran
insists on it: he was only a human, albeit a prophet and the final Messenger of

God for Muslims. In practice, Muslims have often come close to worshiping him, which should hardly surprise anyone because Islam teaches that God spoke to him, not once but again and again over more than two decades. They could hardly consider God's Messenger an ordinary man. Many resolve this matter by calling him the "Perfect Man," a concept honored by millions around the world as they try as hard as they can, in their everyday lives, to be like Muhammad.

Mecca

He was an orphan before he was born. His father, Abdullah, had died on one of the frequent trading caravans from Mecca, their hometown, to Damascus in the north. It was about the year 570.

Alone, the baby's mother, Amina, faced a future of poverty, and not a long one at that as she was in exceedingly poor health. She put him in the good care of a Bedouin shepherd's wife, and thus he began his childhood in the desert—with something to remember Amina by: his tribe dubbed him El-Amin, which means "the faithful." His original name is lost, but later they would call him Muhammad, meaning "highly praised."

The boy lived with the Bedouins until he was six, then was returned to Amina just before she died, making him an orphan in the fullest sense. He would never forget being an orphan, either, even though his grandfather Abd al-Muttalib immediately adopted him—thanks be to God, or so the boy's people would be told in the Koran.

> Did He not find thee
> An orphan and give thee
> Shelter (and care)?   (93:6)

(Note that Koran translators often insert clarifying remarks in parentheses.)

Among his sixteen children and their children, a typical Arabian family, Abd al-Muttalib loved the orphan boy best, but then the grandfather, too, passed away, two years after Amina. Again a caring rescuer was there: Muhammad's uncle Abu Talib, a merchant and politically well connected as collector of the poor tax. It would not be surprising if this orphan thought he was being saved for something; still, those early shocks, the successive losses of love and protection, must have made him an alert and guarded boy, especially given his obvious intelligence. He was made wary, too, by the fact that his parents' clan, the Hashemites, did not share in the wealth of the larger tribe they belonged to, the Quraysh. It was another Quraysh clan, the aristocratic Umayyads, who were the richest and most powerful people in Mecca. Of course, Muhammad's ambiguous position in the community—an outsider as a Hashemite, an insider as a Quraysh—let him see both sides for what they were, and may have planted both envy and ambition, though many would say the Perfect Man could never have harbored such weaknesses.

One day Uncle Abu Talib took the boy—authorities differ on whether he was nine or twelve—on a caravan to Syria, where a monk, Bahira, taught him some Christian ideas. Arab tradition has it that Bahira was astonished to see the mark of a prophet, a mole, on the boy's shoulder. But some Western scholars, such as the British diplomat Anthony Nutting, have held to the early Christian view that Muhammad was the one who was impressed, and that Bahira was "the first man to introduce him to the concept of a belief in one God." Nutting wrote there was evidence "Mohammed returned more than once with his uncle's caravan to consult his Christian mentor and to ply him with searching questions about his faith. One may even wonder just how near Mohammed came to becoming a Christian at this formative age."[5]

To say the Arabian peninsula was ripe for a prophet would be the understatement of the sixth century. Shaped like an arrowhead with its base in the Arabian Sea, it thrust northwest between two warring civilizations, each so vast that it is amazing to realize Muhammad and his disciples would all but erase both with the flick of a sword. The Byzantine Christians, successors to the Romans, ruled from southern Italy to modern-day Turkey, Egypt, and Syria. The rival Persian Empire reached across Iraq and Iran into the edges of central Asia. For the past four decades, their armies had contested the middle region—Palestine, Syria, Iraq—and were only half done fighting, but it was also a battlefield of ideas, all sides firing off questions about competing gods and their even more competitive prophets.

To the south lay the Arabian vacuum. Its Bedouin nomads were hopeless individualists, paying scant attention to their own gods and *jinns,* or evil spirits. In the Koran, God himself would declare in a rare moment of exasperation:

> The Arabs of the desert
> Are the worst in unbelief
> And hypocrisy.   (9:97)

Along the arrowhead's western edge ran the trading route from Yemen in the south, with its frankincense, highly esteemed by the rival religions, and its Coptic Christian rulers from across the Red Sea in Abyssinia, the future Ethiopia. From Yemen the caravans struggled sixteen hundred miles northwest, an incredible stretch when you think of the severity of that desert highway, to the fought-over cities of Jerusalem and Damascus. This was the road that took the life of Abdullah and brought his son to the monk.

Halfway up, in the Hejaz region, it was intersected by the prosperous town of Mecca, a watering hole for the caravans—a truck stop, we would say today—and a destination of the many pilgrims who worshiped at Arabia's main religious shrine, a sanctuary called the Kaaba, just as Muslim pilgrims do today. But the pilgrims then were pagans of all stripes, worshiping idols and images of a confusing multiplicity of gods. Little did they know that the chief of all these gods, named al-Lah (the God), was the one true god, though some did suspect he was the god worshiped by the Jewish and Christian monotheists. At the Kaaba, they kissed the black stone, probably a meteorite, drew water from an ancient well called the Zamzam, and made life-or-death decisions by drawing lots with ritual arrows that stood beside a statue of the moon god. Like watering holes and truck stops through the ages, the pagan Hejaz sank from time to time into gambling, drinking, and orgies, but its source of what seemed like permanent wealth was Mecca's combined caravan and pilgrimage business.

With rare exceptions, Mecca, as the site of the peninsula's principal religious shrine, enjoyed immunity from raids by surrounding powers, including Yemen, Abyssinia, Syria, and Persia, which protection automatically extended to the rich caravans in town. The Quraysh, the tribe to which Muhammad belonged but did not belong, had controlled this gold mine for going on a century and a half, or, rather, the tribe's Umayyad clan controlled it. It gave them a commanding influence over other tribes. Through their trading trips north and south, they also became accomplished travelers and traders, well versed in that world connecting two empires and in its arts, not the least of which was the polishing of the magnificent Arabic language. It all spun before the boy's luminous gray eyes until, in the ancient sources, he virtually disappears. We hear almost nothing about him for several years. Then the young man from the wrong clan reemerges to take a big step.

Like his father, uncle, and it seemed just about everybody else in Mecca, Muhammad began to work in the caravan business; at twenty-five he had built a small reputation as an honest trader, no small thing in that town and time. As a result he won a contract to take some goods north by caravan for a merchant's widow named Khadija, now a well-to-do trader in her own right. It was a major undertaking, calling for both physical courage in the face of constant caravan raids, some-

thing of a national sport in Arabia, and the colder courage of wheeling and dealing with Syrian traders. He succeeded. She was impressed. He was fifteen years
younger than she, and of barely average height, but he more than made up for
it with a kind of powerful but controlled energy. His overly large head, those
dark-pearlescent eyes, that full mouth and bushy black beard—those strong features were all relieved by a surprisingly quiet, most engaging smile. She liked
him, too.

It was the woman who proposed, more than thirteen centuries before such a
thing became almost acceptable in the West. He accepted. Rescued again. And
as the historian Philip Hitti wrote, "As long as this lady with her strong personality and noble character lived, Muhammad would have none other for a wife."
Which would be two more decades, during which time Khadija would give him
three boys, all of whom would die in infancy, and four daughters, although for
some this detail casts doubt on the report that she was as old as forty when she
married Muhammad.[6] In any event the Koran itself would take note of this latest
rescue, reminding him again that it was thanks to God:

> And He found thee
> In need, and made
> Thee independent.   (93:8)

Independent indeed, Muhammad ran Khadija's trading operations through
the turn of the seventh century and into the next two decades, mixing business with
philosophical wanderings in the countryside and seemingly endless thought. Besides his boyhood talks with Bahira in Syria, he would have had contacts with the
few Christian communities north and south of Mecca and with Jewish communities around Yathrib to the northeast. At the southern end of the trading route, there
were important remnants of Jewish Himyarites, who had ruled Yemen before the
Abyssinians (the Himyarite language would survive in Yemen to modern times).
Perhaps he had discussions, too, with Khadija's devout Coptic Christian cousin
Waraqa, a lover of "spiritual lore."

What increasingly interested Muhammad now, actually worried him, was not
trade but the swirling religious questions of the day. Like Christian and Jewish as-
cetics of his time, he would take to the hills to brood upon those increasingly urgent questions. He was distracted, troubled, searching for a truth to live by, a
better answer than the polytheistic confusion of the town.

"O God, if I knew how you wished to be worshipped," he pleaded, in the
words of an early biography, "I would so worship you, but I do not know."[7] Which

would suggest, however, that Muhammad did know one thing: he was a worshiper of one God only, as the Jews and Christians were. As for how to worship him, he was about to borrow another idea from the Jews and Christians. He had picked out a cave among the red granite rocks of Mount Hira a few miles northeast of town. Although Westerners might mock twenty-first-century Afghan and Arab leaders on the run for resorting to a cave, a cave has long suggested something else to students of Islam, something logical, peaceful, productive. It suggests Muhammad. There he would meditate, day and night, sometimes joined by Khadija. It appears he brooded over the outlying Jewish and Christian communities and the one thing they had in common: a holy book.

Here—after the boy's contemplation of the rich Umayyads—is another intimation of envy as the businessman considers the outsiders with their book, a "have-not" analyzing the "haves." This suggestion of "culture envy" would resurface prominently in our own time, although what might seem envy to some is simply productive learning to others. Hitti is most interesting on this point. A Lebanese American from a Maronite Catholic family, he authored the 1937 *History of the Arabs,* which really introduced Americans to the Middle East, used as it was by the military and diplomatic establishments and countless college classes. He founded Princeton's Middle Eastern Studies Department, the model for future university departments in the field. Discussing Muhammad's thoughts at Mount Hira, Hitti put economics first when he wrote:

> Evidently what was primarily weighing on Muhammad's heart was the observation that the Jews had a book, a revelation, and the Christians had a book and were all progressive and prosperous, whereas the Arabians had no book and were comparatively backward.[8]

But Islam's book was about to be released.

The Prophet

One night in his fortieth year, alone in his favorite cave, Muhammad heard voices, according to the early accounts. They sometimes sounded like the reverberating of bells. "Recite!" the voices commanded him.

> Recite: in the name of thy Lord, who created,
> created man from a blood clot.
> Recite: And thy Lord is most bountiful—

> He who taught by the pen,
> taught man what he knew not.   (96:1–5)[9]

The voices became one, that of the archangel Gabriel. In the moment after hearing it, Muhammad felt dazed, empty, terrified. He rushed home to the familiar comfort of his bed. Coming down with chills, he asked Khadija to put more covers over him. Then the angel's voice came again.

> Thou, wrapped in a mantle,
> Arise and deliver thy warning!
> And thy Lord do thou magnify!   (74:2)

Thus, in about the year 610, on what Islam calls the Night of Power, did the orphan, husband, businessman, and searcher after truth become the Prophet, receiving his order to proclaim and spread the Word of God. But who would believe it? Oxford historian Albert Hourani, who in 1991 produced the landmark *History of the Arab Peoples,* said that what happened next is typical in the lives of "claimants to supernatural power," Muhammad's claim being that he was the Messenger of God. "The claim is accepted by some to whom it is told, and this recognition confirms it in the mind of him who has made it." In other words, if even they believe it, it must be true.[10]

The confirmation came from Khadija, who took Muhammad to her Christian cousin Waraqa, who reconfirmed it. Besides Khadija, his few initial converts included a child, his ten-year-old cousin Ali, and a wealthy friend, Abu Bakr, Islam's future first caliph (leader) after the Prophet's death, but other support was slow in coming. Even Muhammad's dear uncle and protector—Ali's father, Abu Talib—was hesitant, as might be expected from a watchful merchant and civil servant.

Muhammad would name his religion *Islam.* Perhaps because it is closely linked etymologically to the Arabic word for peace, *"salam,"* many Westerners mistakenly think *Islam* actually means "peace." This little error can have serious consequences. After the attacks on New York and Washington, many American leaders, trying to separate the terrorists from the religion and protect Muslims from persecution, proclaimed that *Islam* means "peace." One important New York magazine editor thought the same thing and called it a sign that Americans have earnestly absorbed the lesson, among others, of the internment camps for Japanese Americans sixty years ago. "Islam is peace" is the way President

Bush himself put it when he visited the Islamic Center in Washington after the attacks. But what the editor and many other people had not earnestly absorbed was the fact that *Islam* does not mean "peace." [11]

What's in a name? In this case a good deal, because the meaning helps us understand not only Muslims and their faith, but also extremists. *Islam* means "submission," or "surrender." Muhammad chose the name because he was warning all men and women to submit entirely to the will of the one all-powerful God—the same God, as we shall see, that Jews and Christians were worshiping. Hitti suggested that, in deciding on the name *Islam,* Muhammad was inspired by Abraham's total surrender to God in offering to sacrifice his son. As for Muhammad's followers, they would be called "Muslims," or "those who submit."

To the most extreme of the extremists, total submission to God means giving up free will. Throughout the day they frequently remind themselves of the need to surrender, not that there is anything wrong with this, of course. Just as many Christians constantly invoked the saints in our grandparents' day and still find consolation in daily or at least weekly prayer, many ordinary, peaceful Muslims recall their total indebtedness to God several times daily. This point used to amuse imperialist Western travelers like the Orientalist Sir Richard Burton. While sailing to Alexandria in the mid-nineteenth century he carefully observed, with a narrow and narrow-minded eye, an Indian Muslim drinking a glass of water:

> With us the operation is simple enough, but his performance includes no fewer than five novelties. In the first place he clutches his tumbler as though it were the throat of a foe; secondly, he ejaculates, "In the name of Allah the Compassionate, the Merciful!" before wetting his lips; thirdly, he imbibes the contents, swallowing them, not sipping them as he ought to do, and ending with a satisfied grunt; fourthly, before setting down the cup, he sighs forth, "Praise be to Allah!"—of which you will understand the full meaning in the Desert; and, fifthly, he replies, "May Allah make it pleasant to thee!" in answer to his friend's polite "Pleasurably and health!" [12]

Had the Devonshire lad left for Ireland instead of India after Oxford, he might have been equally distracted by grandmothers invoking the Virgin Mary in her many guises.

The religious invocations in the videotapes of Osama bin Laden and com-

pany came off as an obvious fraud upon Muslims. But in the mouths of their un-
derlings—and in the instructions apparently written by a subaltern for the World
Trade Center attack—the pious ejaculations appear to be sincere reminders that
they must accept their own total lack of free will and submit to what they have
been told is God's will.

Just how fanatic one becomes often depends on those teachers who are passing on the religion. Consider a small example of how emphasis can make the difference. In the Washington Islamic Center's Koran, translator Abdullah Yusuf
Ali renders one of God's verse-ending remarks as "For God is never unjust / To
His servants." Whereas the Koran printed by the government of Saudi Arabia,
home to Bin Laden and several of the World Trade Center terrorists, translates it
"Allah is not unjust to his slaves." In their enslavement to orders defined for
them as God's will, the terrorists think they are the ones really fulfilling the
meaning of Islam: submit.

But a correct translation does not solve everything. In periods of Islamic revival or conquest, non-Muslims who do learn the real meaning of the word *Islam*
do not always take it as personal spiritual advice for an individual: "Submit to
God"—which is all that the Koran intended, as it emphasizes over and over.
They take it as a threat: "Submit to us!" Never mind that the Koran itself initiated
a long tradition of recommending compassion and freedom of religion for captured peoples: "Let there be no compulsion / In religion" (2:256).

Of course, it is not difficult to understand how non-Muslims might fail to appreciate this Koranic tolerance when Islamic fundamentalist states, such as the
Taliban's Afghanistan and Saudi Arabia, become aggressively intolerant of other
religions. Try to talk about Saudi tolerance with Americans and others who have
attempted to practice Christianity in the desert kingdom.

In the early 1980s, a friend who is a former Episcopal priest was working for
an American company in Saudi Arabia. He watched as the religious police became increasingly active against practicing Christians, breaking up any meetings
of two or three, just the sort of meetings of Christians that, in the Episcopal prayer
book, ensure God's presence. But the Americans kept holding them, in extreme
secrecy. "An RC priest actually got into the Bechtel [Construction Company]
compound for a long period of time, claiming to be a social worker. How he got his
clerical garb into the kingdom is beyond me!" The Christians just could not be
stopped. "I even celebrated the eucharist with them myself in a few living rooms,
but usually basements—it all reminded me of the early Christians during the Second and Third Centuries in Rome who were doing the same thing, hidden away
from view." By 2003, it was not the fundamentalist religious police but terrorists

who posed the biggest threat to the foreigners' residential compounds. They bombed three of them, killing thirty-four people, including eight Americans.

Fundamentalist, it should be noted, is not quite the right word. It was coined in the 1920s to describe Protestants who interpret the Bible literally, then simply extended to Muslims and sometimes Jews who take a similar approach to their own teachings. It is not quite satisfactory as a description of ultrastrict Muslims, but then neither is *ultrastrict* or *orthodox*. It is the best we can do in English; it has no Arabic equivalent.

Omar Khayyam's Paradise. *Courtesy of Tahrir Iran.*

2

Paradise and Islam's Four Core Beliefs

Just what was it that Muhammad was trying to teach in pagan Mecca? Here are his four main beliefs, or articles of faith, which Islam still teaches today.

1. There is only one God, or, as phrased in the call to prayer from minarets around the world, "There is no god but God!"

This profession of faith is often given as "There is no god but Allah," which is not wrong but has led many Christians and Jews to believe that Muslims worship a different god. For example, in Los Angeles, just as the American invasion of Iraq was getting under way in the spring of 2003, Adrien Brody accepted the best-actor Oscar for his role in *The Pianist* by declaring, "Whether you believe in Allah or God, may he watch over you." And the *New York Times* reported that Brody urged viewers to pray for a swift and peaceful resolution in Iraq, "whatever their deity." [1] But God and Allah are the same deity. "Allah" is simply the way "(the) God" is said in Arabic, just as Germans say "Gott," the Spanish "Dios," the French "Dieu."

Was this saying—there is no god but God—not the First Commandment that God had delivered to the Jews in the Sinai desert a few hundred miles northwest? "You shall not have other gods besides me" (Exod. 20:3). Nor was Allah a new God even for Mecca. As mentioned earlier, he was already worshiped as the chief god at the Kaaba shrine. Byzantine Christian Arabs are also said to have made pilgrimages to the Kaaba to worship this Allah, which may have confirmed for the Muslims that they and the earlier monotheists shared the same God.

Now Muhammad was warning his fellow Meccans that the pagan gods and Allah could not be worshiped together, the others must go, monotheism must en-

tirely replace polytheism—in other words, the Meccans must trash their way of
life (with all its profits from the pagan pilgrimages) and accept only Allah. Non-
Muslims often learn of the triumphant encomium "Allahu akbar!" ("God is
great!") in accounts of terrorist or war operations, but it simply sums up Islam's
first and second articles of faith.

2. God is the all-powerful Creator of the universe
and of every human being.

How close these first two beliefs are, in concept and in priority, to the opening of the Roman Catholic Apostle's Creed, which preceded Muhammad by more
than four centuries. The creed was "the earliest existing summary of the essen-
tials of Christian belief as transmitted by the Apostles," writes H. W. Crocker III
in *Triumph: The Power and the Glory of the Catholic Church, a 2,000-Year History.*[2] But Muhammad, while glorifying God as the Creator, rejected the notion
that Christ was God's son, even while accepting Jesus as a prophet. This stand
was not original, either. A furious fight over the divinity of Jesus had nearly torn
apart the Catholic Church in the years before the Apostle's Creed was confirmed
and enlarged by the Nicene Creed at the Council of Constantinople, still two centuries before Muhammad. Like some of the early Christians before him, Muslims
would edit out the parenthetical phrases in the following lines that open the
Apostle's Creed: "I believe in God (the Father) Almighty, Creator of Heaven and
Earth. I believe in Jesus Christ (His only son Our Lord)."

Here is Islam's crucial difference with Christianity: God is one; neither Jesus
nor Muhammad is divine. Muhammad is placed very high in Islam's profession of
faith—in the call to prayer, "There is no god but God" is followed immediately by
"and Muhammad is His Messenger"—but he most certainly is not divine.

> Muhammad is no more
> Than an Apostle: many
> Were the Apostles that passed away
> Before him.   (3:144)

3. Upon death, each human will face a Judgment Day.

Here again, and in the following belief, Muhammad was following Christian
tradition.

4. On this Judgment Day, those people who reject Islam will be consigned to
the eternal fires of Hell, but believers will be admitted to the glories of
Paradise, or Heaven.

We need to consider these two fates before returning to the life of the Prophet for the answer to the question "What would Muhammad do?"

Hell and Heaven are often forgotten in the secular West, especially during stock-market pops, which seem to render Hell less likely and Paradise redundant. Will one more recession revive them? In Western reporting on Islam, however, Muslim Paradise has been enjoying a comeback because some of the troubled terrorists crave it, and their leaders help by craving it for them, while preferring the cave or a cavelike apartment with kitchenette for themselves. But before we reveal what this Paradise is really like, apparently an incorrect subject for American and college textbooks, we should briefly look in on Hell, because it is rarely discussed in any detail at all, not lending itself to enthusiastic discourse, as witness some of the Koran's many graphic descriptions:

> And thou wilt see
> The Sinners that day
> Bound together in fetters;
> Their garments of liquid pitch,
> And their faces covered with Fire.   (14:49–50)

> As often as their skins
> Are roasted through,
> We shall change them
> For fresh skins.   (4:56)

There was a suggestion of this Hell in the memory of a former Soviet intelligence agent who offered free advice for American troops in Afghanistan after the September 11 attacks. He recalled a KGB file about an incident in 1981, when five Soviet troops—Uzbeks—were ordered to befriend Afghans in a village near Kandahar. First, an exchange of gifts. Then the Uzbeks were invited into a home. But as tea and food were offered, the ex-KGB officer said, "the local guys took our men's guns away, and brought them to the yard, and beat them." If the officer's account, reported in the *New York Times,* was true, then what followed seems as perverted as some of the worst stories to come out of that long-bloodied land. Could it have been inspired by a depraved interpretation of the Koran? The officer said the villagers, while attacking the Uzbek soldiers, "cut their faces, ears, hands and legs, and then they cut them into pieces and put them into pots of boiling water."[3] Had the deranged villagers remembered the Koranic references—there are at least eight of them—to drinking or being scalded by boiling water in Hell?

How did the Koranic Hell differ from the Christian and Jewish Hells? Hell, of course, was a not a new concept by Muhammad's day. The early Jews had believed in a postmortem underworld, the Sheol, Isaiah saying of the king of Babylon: "[D]own to the netherland you go to the recesses of the pit!" (Isa. 14:15). As for Christian Hell, the New Testament envisioned Christ telling the wicked on Judgment Day, "Depart from me, you accursed, into the eternal fire prepared for the devil and his angels" (Matt. 25:41). In another passage, unusually harsh for Jesus, he warned: "If your hand causes you to sin, cut it off. . . . And if your foot causes you to sin, cut it off. . . . And if your eye causes you to sin, pluck it out. Better for you to enter into the Kingdom of God with one eye than with two eyes to be thrown into Gehenna, where 'their worm does not die, and the fire is not quenched' " (Mark 9:43). Gehenna was the site of a pre-Christian pagan cult that offered children in sacrifice.

Still, and in contrast with later Christianity, Jesus most often spoke of Hell "not in terms of bodily torment," as the Catholic writer Anthony Wilhelm puts it in *Christ among Us*, "but as rejection, eternal isolation."[4] And one concept of Hell in Christ's time was not necessarily eternal, including as it did a Limbo into which the souls of the just are cast temporarily. This notion might help explain an early version of a line about the crucified Jesus in the Apostle's Creed: "He descended into hell. On the third day he rose again." A century before Muhammad, Christian theology had settled on Hell as the place of punishment of Satan and all who die unrepentant of serious sin, and the Koran's graphic descriptions of it would resemble medieval Christianity's.

Today, Wilhelm writes, "one in hell is seen as eternally alone. It is complete alienation. There is no love, no sympathy, no sense of companionship, only emptiness and hatred." And "God makes it clear that no one will go to hell except one who, with full awareness, fundamentally and permanently rejects God with his total being."[5] Still, the whole concept remains controversial among Christians, some rejecting the belief that Hell involves physical torture, or is eternal, and some rejecting the doctrine of Hell altogether.

The Terrorists' Paradise

Meanwhile, Paradise, or Heaven, gets more attention than Hell in the Koran and a lot more in recent headlines. Oddly, though, it figures hardly at all in college courses or recent Western books on Islam. Why do scholars have little or no time for Paradise when it appears again and again in the Koran, not to mention in the actual instructions to the World Trade Center terrorists? Is Paradise irrelevant? Is it politically incorrect?

What, indeed, is this Paradise that drives young terrorists wild but that our students are not supposed to hear about in detail? The Koran notes that men do covet treasures on earth, such as "women and sons; heaped-up hoards of gold and silver; horses branded (for blood and excellence), and cattle and well-tilled land." But something far better, and eternal, awaits righteous Muslims: "Gardens in nearness to their Lord, with rivers flowing beneath" . . . "shade, cool and deepening" . . . "beautiful mansions." These pleasures dominate the Koranic Paradise. Of course, many of the world's Muslims as well as Christians do not accept the literal Paradise, or Heaven, presented in their holy books, but others do. The Koran's rivers, shade trees, stately mansions must seem like the pleasures we would all enjoy at a certain age. Is that all there is? What else attracts the disturbed young men who seek Paradise through suicide attacks? We find one answer in a Koranic picture of the believers who get to Paradise, verses that celebrate the exotic Damascus trade and more:

> Among Gardens and Springs;
> Dressed in fine silk
> And in rich brocade,
> They will face each other;
> So; and We shall
> Join them to Companions
> With beautiful, big
> And lustrous eyes.   (44:52–54)

Those riveting eyes reappear in the Koran (and throughout the real Middle East), and although the translator of the Washington Islamic Center's edition, Yusuf Ali, explains that the "symbolic words" in the above verses are not meant to connote "any physical things," translation is everything, or at least a lot. In the English Koran published by the Saudi Arabian government, the last lines above become: "And we shall marry them to *Hur* with wide, lovely eyes." As the editors note, *hur* ("houris" in English) are "very fair females created by Allah as such, not from the offspring of Adam, with intense black irises . . . and intense white scleras."

Nor is it just about the eyes. There is more to Paradise, and better—which is the point, because it was meant to lure the righteous. Another look will show how essential it is to consult more than one translation of the Koran. Just as there are

many ways to interpret the Old and New Testaments, the Koran is wide open for
interpretation (fundamentalists would not agree). We have already seen in the
above lines that Yusuf Ali's "Companions" seem less vivid than the Saudi editors' *hur,* although it was the latter who made the safer choice of "marry" over
"join." Exegetes of Muhammad's book will never solve its mysteries in translation, however because such translations are not the Word of God. The only true
Koran is the original Arabic version.

But why dwell on the dark-eyed *hur* when there is more to Paradise and when
Western scholars have chosen to ignore Paradise altogether? Precisely because
modern Western academics have censored the *hur,* and for many other reasons:
because the Koran itself often returned to them; because they help us understand
some of the Paradise-bent terrorists; because they might shed light on how, in
some poor communities, women are viewed on earth; and finally because Paradise
is also on the minds of millions of peaceful Muslims around the world, whom, given
current population trends, we should be getting to know as well as we can. And although most recent writers have not been interested in Paradise, the Nobel laureate V. S. Naipaul, a non-Muslim who has traveled extensively in Muslim countries,
thinks Paradise is the single biggest motivator of Muslims. "The idea in Islam, the
most important thing, is paradise," he said recently. "No one can be a moderate in
wishing to go to paradise." For tough-minded Naipaul, Paradise makes fundamentalists of all Muslim governments. "The idea of a moderate state is something
cooked up by [its] politicians looking to get a few loans here and there."[6]

Other verses are still more descriptive of Paradise, depending on who is
reading them. The Islamic Center's Koran for American readers offers

> A fulfillment of
> (The Heart's) desires;
> Gardens enclosed, and Grapevines;
> Companions of Equal Age;
> And a Cup full
> (To the Brim).   (78:31–34)

On the other hand, another prominent translator, Maulana Muhammad Ali, says
the Arabic word for the "Companions" (*kawaib*) means "showing freshness of
youth." Moving on, the well-known British translator Kenneth Cragg gives us
"sheltered gardens and vineyards, buxom companions and a cup of overflowing
delights." More enthusiastic still is the Saudi government translation, impres-
sively executed and annotated by two former professors at the Islamic University

in Medina, Muhammad Taqi-ud-Din Al-Hilali, a Sudanese, and Muhammad Muhsin Khan, a Pakistani. Here is the Paradise awaiting Saudi readers:

> Gardens and vineyards,
> And young full-breasted (mature) maidens of equal age,
> And a full cup (of wine).[7]

Setting aside the wine for a moment, it should be pointed out that the next Koranic line says: "No Laghw (dirty, false, evil talk) shall they hear therein"—a reminder, perhaps, that we are hearing the Word of God, not to be denigrated or besmudged by human thoughts. Also, it doubtless should have been remarked here already that there are no male equivalents to the women of Paradise, although the Koran makes it clear that women are every bit as eligible for entrance as men.

Certainly, the vast majority of Saudis are not as crude, sexist, and sexually obsessed as some of their ignorant local religious leaders must be, to judge from the Saudi translation, which leads one to wonder: Who is their audience? Doctors? It might seem so as the Saudi government interpreters resort to clinical terms to emphasize the "purity" of the women of Paradise, by which they mean "having no menses, stool, urine, etc." The translators are equally unromantic in describing these ladies' virginity. When the Washington Koran's notes discuss the Koran's Chaste Maidens "Whom no man or Jinn / Before them has touched," they point out that the verse refers to "the symbolic meaning of female Companionship, in terms of grace, purity, innocence and beauty." The more literal Saudis, though, translate it "with whom no man or jinni has had *tamth* before them," explaining in a note: "Tamth means: Opening their Hymens with sexual intercourse." At still another point, however, the Saudis simply call them virgins, and add a few confusing parenthetical remarks:

> Verily, We have created them (maidens) of special creation.
> And made them virgins.
> Loving (their husbands only), (and) of equal age.

Whereas many of our professors and other experts try hard to protect America from such visions, a letter containing another glimpse of the women of Paradise was smuggled in inside the luggage of the Egyptian Mohamed Atta, who flew into the north tower of the World Trade Center. This strange letter, to be considered later in more detail, gave instructions to the hijackers, with their fevered, untreated minds. "Know that the gardens of paradise are waiting for you in all their beauty," the letter said, "and the women of paradise are waiting, calling out,

'Come hither, friend of God.' They have dressed in their most beautiful cloth-ing."[8] I have found no houris in the Koran calling, "Come hither."

In world art and literature, these lovely dark-eyed *hur* would be much more respected than in Saudi Arabia with all its religious pretense. They would be celebrated as "the beautiful virgins of the Koranic Paradise," and the term *houris* would be adopted as an affectionate compliment for dancing girls of earthy Middle Eastern cabarets. In what might be called Iran's second pre-Islamic period—the late shah's era—the belly dancers at a dark club on Istan-bul Street in Tehran were cheerfully dubbed houris, though they must have deeply offended the shah's future Islamic successors. They were not strippers, however, like the troubled "girls" of the Western-topless-clubs sort preferred by terrorists in repose, who seem to find in these attractions a satisfying confirma-tion of the West's degeneration, even as they join in (or, as they might tell their mullahs, blend in).

For some fourteen centuries Arabia's houris have haunted the fantasies not only of Muslim men but of—artistic? sensual? jealous? repressed? puritanical? all?—non-Muslim men as well. Shocked them, too. Though the idea of chaste houris in heaven may seem perfectly wholesome and delightful to many Mus-lims, and not a few non-Muslims, although not including the more puritanical Americans, it was certainly a sharp break with Christianity. In the shock of the World Trade Center attacks, and the terrorists' own references to women in Par-adise, the houris would be cited by some Christians as another contrast between Muhammad and Jesus, between celebration of the flesh (never mind that the paradisiacal *hur* were not fleshly but divine) and its renunciation by the celi-bate Jesus. And though it is true that such comparisons often stem from bias, it is also a fact, for what it's worth, that there are not a lot of houris in the Bible.

Again, Koranic heaven is even more about running springs and gardens of delight, rich carpets, and thrones of gold and precious stones—and, most impor-tant of course, eternal bliss in the presence of God—than it is about come-hither women or Companions of Equal Age, buxom companions, or any of the ladies first conjured by the nervous Christian enemies of Islam during the Dark Ages and in occasional reruns since that September morning. Moreover, Paradise's al-luring reputation did not seem to bother the Washington Islamic Center's conser-vative translator in the least. "Carnal sex has, of course, no place in Heaven," Yusuf Ali says. At the same time his notes seem to suggest there is nothing wrong with believers thinking about sex when they think about Heaven. He puts it this way: "Sex in our constitution here has a mental and psychological value, which we can picture in our transformed and perfected Love above."

The Wine of Paradise

A bit about the wine, which "immortal boys" pass around. Some will say there is no contradiction here with the Koran's ban on alcohol because this libation is not the forbidden wine of mortals, but rather a heavenly drink. The Saudis put it more bluntly, saying simply that in Paradise (as opposed to Saudi Arabia) drinking will be legal. The wine will be "white, delicious to the drinkers," with "the smell of Musk," sometimes "mixed with Tasnim: / A spring whereof drink those nearest to Allah." But in a line revealing the trouble some seventh-century Arabians were apparently having with the earthly stuff, the Koran says of drinkers in Paradise: "Neither will they have *Ghoul* (any kind of hurt, abdominal pain, headache, a sin) from that, nor will they suffer intoxication therefrom." By the eleventh century, the independent-minded Persians had taverns, though few would go so far as the poet Omar Khayyam, who in his well-drenched *Rubaiyat* had a representative from Paradise stop by:

> And lately, by the Tavern Door agape,
> Came stealing through the Dusk an Angel Shape
> Bearing a vessel on his Shoulder; and
> He bid me taste of it; and 'twas—the Grape![9]

On the issue of wine, women, and Paradise, the rebellious Muslim Khayyam pushed Islam to its limits. Again from Edward Fitzgerald's famous translation (in which *enough* becomes the rhyming *enow*):

> A BOOK of Verses underneath the Bough,
> A Jug of Wine, a Loaf of Bread—and Thou
> Beside me singing in the Wilderness—
> O, Wilderness were Paradise enow!
>
> Some for the Glories of This World, and some
> Sigh for the Prophet's Paradise to come;
> Ah, take the Cash, and let the Credit go,
> Nor heed the rumble of a distant Drum!

Long suppressed by Islam, Persia's oenophilia reaches back to the wine country around Shiraz, the ancient capital of Iran's Fars province, as early as 600 B.C.E. and maybe thousands of years before then, to judge from the jugs that have been unearthed. It seems impossible to eradicate. If Omar the Tentmaker is a sticky

enough memory for modern Iran's Islamic rulers, what must they have thought of
the recent worldwide success of a grape named, in tribute, Shiraz?

Women and wine aside—indeed, they are viewed as purely allegorical by
Yusuf Ali and many other Muslim writers—the wonders of Paradise exert a powerful pull among those believers who have little hope of worldly prosperity, or
even much comfort. Moreover, they can be proud to have paid for Paradise with
their own lives and property:

> God hath purchased of the Believers
> Their persons and their goods:
> For theirs (in return)
> Is the Garden (of Paradise).   (9:111)

As for the military route to Paradise, namely, martyrdom, which has so attracted
the disturbed terrorists, we will take that up in chapter 5, along with early Christian and Jewish views on martyrdom.

How does Muslim Paradise compare with Christian Heaven? Some American professors find the question rude, even shocking, as if we are approaching
politically forbidden territory. They are a little out of sync, however, with the
American public, which found the subject featured in two recent *Newsweek* cover
stories, one emblazoned with the headline "Visions of Heaven: How Views of
Paradise Inspire—and Inflame—Christians, Muslims, and Jews" and almost
pushing off the cover a smiling little picture of an American houri with the headline "Lost Photos of Marilyn Monroe." [10]

In contrast to the Koranic Paradise, a very physical, knowable place, the
Bible and early Christianity offered little physical detail of Heaven. "We can de-
duce next to nothing about the next life from scripture," the Catholic writer Wilhelm comments. "It was not part of Christ's mission on earth to describe eternity,
but rather to announce the good news of God's kingdom." Apparently feeling
pressed to come up with something, Wilhelm offers: "[W]e will . . . know all
those we have known and loved in this world, the saints and all the great people
of history. In fact, we will be strangers to no one, and we will delight in one
another's perfections and in our mutual love." But Heaven "is not a place, not
'here' or 'there,' " Wilhelm says. [11]

Rather, the predominant Christian view today is close to the view of many
moderate Muslims. Heaven is "a state in which . . . we will be caught up into the
infinite God," one of eternal "incredible, unimaginable happiness," with "no
sorrow, no pain, no hardship, no struggle or temptation of any kind." Further-

more, the only thing that can keep people from Heaven "is deliberately turning away from God."

Interestingly enough, the constant attention that the Koran gives Paradise reminds us of the even greater importance originally accorded to the Kingdom of Heaven by Jesus and virtually abandoned by his churches. That Christians, as opposed to Christ, should evince little interest in the Kingdom of Heaven is perhaps no surprise, as it seems too difficult a prophecy even to entertain. But listen to the British thinker H. G. Wells: "The doctrine of the Kingdom of Heaven, which was the main teaching of Jesus, and which plays so small a part in the Christian creeds, is certainly one of the most revolutionary doctrines that ever stirred and changed the world. [It] was no less than a bold and uncompromising demand for a complete change and cleansing of the life of our struggling race, an utter cleansing, without and within."[12]

By "our struggling race," Wells meant, of course, the human race. There would be no chosen people in the Kingdom of Heaven, not the Jews or anyone else. Christians would criticize Muhammad's obsession with Paradise? Well, Jesus was "obsessed" with the Kingdom of Heaven, and it went far beyond Muslim Paradise, allegorical or not. There would be no Jewish, Christian, Muslim, or any other exclusive heaven. What Jesus actually taught, Wells wrote, was that "God was the loving father of all life, as incapable of showing favor as the universal sun. And all men were brothers—sinners alike and beloved sons alike—of this divine father. . . . From all, moreover, as the parable of the buried talent witnesses, and as the incident of the widow's mite enforces, he demands the utmost. There are no privileges, no rebates, and no excuses in the Kingdom of Heaven."

Family affections and loyalties would disappear in the "great flood of the love of God." Furthermore, the teaching of Jesus "condemned all the gradations of the economic system, all private wealth, and personal advantages." What church would dare hold up that ideal? As Mark famously quoted Jesus: "It is easier for a camel to go through the eye of a needle than for a rich man to enter into the Kingdom of God." As for Wells, he wound up with a slap at organized churches: "Moreover, in his tremendous prophecy of this kingdom which was to make all men one together under God, Jesus had small patience for the bargaining righteousness of formal religion."

Medina. *Courtesy of Aramco World.*

3

The First Islamic State

The four core beliefs of Islam—in the one indivisible God, in his power as the Creator, in Judgment Day, and in an eternity of Paradise or Hell—hardly sum up the Koran. No one has done that better than the Oxford historian Albert Hourani, a Syrian British Catholic, who describes it as a book "which depicts in language of great force and beauty the incursion of a transcendent God, source of all power and goodness, into the human world He has created." [1]

Muhammad preached the simple human virtues that would lead to salvation. As the Washington Islamic Center's translator, Yusuf Ali, lists them, they are:

> Faith, hope, and trust in God.
> Devotion and service in worldly life.
> Love of truth.
> Patience and constancy.
> Humility and self-denial.
> Attention to God's message.
> And the great Arabian tradition of charity.

The continuing revelations came to Muhammad as quick, painful bursts of light, startling epiphanies that knocked the breath out of him. Even in English you can almost feel the staccato stabs in Kenneth Cragg's translation: "O you who believe, hold God in awe. Let a soul look to what he has forwarded for a morrow. Hold God in awe. God is cognisant of all you do. Do not be like those who forgot God and God caused them to forget themselves" (59:18–24). And they came in Arabic, as the Koran itself explains:

27

> Lo, We have made it
> A Quran in Arabic,
> That ye may be able
> To understand (and learn Wisdom).   (42:3)

This made the Arabic version the only official one, the Word of God, for centuries, a status enhanced by the appeal of its poetry, for which Muslims also give God the credit.

To some writers, three cs and an a sum up Islam's highest contributions to the arts—calligraphy, ceramics, carpets, and architecture—but the rolling, complex poetry that is the recited Koran was Islam's first gift, and a weapon, too. It was the poetry alone that converted one of Muhammad's fathers-in-law, the future second caliph and great conqueror Umar ibn al-Khattab. "When I heard the Koran," he said, "my heart was softened and I wept, and Islam entered into me."[2] The book's empowering rhythms were an inspiration to Arab warriors, who carried small copies of the Koran to the far reaches of the world (just as many traveling Muslims do today) and planted Arabic permanently throughout most of the Middle East and far across North Africa.

Not that Muhammad and his followers introduced Arabic poetry to the peninsula. It dated back at least a century, perhaps further—no one knows just how far because it was spoken and rarely copied down. Not only for the Arabs but also for the earlier Jews, Christians, and others, verse did not have to be copied down because it was its own recording system, easily memorized and disseminated. Long before Muhammad, spiritual poetry had attained the level of the taunt-song against the king of Babylon in Isaiah and, of course, the Psalms. In Bedouin desert encampments, love poems and poetic storytelling became a cherished tradition, with poets vying to read at festivals, which in turn led to competitive recitals in the towns and to bigger "poetry fairs." These could get out of hand, one in the Hejaz settlement of Ukaz, according to an Arab historian, becoming "a rendezvous of unspeakable vice." The spirit of popular poetry lives today in the Middle East, as ingrained in the desert as it is in the Ould Sod. Arab television news crews driving back to Beirut from a hard day's assignment in the countryside are as likely as not to break into rollicking, joyous, soul-satisfying verse.

Although pre-Islamic Bedouin poetry is all but lost, scholars having fought for years over the authenticity of a few alleged remnants, the Koran's verses were apparently quite traditional because they were delivered, as Muhammad reported, "so that ye may understand." Thus also today, from the minarets of neighborhood mosques around the world, albeit more often via recordings and loudspeakers than by the chanting muezzin himself, ancient Arabian poetry still summons Muslims musically, to come and pray, beginning with: "La ilaha illa Allah! Muhammadun rasulu Allah! / There is no god but God! Muhammad is His Messenger!"

The Flight

When Muhammad first preached his four core beliefs to pagan Mecca, he knew that much of it had already been heard from the Jews and Christians (it was his later teachings that would depart more sharply from theirs). He not only acknowledged this fact, honoring the Jews and Christians as "people of the Book," but also emphasized his debt to them, especially to the prophets Moses (mentioned in thirty-four suras, or chapters, of the Koran) and Abraham (twenty-five suras, including one dedicated to him), and to the Old Testament as a whole.

The debt was considerably greater to Judaism than to Christianity. "Abraham's religion was the mother of Islam," wrote Hitti, as he explains Muhammad's position. "Abraham himself was the father of the Arabians through Hagar and Ishmael. It was he who rebuilt and purified the Kaaba as 'the house of Allah' "—before pagans moved in to set up their false gods alongside him. Jews, Christians, and Muslims were all—and still are, Middle East peacemakers like to proclaim—"the children of Abraham." Most of the prophets accepted in the Koran are also from the Old Testament; only a few New Testament figures are emphasized, among them Jesus, Mary, and John the Baptist. It is clear that Muhammad hoped to establish his religion within the framework of the other two monotheisms.

The Meccans laughed in his face. The diplomat/historian Anthony Nutting imagined the scene:

> "If you're a Prophet," they shouted, "then perform miracles like Moses and Jesus!"
> He replied, God's Word is sufficient.
> At which they all laughed again.

At first, the Koran tells us, the lone prophet was merely mocked as "possessed by jinn," "a falsifying magician," "a soothsayer," but over the next few years the pagans increasingly saw him as dangerous. As he attracted the poor, slaves, craftsmen, and some of the younger Quraysh and weaker clans, the authorities tried to get his uncle to stop him, but Abu Talib courageously refused to sell out Muhammad. The authorities felt threatened, and they were right. Doing away with the pagan gods would not only embarrass their own fathers but consign them to Hell, too. Worse, to be realistic about it, it would cut off the money the Umayyads and others were making off the pilgrimages. This prophet was beginning to look like a revolutionary of the dangerous middle-class sort that would become familiar to history. He preached not only protection of orphans, a favorite personal cause, but even the right of the beggars and the poor to share in the wealth, a revolutionary concept to many even today but "a recognized right," said the Koran fourteen centuries ago, "for the needy one who asks and for him who is prevented (from asking, for some reason)" (70:24).

It was not long before Muhammad's followers were being taunted, boycotted, and sometimes beaten by bands of pagans led by the Muslims' chief persecutor, to be known as Abu Jabl (Father of Lies). They hectored Muhammad himself even about the deaths of his two infant sons, but the worst of it was saved for converted slaves, who were bound and left under the Arabian sun. Within five years after the Night of Power (a strikingly modern phrase that begins to sound like "Power to the People"), eleven newly converted Muslim families escaped across the narrow Red Sea to monotheistic Abyssinia, where the Christian emperor, the negus, gave them asylum. This was Islam's first expansion, however unwilling, beyond Arabia. It made modern Ethiopia the home of Islam's second oldest community. The eleven were followed by another eighty-three in 615. The negus refused to give them up to their pursuers. More important, back in Mecca, Abu Talib, who could still deal with the authorities despite his connections with the Muslims, refused to turn over his nephew, but Muhammad was virtually a captive in Mecca anyway, shunned and boycotted by the entire Quraysh tribe, which is to say most of the town.

It was a brutal economic and social boycott that strangled Muhammad's tiny band for about three years. The Quraysh banned intermarriages and refused to trade with them, threatening the Muslims with famine. In the midst of this, the prophet was badly shaken yet again by two deaths in about the year 620, Abu Talib's and Khadija's. Abu Talib, whom he needed more than ever, had been his surrogate father and crucial political protector during the persecution, which was only getting worse. In fact, the cutoff of food supplies may have had a part in Khadija's final illness. She had been his only wife, great love, first convert, employer, adviser—one of the many strong women in early Islamic history. "Khadija the Great," as she is known in Muslim lore, was one of the first women in history to be accorded that honorific. Yusuf Ali's obituary:

> (She) befriended him when he had no worldly resources,
> Trusted him when his worth was little known,
> Encouraged and understood him in his spiritual struggles,
> Believed in him when with trembling steps
> He took up the Call and withstood obloquy,
> Persecution, insults, threats, and tortures,
> And was a life-long helpmate till she was gathered
> To the saints in his fifty-first year,—
> A perfect woman, the mother of those that believe.[3]

His twenty-five years of monogamous bliss with Khadija had been a rare thing among men of his position, but as we shall see, the Prophet, too, would have several more wives in the coming years, more than he would allow any other Muslim. First in his heart, it would seem, was the one who joined him soon after Khadija's death, Aisha, the young daughter of his friend, the wealthy Abu Bakr. Before we return to the subject of Muhammad's harem and how it grew, however, we need to rejoin the Prophet as he made a crucial, possibly life-or-death decision. Harassed, threatened, his people boycotted, their food supplies running out, he decided to get out of Mecca.

He moved first to the Quraysh resort of Taif, seventy-five miles to the southeast, where he thought he could get help from the Thaqif tribe, but he was not only unwelcome in Taif, he was stoned by mobs. So it was back to Mecca, though only a matter of months before Allah would allow his Messenger to make a truly spectacular escape. This was his amazing night journey in 621, when he was magically transported from the Kaaba—which Muhammad was already calling the Sacred Mosque, though the pagan idols still thrived there alongside Allah—to Mount Moriah in Jerusalem, near where Solomon's Temple had stood and where Abraham had prepared to sacrifice his son Isaac.

Given Jerusalem's holiness to both Jews and Christians, Muhammad must have felt his sudden appearance there would add considerable status to his own movement. That he wanted to be part of the glory of Jerusalem was also evident in his original requirement that Muslims face toward that ancient holy city, not Mecca, when praying. This, too, he borrowed from Judaism, in which, as could be seen four centuries earlier inside the synagogue at far-off Dura in Iraq, the reader of the Torah faces Jerusalem. (The writer Karen Armstrong suggests that Muhammad made Muslims look toward Jerusalem so they would turn their backs on pagan Mecca, but in fact, a few years later, when he changed his mind and had them face Mecca, the pagans were still very much in charge there.) The Koran on Muhammad's night journey:

> Glory to (God)
> Who did take His Servant
> For a Journey by night
> From the Sacred Mosque
> To the Farthest Mosque,
> Whose precincts We did
> Bless—in order that We
> Might show him some
> Of Our signs: for He
> Is the One Who heareth
> And seeth (all things).   (17:1)

Mosque, or *"masjid,"* simply means place of prayer, and Mount Moriah in Jerusalem was apparently called the Farthest Mosque, or *masjid-ul-Aqsa*, in the Koran because of its distance from Mecca. The People of the Book who had prayed there to date were only the Christians and Jews, but Muhammad had his own ideas.

Most modern writers ignore this most remarkable journey, called *al miraj*, because it is too strange and does not help them explain Islam in the cold, practical terms they prefer. It does offer a neat comparison between Muhammad's ascension into Heaven from Jerusalem that night and Christ's permanent ascension after he was crucified in Jerusalem, but that contrast does not help much, as Muhammad was not supposed to be capable of such miracles. The Koran does not help much here, either, providing few details on this adventure, but the hadiths, the sayings of the Prophet as remembered by his surviving friends and family, fill in some.

According to one tradition, the Prophet rose on a white winged horse with a woman's face and a peacock's tail from what today is known as the Wailing Wall, the presumed remnant of Solomon's, Herod's and Hadrian's Temples, to the highest heaven, equivalent to the seventh of the heavenly spheres envisioned by Jewish mystics. This story would much influence medieval Christian writers, especially, it is said, Dante Alighieri as he was feverishly dreaming up *La divina commedia* and throwing Muhammad into Hell. It apparently had less effect on Aisha, who according to tradition reported that her husband seemed to have slept quite soundly until morning.

If Muhammad's journey reflected his deep desire that Islam be represented in Jerusalem, could it have been prompted by the fact that the city had become, once again, a mixed-up place, having been captured a few years before (in 614) by the Persians? Whatever its inspiration, the heavenly transfer foretold remarkable earthly events. Sixteen years later, four years after the Prophet's death, his father-in-law Umar ibn al-Khattab would walk across the Temple Mount as its latest conqueror and choose a site for a mosque; within a century, the Muslims would build there the gleaming Dome of the Rock and the Al Aqsa Mosque.

◆ ◆ ◆

The *miraj* tradition comes with bloody footnotes. One and one-half millennia later, Israeli troops would capture the "Old City" of Jerusalem from Muslim Jordan and make their way through the wartime rubble on that same Temple Mount. It was in the middle of the Six-Day War—June 5–10, 1967—when Israel, led by its lightning air force, seized and occupied the Egyptian Sinai, Jordan's West Bank, and Syria's Golan Heights. Rifles slung over shoulders, curls fighting yarmulkes, the young conquerors slipped through a narrow passageway alongside the temple's presumed remnant. I watched as they leaned toward their long-lost Wall, dissolving into tears and prayers, and listened as the poor Arabs inside their mud homes by the Wall spoke of their worries for the future—these wrenching scenes to be succeeded by the Israelis bulldozing the mud homes to create a decent-size terrace in front of the Wall.[4]

Jerusalem was as confusing as ever in 1967, as mixed-up as in the days of *al miraj*. A frightened Arab policeman halted me at gunpoint near the point of Muhammad's ascent. The rifle shook in his hands as he confronted this stranger on the still-hot battlefield, which welcomed snipers and was surrounded by angry Palestinians. Should he shoot or not? he seemed to wonder. Would he shoot or not? I definitely wondered. No one would have cared. Nor was he the only one who was confused. Amid the rubble lay a wooden ammunition box, labeled U.S. Aid, which was symbolized by a drawing of two men shaking hands, or rather just their hands. There was no way of knowing if this aid was for the Israelis or the Jordanian Arabs. America was arming both.

Al miraj, the Muslims' first (if mystical) arrival in Jerusalem, would leave peaceful footnotes, too. Six years after the Six-Day War, another Arab-Israeli war broke out, in which Israel got more Syrian territory and more out of Egypt than it lost.[5] The following summer President Nixon set off on an unprecedented peacemaking tour of the Middle East, but he had a very big problem with his itinerary: flying from Saudi Arabia to the enemy land of Israel was unthinkable. But a way was found to bring Jerusalem a lot closer to Arabian desert, just as Muhammad had. The solution was not quite a white horse with a peacock's tail but something close—Henry Kissinger and his current proud invention, shuttle diplomacy.

First, Nixon, Kissinger, and our press plane, with its own peacock tails in the form of Walter Cronkite, John Chancellor, Dan Rather, Connie Chung, and Pierre Salinger (Diane Sawyer was along, too, but as a Nixon aide), et al., flew out of Jeddah, "Gateway to Mecca," where on that earlier night Muhammad was supposed to be sleeping. Then we shot north, but veered around Israeli airspace, to the Syrian capital. From there, flying into enemy territory was not quite as verboten as from Muhammad's homeland, so after a stop in Damascus, *Air Force One* and its press caravan flew back through the unfriendly but negotiable skies to Jerusalem, where Muhammad had ascended into Heaven.

In his revelatory dream Muhammad solved more than just the transportation problem by getting to Jerusalem his way. He also solved a communication problem by being beamed to the heavens to be welcomed by the God of the Muslims, Jews, and Christians, "the One Who heareth / And seeth (all things)." Translator Yusuf Ali says Muhammad's ascension was a reflection of God's ability to see and hear all "without any curtain of Time or any separation of Space." The dreaming Muhammad almost seems here to foretell the shrinking of the globe, which was actually happening when the Nixon-Kissinger peace caravan hit the tarmac at Jeddah. Dan Rather dashed for the phone bank, and when I, a fellow CBS-er, found him a few minutes later he was about to beam his clipped, staccato voice up to a satellite in the heavens, then down to our radio headquarters in New York. The excitement of the moment was not about the news itself, but about conquering time and space, delivering the news live from steaming Arabia to steaming West Fifty-seventh Street. What, indeed, had God wrought?

But that event was nothing for Rather (whose speed and resourcefulness on the road Muhammad would have appreciated). In Egypt he outmaneuvered all of us by skipping the presidential motorcade, crossing Cairo's teeming streets and charging up the rickety stairs of the portable satellite ground station outside Anwar Sadat's presidential palace—planning to call radio in New York and score another world beat. But instead, when this broadcasting neophyte got there, Rather handed me the phone with his usual elaborate Bedouin (Texas) courtesy and let me get the credit in New York, though Dan still glowed with boyish satisfaction that he had once again smote the necks of the infidels at NBC and ABC. Of course, from the ground station Rather could beam not only his voice but also his face, and his pictures of the world, up to heaven, then back to the land of the unconverted. You can see how reading the Koran can get you thinking.

So Muhammad's ad hoc ascension to see God's signs in the heavens, defeating Time and Space, reminded me of those ad hoc satellite ground stations I came to know in the Middle East. They included one from which the image of man ascended into orbit from the town of Herzelia in Israel, not far from the Dome of the Rock.

Medina

Muhammad's heavenly journey helped prepare Muslims for another trip the following year, a real trip—the most important one of his (and their) lives. It was arranged on the sidelines of a poetry-reading contest during Mecca's big fair of 622. But Muhammad's business this time was critical: a prearranged meeting with more than seventy men from two tribes in the town of Yathrib, about 250 miles north-northeast (a bit more than a four-and-one-half-hour drive from Mecca today). They were asking Muhammad to relocate. Even amid the persecution, he had become known for his unusual talents as a community conciliator and arbiter—a superb peacemaker—and now Yathrib's pagans needed someone to arbitrate their tribal disputes.

Some Arab historians have also said the town's three Jewish tribes—which maintained a well-armed fighting force of their own—had convinced the two pagan tribes to accept a new teaching based on a holy book and a prophet. These historians have even speculated that the Jews thought Muhammad might be their Messiah. In any event, according to ancient records, he and the pagans agreed that each group would adhere to its own laws, with disputes to be decided peacefully by "God and Muhammad," which obviously raised the arbiter to the status of leader. It has also been noted that Muhammad could have been attracted to Yathrib because it was his mother's hometown. So the first agreements were made, and the much scorned Prophet of Mecca prepared to set up a new headquarters in Yathrib.

The historic Muslim migration of 622 got under way fast, for security reasons. Some two hundred disciples quickly escaped the Quraysh police and made their way to Yathrib, becoming the first of those known in Islamic lore as the Emigrants. They left their fifty-two-year-old leader back in Mecca, where his cousin Ali, who was twenty-two, volunteered to stay in the Prophet's house to face the police. Muhammad himself and one companion, his father-in-law Abu Bakr, hid out for three nights in a cave at Thaur, three miles from town, as pagan soldiers prowled outside. "We are only two," said Abu-Bakr. "No," said Muhammad, "God is with us." They reached Yathrib soon afterward, and although Abu Bakr would become Islam's first caliph—Muhammad's first successor—he wore no prouder title than "the second of two."

Thus, two of Islam's grandest moments, the first revelation and the flight from Mecca, had begun in caves. So the president of the United States did not necessarily win the sympathy of Muslims when he declared of Bin Laden and the Taliban, "They hide in shadows, they hide in caves"; to Muslim ears, this sounds just like a typical pagan. Of course, Bin Laden knew the caveman image only helped them among many Muslims in the street, but he was finally exposed, or rather should have been (nobody noticed), when a Pakistani reporter said he had met him in an "artificial cave." An artificial cave is worthy of a Middle Eastern Madison Avenue, taunting insecure Westerners with the notion that they had been humiliated by a caveman while at the same time wooing those Muslims who regard caves with the reverence Christians save for the manger.

The migration from Mecca opened Islam's triumphant era, to be known forevermore as the *hijra*. It means "flight"—not only in the negative sense of a flight *from* a place but also in the positive one of a flight *to* a better place, indeed, in this case a flight to the future, for A.D. 622 would become the first year of the Islamic lunar calendar, or Year 1 of the *hijra*. In European languages, Islamic years are designated A.H. (anno Hegirae). Each Islamic year of twelve lunar months averages about eleven days fewer than the solar years of the Christian era, now known to scholars as the Common Era, or C.E.. Thus, the two calendars overlap irregularly. Part of the year 2005 anno Domini, or C.E., would translate to A.H. 1426. As for Yathrib, an obscure oasis town south of the Byzantine Empire's juncture with the Persians, the Muslims gave it an ambitious new name: al-Madina, or Medina, meaning simply "the City."

It was here that Islam itself took flight. The Prophet was transformed into a statesman and the commander of Islam's first army—a chief of state. His enlarged civilian role is clear in the new revelations he brought, which dealt less with personal redemption and more with peace, community rules, the roles of wives and women, women's dress, religious rituals, marriage, property, and inheritance. It was here, finally, that Muhammad formed the *ummah*—Muslim community or nation—which was, in practice, the first Islamic state. Less than a year and a half after the *hijra*, Muhammad declared his community's spiritual independence by switching the direction toward which Muslims should pray, from Jerusalem back to the Kaaba in Mecca, where Allah was still surrounded by the pagans and their idols. Mentioning this, the Koran states:

> To God belong both East and West:
> He guideth whom He will
> To a Way that is Straight.
> Thus have We made of you
> An Ummah (nation) justly balanced.   (2:142–43)

The *ummah* was dedicated to social justice, which Karen Armstrong calls "the crucial virtue of Islam." In recent years extremists have returned to reveries of a worldwide *ummah,* and as we shall discuss in chapter 12, they might one day find themselves confronting one of "the crucial virtues" of the secular West: separation of church and state.

Indeed it was right there in Medina that the Prophet's teaching became "more universal," as the historian Albert Hourani puts it, "directed to the whole of pagan Arabia and by implication to the whole world." That Islam dreams of such global bliss as an ideal is doubted by few scholars, Muslim or non-Muslim, and in chapter 7 the reader will find the Koranic evidence. It is good to keep in mind that evangelical Christians, among others, have similar hopes, if no shock troops at the moment, the president of the United States having put out the word that he did not really mean it when he spoke of another Crusade.[6]

At Home, Damascus. *Courtesy of the author.*

4

The First Women of Islam

What was the role of women in the first *ummah*, or Muslim community? A good place to start is with Muhammad's wives. As we mentioned earlier, he not only remarried but did so many times. Here again some Christians contrast the celibate Jesus with the much married Muhammad, though it is almost apples and oranges because Jesus is divine to Christians whereas Muhammad is divine to no one, including Muslims. It is more enlightening to look first at Muhammad's times. Islam was not inventing polygamy; it was reining it in. Until then, in what Muslims came to call "the Times of Ignorance," as the Koran translator Yusuf Ali notes, Arabians could have an unlimited number of wives. The Koran limits Muslims to four wives and then only if they can really provide equally for each. Even that allowance was the result of war, the Battle of Uhud, in which the Muslims were defeated by the pagans from Mecca and Muhammad himself was wounded.

The fight left the Medinese Muslims with many orphans and widows on their hands. Polygamy became a practical, humanitarian solution to the plight of the orphans, still a deep concern of the orphaned Prophet. Far ahead of its time, the Koran warns the Muslims to restore the orphans' property when they come of age:

> Nor substitute (your) worthless things
> For (their) good ones; and devour not
> Their substance (by mixing it up)
> With your own.

Then:

> If ye fear that ye shall not
> Be able to deal justly
> With the orphans,
> Marry women of your choice,
> Two, or three, or four;
> But if ye fear that ye shall not
> Be able to deal justly (with them),
> Then only one, or (a captive) . . .   (4:3)

Thus, Muslim polygamy was instituted in about 625 so that Medinese men could marry and care for those children orphaned by the Battle of Uhud. From that day polygamy became a general Muslim practice, as did the requirement that the wives be treated equally, not only in "material things" but also "in affection and immaterial things," as Yusuf Ali writes. He adds this critical point: "As this condition is most difficult to fulfill, I understand the recommendation to be towards monogamy." No one in Saudi Arabia at the time, or anywhere else recently, campaigned for another solution: allowing women to take several husbands.

In a rare departure from his own teachings, the Prophet himself would have ten or eleven more wives. Many of Muhammad's marriages were political. He was fifty or fifty-one when Khadija died, "most abstemious in his physical life," and probably would not have married again, thinks Yusuf Ali, except for a practical reason that Ali believes superceded even politics. He needed a hand. So he set a precedent followed by certain American presidential couples. The wives could lead other women in the *ummah*, who were quite an active group of social workers, fortified by the fact that they shared equal rights with men in many spheres; for instance, they could help train Muslim women for community service. Like presidential wives today, some of Muhammad's adopted favorite causes. Zainab, devoted to the underprivileged, became known as the "Mother of the Poor." Another Zainab also provided for the poor, from the proceeds of her own leather craft.

These first ladies were called Mothers of the Community or Mothers of the Believers. "Theirs were not idle lives, like those of Odalisques, either for their own pleasure or the pleasure of their husband," says Yusuf Ali. If they were guilty of any misconduct, they were to be doubly punished (not that any of them ever had to be). Unlike the wives in later Muslim households, the Prophet's wives were not confined to one part of one house—the harem, or sanctuary; instead, the Koran indicates the Prophet had a number of houses out of which the wives ran their social projects. If any one of them did not want to work, Muhammad would simply set her free, putting her up comfortably. Not one took him up on it.

Still, the overriding factor in most of the Prophet's marriages was not the need for help—there would have been a lot of volunteers—but politics. Consider the evidence. After Khadija died, Muhammad's most prominent wife, the first lady among the first ladies, was Aisha, daughter of the rich and influential Abu Bakr, Islam's future first caliph. One of Islam's best-remembered women, Aisha would be at Muhammad's deathbed, would contribute to the hadiths, and would go on to prominence in her own right in both politics and war. Another wife, Hafsa, was the daughter of Umar ibn al-Khattab, who would succeed Abu Bakr as caliph. And Muhammad's daughters married Uthman ibn Affan and Ali, the third and fourth caliphs. So by marriage the Prophet strengthened his relationships with four loyal and powerful men, who would become Islam's much venerated "Rightly Guided Caliphs," the four founding fathers, so to speak, after the Prophet's passing.

Muhammad Fights Gossip

These powerful women could be difficult. There was the time Aisha, according to tradition, let herself become the center of an alleged scandal that made Muhammad so angry he refused to talk with any of his wives. The Muslims were returning from a military expedition with some of their wives. They did not notice until the next halt that Aisha's veiled litter was empty. She had left her tent before the Muslims broke camp to go look for a valuable necklace she had lost. When she got back and saw nobody around, she sat down to wait for someone to come and get her. As night came on, she fell asleep. The next morning she was found by Safwan, who had been left behind specifically to collect anything that had been forgotten. He put her on his camel and brought her back, leading the camel on foot.

One can imagine the scandal, which the Muslims' enemies in Medina were delighted to spread, and the Saudi government's English Koran, subtle as usual, does not hide the slanderous charge that was made against the Prophet's own wife: "illegal sexual intercourse." Tradition has it that Muhammad defended both Aisha and Safwan and said: "By Allah, I am not aware of anything with regard to her but good. They mentioned a man of whom I know not but good." He went to speak to Aisha at her father's house. "If you are innocent, then Allah will acquit you, and if you have committed a sin, then seek pardon of Allah and turn to Him." Aisha was innocent. It was the gossiping more than anything that outraged Muhammad, and he brought several revelations, stretching over no fewer than fifteen verses, threatening the gossipmongers with immediate and future penalties. Magazine and television editors might not want to read the following verse:

> Those who love (to see)
> Scandal published, broadcast
> Among the Believers, will have
> A grievous Penalty in this life
> And in the Hereafter.   (24:19)

The usual punishment for anyone who unjustly accused chaste women was eighty stripes. For actual adultery by a man or woman, it was stoning to death.

As a result of the "imprudence of Aisha," as Yusuf Ali puts it, meaning letting herself become a target of scandal, "the holy Prophet's mind was sore distressed, and he renounced the society of his wives for some time." It was especially difficult for him "because she was a daughter of . . . Abu Bakr, one of the truest and most intimate of his Companions and lieutenants." But if Aisha was trouble at that particular time, Aisha and another wife, Hafsa, could be double trouble, according to the Washington Islamic Center's Koran notes. "Hafsa was also sometimes apt to presume on her position, and when the two . . . discussed matters and disclosed secrets to each other, they caused much sorrow to the holy Prophet . . . who treated all his family with exemplary patience and affection."[1]

Politics was mixed with compassion in some of Muhammad's marriages. In those cases he wanted to provide for older women, some of them, such as the poor widow Sauda, having children by a previous marriage, and some also kin to tribal chiefs dealing with the Muslims. In addition, Muhammad's harem included a Coptic Christian concubine named Mary, "sent to him as a present," as Yusuf Ali writes, by a Christian community in Egypt. Mary was the mother of Muhammad's deeply lamented last son, Ibrahim, who died in infancy, just as Khadija's two sons had.

In the domain of marriage and the status of women, as in so many others, Islamic extremists are far behind the Prophet and his wives, who could easily be imagined marching for women's rights today. When all was said and done, Muhammad liked women, especially strong, intelligent women, and having no male servants in his household, he was happily surrounded by them. "Muhammad was one of those rare men who truly enjoy the company of women," as Karen Armstrong notes. "Some of his male companions were astonished by his leniency towards his wives and the way they stood up to him and answered him back. Muhammad scrupulously helped with the chores, mended his own clothes and sought out the companionship of his wives."

And what about the covering of women—from the *abaya* of Saudi Arabia, to the chador of Iran, to the *burka* of Afghanistan, to what is actually prescribed in the Koran? To cover or not to cover, that is the question, and it stokes heated debate even within Muslim families, so it is understandable so many non-Muslims have made wrong assumptions about it. But no one can doubt that it has now become a major issue among Arabs. One day in the heavily guarded Saudi Arabian Embassy in Washington, an official was discussing such issues with me when an assistant walked in, and the conversation went like this:

"Brian Williams' producer is on the phone."

"Who's Brian Williams?"

(I tried to explain that he was the principal news "anchor" of the MSNBC television network, but nobody cared, and the conversation continued.)

"They want to know if you'll go on the show to talk about *burkas*."

"No, *burkas* are Afghan. We don't have anything to do with that."

Tripping on the Veil

Even experts trip up on the veil. Karen Armstrong notes that Muslims first adopted the veil in the century after Muhammad's death, copying the Byzantine Christians, but this assertion is a bit off base. Not only did the Koran call for the veil in Muhammad's time, but the tradition was already ancient, dating back at least to the Assyrian Empire in the seventh century B.C. (or B.C.E.), the Greeks, the early Christians (Mary is invariably portrayed in a head covering), and many other ancient peoples, among them almost certainly the pre-Islamic Arabians. As a matter of fact, the covering of women in many parts of the world even today has nothing to do with Islam. But let us open our Korans again. We find God telling Muslim men how to act in Muhammad's houses:

> . . . when ye
> Ask (his ladies)
> For anything ye want,
> Ask them before
> A screen: that makes
> For greater purity for
> Your hearts and theirs.   (33:53–55)

This sura contained two messages. It advised the local men not to gaze upon one of Muhammad's wives if she was not wearing a "screen," which Yusuf Ali interprets as a facial covering. And it reminded the Prophet's wives to have one on when receiving male visitors or non-Muslim women, except for close male relatives and slaves. If this strict "screening" requirement did not sound like the original Muhammad in the days of the strong Khadija, it was not. The facial covering appeared later, in Medina, says Yusuf Ali, as "a special feature of honor for the Prophet." It was introduced "about five or six years before his death."

But when the Koran prescribes the covering for *all* the women of the *ummah*, it does not call for a facial screen indoors. For Muslim women today, Yusuf Ali would say forget the face mask, the Koran states only that, while indoors, women should wear a veil covering the bosom and adopt general modesty in dress:

> . . . they should lower
> Their gaze and guard
> Their modesty; that they
> Should not display their
> Beauty and ornaments except
> What (must ordinarily) appear
> Thereof; that they should
> Draw their veils over
> Their busoms and not display
> Their beauty except
> To their husbands.

. . . and other close male relatives. Even though the Koran does not require that women indoors wear a facial screen, it does seem to say that their lower legs must be covered:

> . . . they
> Should not strike their feet
> In order to draw attention
> To their hidden ornaments. . . .   (24:31)

Ali, interpreting this sura, says: "It is one of the tricks of showy or unchaste women to tinkle their ankle ornaments, to draw attention to themselves." The Saudi translators, though, appear to be thinking not so much of ankle bracelets as of the beautiful, jangly tribal jewelry still collected today: "And let them not stamp their feet so as to reveal what they hide of their adornment."

The Koran makes clear that Arabian women and their baubles were a moving sight to the rough male citizens and soldiers of the desert peninsula. One gets a sense of just how moving it was—and is—in the following Saudi government translation. Note again that any parenthetical remarks were inserted by the translators; in this case, they seem to suggest that the Saudis are more worried about sexual misconduct than moderate Muslims elsewhere. The Saudi Koran tells women:

> to lower their gaze (from looking at forbidden things) and protect their private parts (from illegal sexual acts) and not to show off their adornment, except only that which is apparent (like both eyes for necessity to see the way, or outer palms of hands or one eye or dress like veil, gloves, head-cover, apron, etc.), and to draw their veils all over *Juyubihinna* (i.e., their bodies, faces, necks and bosoms) and not to reveal their adornment except to their husbands . . . or old male servants who lack vigour, or small children who have no sense of feminine sex.

The huge families created by polygamy meant that Arabian women were (and are) not quite as isolated as Westerners might think. Reading the Koran's list of the many males who could visit with unveiled women, one sees that they could easily number in the hundreds: their husbands, fathers (which includes uncles), husbands' fathers, their sons and husbands' sons, their brothers and brothers' sons, their sisters' sons, male servants "free of physical needs," and children. Add Muslim women, and you have a large, if closed, society, something you could perhaps get used to in the seventh century.

Although Muslims disagree over how much women should cover up indoors, even Yusuf Ali's moderate translation for the Washington Center calls for full coverage outside:

> they should cast
> Their outer garments over
> Their persons (when abroad).   (33:59)

This verse also shows that in Muhammad's day there was nothing wrong with women actually going outside and that, as Yusuf Ali notes, "it was never contem-

plated that they should be confined to their houses like prisoners," even though
in some extremely backward Muslim areas, such as rural Afghanistan under the
Taliban, women have been virtual prisoners in their homes. As for the Saudi government translators, they again call for the most enveloping outer garments for
outdoors, adding parenthetically that the verse means women should screen
themselves completely except "the outer palms of hands" and the eyes, or one
eye, "to see the way."

The Koranic word for the full-length "outer garment" recommended for
outdoors is *"jilbab,"* a word still used by Muslims in many countries today, including the United States. In Iran it is called a chador in Farsi, in Afghanistan
a *burka.* In Saudi Arabia it is an *abaya,* worn with a *hijab,* a head scarf with an
attached bib covering the bosom, making for a tip-to-toe gown in black. The
current battle over the *abaya* has gone a bit beyond the old squabbles among
American women over whether Paris could dictate length. It is explosive, and
the Saudi government is both caught in the middle and divided within.
Whereas the conservative translators at the King Fahd Complex for the Printing
of the Holy Koran call for women to screen the whole body except when they
are with women or close male relatives, the Saudi Embassy in Washington says
otherwise.

The Koran calls only for a head scarf, a veil over the bosom, and general
modesty, which is all that is required in Saudi Arabia, insisted an embassy official. To dramatize the point, he called in a staffer of the busy Information Section, crowded with men. This tall woman marched in wearing, indeed, a *hijab,* a
head scarf with a short veil, her friendly face unobliterated by any "screen." But
she did not look the visitor in the eye, and to most Americans her outfit would
have seemed a bit dismal for such a good job. This was not Riyadh, it was Washington; in many American offices, the other women would have told her (or would
have been dying to tell her), "Wake up, girl!" In this case, though, the inter-
viewer also "averted his gaze," as the Koran advises when looking at either
women or men (and as the Saudi man at the reception desk had averted his gaze).
The pleasant woman said little, then went back to her work, which was piling up
at the harassed embassy, a target of hate mail since the attacks on New York and
Washington.

But what about that stunning woman in a picture in the embassy lobby, her
face completely screened by a bright-red mask yet all the more beautiful with
"beautiful, big and lustrous eyes" peeking through a wide slit in the mask?

"Oh, that's a Bedouin," said the official. (I am quoting from memory.)

"So her covering was an Arabian desert tradition not connected with Islam?"

"Right."

Women for the Veil

When Westerners questioned an anti-Taliban Afghan about women being free now to pack away their head-to-toe *burkas*, the man said to leave that issue alone; getting rid of the Taliban did not mean getting rid of the *burka*. He could have found a great many rural and not a few city women to agree with him. Failure has greeted several efforts to get rid of the veil, of whatever length, in a number of Muslim countries around the world, notably during the reign of the last two shahs in Iran, and in some non-Muslim countries, too, including the United States. Why? Because the conditions that led to the veil still obtain in many areas.

Think of why the Koran calls for any covering in the first place: security. These dress codes were being promulgated in seventh-century Medina in the midst of intense civil strife; moreover, there was the threat of rape. Kenneth Cragg's is one of the clearest translations of the verse telling exactly why women should draw their veils around them when they go outside: "This will facilitate their being identified for who they are and will save them from molestation." The next verse, warning of "those in whose hearts is a disease," is widely taken as reference to an actual outbreak of sexual attacks, or threats, on Medinese women at the time. So there really was a threat of molestation. What American does not remember hearing, in fact or fiction, "She asked for it!" when a "provocatively" dressed woman or girl was attacked?

Millions of women think there are things that can be said for keeping the veil. Vast numbers of Muslim women believe that God and their religion want them to wear it. And what feminist would recommend that all Afghan villagers today leave their *burkas* at home, given some of the characters that pass for men there? How safe would Saudi women be, suddenly *sans abaya*, if Arabian men really are as lustful as their government's reading of the Koran implies? Besides, as Yusuf Ali points out, distinctive dress in public—such as a veil—has actually been considered a badge of respect, honor, distinction, or beauty in many cultures. It has been proudly worn in the past by American women at church, in recent times by Philippine Catholics at mass, and today by many American Muslim women. And what about the bridal veil?

In some ancient societies the veil was such a symbol of honor that they actually prohibited slaves and "women of ill fame" to wear it. Still, East is East and West is West, and as one unreconstructed American male put it, "These supposed advantages of the veil/*burka* are romantic and all that, but it's still a humiliating, oppressive, backward custom, and women aren't given any choice in the matter. This is the real point, rarely made clear. Do all Muslim women advocate a veil requirement, or do they just make use of the veil?"

Christians and Jews

It was in Medina, too, that Islam established its earliest relations with a Jewish community. At first, close ties based on mutual respect seemed in the offing. In important verses the Koran considers Jews and Christians fellow "People of the Book." At one point it even chides pagan Arabs for rejecting what Moses, "a witness from among the Children of Israel," had already accepted:

> And before this, was
> The Book of Moses
> As a guide and a mercy:
> And this Book confirms (it)
> In the Arabic tongue.   (46:12)

Thus, Islam is presented as fulfilling a revelation of Moses. To the Koran translator Abdullah Yusuf Ali, this sura recalls Jesus remarking, "Think not that I am come to destroy the Law or the prophets: I am not come to destroy but to fulfill." To honor the debt as clearly as possible, God has Muhammad admit:

> I am no bringer
> Of new-fangled doctrine
> Among the apostles.   (46:9)

Muhammad did more than recognize Islam's debt to the Jewish teachings. It appears he was even trying to establish Islam within the framework of Abraham's religion. The Koran:

> And remember Abraham
> And Ismail raised
> The foundations of the House.   (2:127)[2]

But then we hear something else. Note in this context that it is always hazardous to quote the Koran briefly (which, as the reader may have noticed, has been going on all day). One needs to be mindful of this fact because, just as in the Old and New Testaments, one passage often leads to another that seems to contradict it. The fourth sura speaks of "the iniquity of the Jews," apparently meaning all of the Jews, for it says God has punished this iniquity by making certain "good and wholesome" foods unlawful for them. But soon after it appears to distinguish between believers and unbelieving Jews.

In a ten-verse catalog of the Jews' "iniquity," the unbelievers are accused of breaking their covenant with God, murdering God's Messengers, claiming Mary was unchaste, practicing usury, and falsely "boasting" that they killed Jesus (there is no reference here to the Romans, and in any event the Koran denies that Christ was killed or crucified). This Koranic jeremiad might seem enough to fuel centuries of anti-Jewish hatred among Muslims, yet it did not have that effect. Future Muslim-Jewish relations would often be cooperative and productive in many areas, reaching their height, perhaps, in the enlightening centuries of Al-Andalus, or Muslim-controlled Spain. This is not to deny that the Muslims took some restrictive measures against Jews (as well as Christians) in future eras or that anti-Zionism boiled over into anti-Jewish hatred in the twentieth and twenty-first centuries, but these events ran against the broader current of history. Nor did the Koran's complaints about the Jews lead to any future epidemic of anti-Muslim hatred among the Jews. Meanwhile, there was enough in Christianity's early teachings, history, and practice to fuel far more violent anti-Jewish hatred over the millennia. On the whole, it can be said, Muslim-Jewish relations were much friendlier than Christian-Jewish relations down to the twentieth century.

In yet another quick shift, after its criticisms of the Jews, the Koran goes on to say: to the believers among the Jews "shall We soon give a great reward." Muhammad himself would establish peaceful relations of a sort with Arabian Jewish and Christian communities. (We might note, in this regard, the odd career of the word *anti-Semitism*. In the West, it has come to refer only to Jews, but both the original Jewish and Arab peoples were Semites—cousins—as were the earliest Christians. As so often happens, however, constant misuse has defeated logic, so that *anti-Semitism* never refers to abuse of the Arabs; we would not hear of movie producers who create hostile stereotypes of Arabs being accused of anti-Semitism. Still, it seems especially odd to see the Arabs—Semites—accused of it. The problem came over on the boat, so to speak, the term itself dating to the 1880s in the United States, when Jewish newcomers were far more numerous than Arab arrivals and ran into massive discrimination. By 1928, *Webster's* defined *anti-Semitism* as "opposition to, or hatred of, Semites, esp. Jews." By the present day, *Webster's*, in its latest corporate form, reports that the Semites still include descendants of not just the Hebrews, but "Akkadians, Phoenicians, Hebrews, and Arabs." By now, though, it drops the other Semites altogether when it comes to defining *anti-Semitism:* "hostility toward or discrimination against Jews." That sense is, after all, the only way it is used. One might still hope that the popular media would find *anti-Jewish* more accurate, but one is not advised to hold one's breath.)

What were Muhammad's views on Christianity? He likely had many more contacts with Jews and certainly devoted far more attention to the Old Testament and its prophets than to the New, citing the Gospels only eleven times. Many Christians will be surprised to learn, however, that Islam does accept the virgin birth of Jesus. The Koran:

> Behold! The angels said:
> "O Mary! God giveth thee
> Glad tidings of a Word
> From Him: his name
> Will be Christ Jesus."
> . . . .
> She said: "O my Lord!
> How shall I have a son
> When no man hath touched me?"
> He said: "Even so:
> God createth
> What he willeth."   (3:45–47)

But the Koran does not accept that Jesus was killed or crucified, "Nay, God raised him up" (4:158). Nor does it buy his divinity. Although he was born supernaturally, Jesus was not the Son of God, Islam teaches. Like Muhammad and the other apostles, he was only a man. These, of course, are no small matters. The Saudi government precedes its English Koran with a section called "Finality of Proofs on the Fabrication of the Story of the Cross," which concludes, "Whoever believes that Jesus is God has indeed blasphemed against Allah and betrayed Jesus and all the Prophets and Messengers of Allah."

Muhammad had his most serious problem with the Christian doctrine of the Trinity—the Father, Son, and Holy Spirit—because it challenges the single most important belief of Islam, the oneness of God. Here again Muhammad was hardly inventing anything as arguments over the Trinity had rent all of Christendom. H. G. Wells pursued the arguments into the twentieth century in *Outline of History,* insisting, "There is no evidence that the apostles of Jesus ever heard of the Trinity—at any rate from him." Indeed, Wells thought so much was later tacked onto the actual teachings of Jesus that he was moved to quote (with apparent approval) those skeptics who "had the temerity to deny that Jesus can be called a Christian at all." [3] In the same vein, many Muslims resemble Muhammad not at all.

So there was nothing revolutionary about the Koran's advice to Christians:

> Say not "Trinity": desist:
> It will be better for you:
> For God is One God.   (4:171)

Nor does the Koran raise Mary to the level she attains in Roman Catholicism as "the Mother of God." (Neither, says Wells, did Jesus.) Although God purified her, Muhammad taught, and chose her "above the women of all nations," Mary, too, must pray. To expand on a point made earlier, the great Arabist Alfred Guillaume once made a useful comparison to show how Islam confirms basic points in the Catholic Apostle's Creed while it also rejects much, as follows (the portions of the creed rejected by Islam are in parentheses):

I believe in God
(The Father)
Almighty, creator of heaven and earth.
I believe in Jesus Christ
(His only son, our Lord).
He was conceived by the power of the Holy Ghost and born of the Virgin Mary.
(He suffered under Pontius Pilate, was crucified)
Died?
(And was buried. He descended to the dead. On the third day he rose again.)
He ascended into heaven
(and is seated at the right hand of the Father.)
He will come again
(To judge the living and the dead.)
I believe in the Holy Ghost;
(The Holy Catholic Church, the communion of saints),
The forgiveness of Sins:
The resurrection of the body, And the life everlasting. [4]

After Islam had survived more than thirteen centuries, the Franco-British writer Hilaire Belloc was still arguing it was only Catholic heresy. This hostile, conservative Catholic insisted on this, even though Islam accepted more from the Jews than it did from the Christians and recognized more of the Jewish prophets. Muhammad, Belloc said, "sprang from the pagans. But that which he taught was in the main Catholic doctrine, oversimplified. It was the great [Byzantine] Catholic world—on the frontiers of which he lived, whose influence was all around him and whose territories he had known by travel—which inspired his convictions. . . . [T]he very foundation of his teaching was that prime Catholic doctrine, the unity and omnipotence of God." Unity? Or Trinity? In any event, where Muhammad broke off from the Christians was in his rejection of Jesus as divine, as Belloc accurately notes. To Muhammad, Christ was "only a prophet: a man like other men. He eliminated the Trinity altogether. With that denial of the Incarnation went the whole sacramental structure."[5]

By the second half of the twentieth century, however, the Roman Catholic Church itself would be welcoming its fellow monotheists. The 1962–1965 Second Vatican Council, convened under Pope John XXIII, asked Christians to open their hearts:

> Upon the Muslims, too, the Church looks with esteem. They adore one God, living and enduring, merciful and all-powerful, maker of heaven and earth and Speaker to men. They strive to submit wholeheartedly even to His inscrutable decrees, just as did Abraham, with whom the Islamic faith is pleased to associate itself. Though they do not acknowledge Jesus as God, they revere Him as a prophet. They also honor Mary, His virgin mother; at times they call on her, too, with devotion. In addition they await the day of judgement when God will give each man his due after raising him up. Consequently, they prize moral life, and give worship to God especially through prayer, almsgiving and fasting.[6]

Many Muslims today cherish the communality they find in the three religions of their book. And they are quick to point out that Muhammad was only one of the prophets, albeit the last one, the "seal" of the apostles. The Koran has God saying to Muhammad:

> We have sent thee
> Inspiration, as We sent it
> To Noah and the Messengers
> After Him: We sent
> Inspiration to Abraham,
> Ismail, Isaac, Jacob
> And the Tribes, to Jesus,

> Job, Jonah, Aaron and Solomon,
> And to David We gave
> The Psalms.   (4:163)

Again, Muhammad would be the final apostle, their seal. His teachings would complete the three monotheisms and make them one. Toward that end, as Yusuf Ali says, Islam postulates that "All who have faith should bow to the Will of God and be Muslims." The book quotes Abraham and Ishmael as praying:

> Our Lord! Make of us
> Muslims, bowing to Thy (Will),
> And of our progeny a people
> Muslim, bowing to Thy (Will).   (2:128)

It was not going to happen in Medina. Contrary to any rumors, the Jewish community there was not about to become "a people Muslim," nor for that matter could they accept this Messenger as their Messiah. Nor, wrote historian Philip Hitti, did they want to help pay for relocating the arriving Muslims and for a new item in Muhammad's budget: military preparations. The two minorities fell to quarreling, and Muhammad's relationship with the Medinese Jews, or rather the possibility of actually having one, collapsed.

By one Arab account, the trouble began with a minor dispute in 624 between a Jewish merchant and a Muslim woman customer, which brought on a bloody communal fight. Several members of one Jewish tribe were wiped out, the rest were forced north into Syria, and the Muslims confiscated the Jews' weapons and other property in this ancient precedent of the endless modern Middle Eastern war. And relations with the Jews were about to get even worse in the midst of a historic battle between the Medinese Muslims and the pagans back in Mecca.

A Caravansary, Asia Minor, by Thomas Allom. *Courtesy of the author.*

"General" Muhammad and the First Jihad

From the beginning, Islam has called for fighting for the faith, but only in self-defense.

> Fight in the cause of God
> Those who fight you,
> But do not transgress limits:
> For God loveth not transgressors. (2:190)

Islam's first jihad opened with the Battle of Badr in 624. It is the centerpiece of the Koran's passages on war, many of them found in what are sometimes called the war suras, Koran chapters 8 and 9. Until now, to dwell on these suras about seventh-century warfare has been considered indelicate, undiplomatic, politically incorrect, especially on our university campuses. After all, we are talking about religion here. Don't other holy books have their carnal moments, especially the Old Testament? It hardly seems fair to take them out of their ancient context. So these suras have been ignored or downplayed in the West, even after the September 11 attacks, to which one of the first reactions was: "It's not about religion."

"This is not a war with Islam," Prime Minister Tony Blair told the British nation as he defended the American-British bombing of Kabul and Kandahar within a month of the September 11 attacks (some two hundred Britons were killed at the World Trade Center, which Blair called "the worst terrorist outrage against British citizens in our history"). On Islam, Blair continued, "It angers me, as it angers the vast majority of Muslims, to hear bin Laden and his associates described as Islamic terrorists. They are terrorists pure and simple. Islam is a peaceful and tolerant religion, and the acts of these people are contrary to the teachings of the Koran." [1]

But it is not that pure and simple. "The terrorists' strain of Islam is clearly not shared by most Muslims and is deeply unrepresentative of Islam's glorious, civilized and peaceful past," as the Washington journalist Andrew Sullivan wrote in the *New York Times* within a month of the attacks. "But it surely represents part of Islam—a radical, fundamentalist part—that simply cannot be ignored or denied." [2]

To put it more bluntly, Osama bin Laden and the majority of the terrorists in the attacks on the World Trade Center and the Pentagon were brought up on the Koran and on the teachings expressed in the Saudi government translation acquired by the author. And even if our universities' anti-intellectual, censorious stand against discussing the Koran's war suras could actually be defended, it no longer has to be, because the terrorists have put those suras back into context, a twenty-first-century context.

Yet even after the attacks, when the University of North Carolina decided it finally had to introduce its incoming freshmen to Islam in the fall of 2002, it chose for its text Michael Sells's *Approaching the Qur'an*. This work really is lovely as far it goes, but because it was written before the attacks, it does not go so far as to discuss the revelatory war suras, not to mention the politically incorrect women of Paradise, who seem to have inspired the terrorists almost as much as the war chapters. (As it turned out, poor UNC could not win either way. Christian evangelists and others attacked it in the courts and over the airwaves for including even the Sells book in its freshman orientation program.) [3]

Yet the terrorists themselves have found the war suras quite politically correct, even if Western scholars ignore them or give them short shrift. Indeed, they were required reading not at UNC or Harvard or Yale but in certain training camps in the Middle East. In fact, though many well-meaning Western scholars and writers had decided to ban the Koran's long-"outdated" comments—on the ancient Battle of Badr, for example—these same passages were being lovingly shared among the World Trade Center terrorists.

It is true that Islam opposes war, even if, like Christians and Jews, Muslims frequently fail to live up to this ideal. But Islam allows for a difference between ordinary war—such as wars for commerce, territory, influence, revenge, or what the Koran calls "the temporal goods of this world"—and a jihad, which is nothing less than a fight between good and evil. President Bush understood this distinction when he assured the Muslims of the world about his own "War on

Terrorism": "This is not a war against Islam, it is a war against evil." The Koranic jihad is a war against pagans, or infidels, or "disbelievers," or "unbelievers"—words extremist Muslim groups find applicable to the West.

The first jihad gave us Muhammad in his debut as a general. It was fought during Ramadan, one of the four sacred months when fighting was forbidden, except in self-defense. But were these first Muslims really fighting in self-defense? Yusuf Ali says they most certainly were, because they were "constantly in danger of being attacked by their Pagan enemies of Mecca. . . . The design of the Meccans was to gather all the resources they could and, with an overwhelming force, to crush and annihilate Muhammad and his party."

But the Arab-American historian Philip Hitti suggested it was Muhammad's forces who made the first move, "taking advantage of the periods of 'holy truce.' " It would hardly be the first time that the ban on fighting during Ramadan was interpreted broadly. When the Egyptians and Syrians attacked Israeli forces in October 1973, the Israelis called it "the Yom Kippur War," but many Arabs openly called it "the Ramadan War," and there was, of course, no religious debate. On the other hand, in the wake of the World Trade Center and Pentagon attacks, the world debated whether the United States should bomb terrorist and Taliban targets in Afghanistan during Ramadan (it did). But why would the weak Muslims have been the attackers at Badr? One reason would be to help the latest Muslims arriving from Mecca, who needed housing, food, and cash. The campaign to assist them established an important requirement of Islam, derived from the Bedouins: hospitality. One welcomes and honors guests, especially brother Muslims. This cardinal rule was evoked when the Taliban first declined to turn over Osama bin Laden, then referred it to a religious council, the *ulama*, which agreed that handing over Bin Laden would violate Islamic tradition. Other Muslim countries dared not object, which confounded many Westerners (a religious council harboring a terrorist?), who suspected the real reasons were the millions of dollars Bin Laden gave the Taliban and its own fate if he were taken.

How could Muhammad's men help the new arrivals from Mecca? By resorting to an old Bedouin tradition known as the *ghazu*—the piratical raid. It was not really warfare; it had nothing to do with offensive or defensive issues. Rather, it was "one of the few manly occupations," said Hitti. "Christian tribes, too, practiced it . . . a sort of national sport." He quoted an ancient poet: "Our business is to make raids on the enemy, on our neighbor and on our own brother in case we find none to raid but a brother!" With one exception: blood was not to be spilled "if possible," or as they say in the Middle East, *inshallah*, "God willing"—a little Arabic expression that is actually a gaping hole in the desert.[4] Blood was certainly going to flow at the Badr oasis.

A Fabulous Train

The first jihad began when a long, lazy—but not so lazy as it looked—richly laden caravan lumbered past Medina on the way to Mecca, loaded with cash and Byzantine baubles lashed to a thousand camels. This fabulous train was protected by only forty guards, and they were quite pathetic, with few weapons among them. On the other hand, the caravan chief was not pathetic. He was none other than Abu Sufyan, the Umayyad chieftain who was Mecca's military commander. Of course, nobody knew better than that veteran caravan man Muhammad himself that Abu Sufyan would pause at the oasis fifty miles southwest of Medina, to water and prepare for his phony grand welcome back.

Somehow, though, Abu Sufyan had gotten wind of danger around Medina, or maybe even expected it, and sent on to Mecca for help. Over the next few days he was joined by some of the toughest fighters of the western desert, among them the notorious Abu Jabl, the hyperactive persecutor of Islam. The Prophet's own uncle Al-Abbas, keeper of the Zamzam well, came out to help the Meccan commander. All told, the Quraysh enemy numbered about a thousand—"accompanied by female singers to spark the fighters' enthusiasm" (which may not have been a good idea). And the Prophet's army? Only about three hundred recruits, ranged on a northward hillside looking down on the caravan and beyond it the great Quraysh cavalry that had come to Abu Sufyan's rescue. Some Muslim writers have said Muhammad had no intention of raiding the train but actually planned to leave the loot aside and march out to meet the threatening Quraysh, having no idea of their strength.

It started with challenges between individual champions, then went into the pitched battle, with the Muslims outnumbered some three to one, yet when the last pagan had been run through, stoned, or captured, Muhammad's little band had won. Seventy pagans lay dead or dying, among them Abu Jabl, the others captured or in flight, the fate of the not-very-helpful female singers still unclear. Among the prisoners was Uncle Abbas, who soon became a convert, then founded a long line of caliphs known as the Abbasids. Fourteen Muslims were killed—"Islam's first martyrs." How did three hundred beat a thousand? Allah was with them. When they prayed, according to the Koran, he replied,

> I will assist you
> With a thousand of the angels,
> Ranks on ranks.   (8:9)

That unseen angels joined the battle is not questioned by Yusuf Ali, translator of the Washington Koran, although he writes that a thousand angels "is probably not to be taken literally, but to express a strength at least equal to that of the enemy." The angels were tough:

> If thou couldst see,
> When the angels take the souls
> Of the Unbelievers (at death),
> (How) they smite their faces
> And their backs (saying):
> "Taste the Penalty of the blazing Fire—"   (8:50)

We are now in the midst of the widely ignored (in the West) eighth sura, which brings us God's enlightenment on this first Muslim jihad. We might pause to note, though, as so little attention has been paid to it, that in fact the Jews and Christians preceded the Muslims in holy war. For contrary to the fears of the first frightened Westerners who would confront them, the Muslims did not have a monopoly on a fighting God, or on beating the odds.

Moses had declared in the Old Testament's Book of Deuteronomy: "When you go out to war against your enemies and you see horses and chariots and an army greater than your own, do not be afraid of them, for the Lord, your God, who brought you up from the land of Egypt, will be with you" (20:1). As for the Christians, as the popular historian James Reston Jr. notes in his *Warriors of God*, Augustine had written three centuries before Muhammad that a war to defend Christianity could be just, even holy, and that the fighters would be soldiers of God. In future centuries, as Reston also points out, Charlemagne, and later the popes preaching the Crusades, would call in heavenly artillery against the Muslims.[5]

Battlefield Terror

The Koran's verses on the Battle of Badr also provided tactical advice—and now we have the word *terror:*

> I will instill terror
> Into the hearts of the Unbelievers:
> Smite ye above their necks
> And smite all their
> Finger-tips off them.   (8:12)

About the smiting, the Washington Center's Koran helpfully notes: "The vulnerable parts of an armed man are above the neck. A blow on the neck, face, or head, finishes him off. If his hands are put out of action, he is unable to wield his sword or lance or other weapon, and easily becomes a prisoner." The Saudi government translation is a little more specific: "strike them over the necks, and smite over all their fingers and toes."

As for *terror,* here it simply means striking fear on the battlefield. This sense is confirmed a few verses later when God adds, in the Saudi translation, "O, you believe! When you meet those who disbelieve, in a battlefield. . ." But a twenty-first-century terrorist pilot did use this passage to justify flying into the World Trade Center. Several verses later, the Koran tells its holy fighters:

> . . . make ready
> Your strength to the utmost
> Of your power, including
> Steeds of war, to strike terror
> Into (the hearts of) the enemies,
> Of God and your enemies,
> And others besides, whom
> Ye may not know, but whom
> God does know.   (8:60)

The Saudi translators make this "steeds of war (tanks, planes, missiles, artillery) to threaten the enemy of Allah." This reference to airplanes, missiles, and other modern war machines seems a novel way to update a holy book, but it is also a signal from Saudi Arabia, the most powerful Muslim state, to the world and perhaps most fatally to other Muslims, that the Koran's words are still fighting words.

We are left with that scary seventh-century threat to "others besides, whom /

. . . God does know." In the terrorists' minds, such as they are, does that take us off the battlefield and into a random population? And if they make that leap, whose necks will they aim at after hearing God tell them to smite above the necks of the Unbelievers?

"The beauty of the Koran," a spokesman for an American-Islamic group in Washington told me, is that you can interpret it many ways, just as you can the Bible and other great literature. He was referring to the Koran in general, not the war suras, in which the possibilities are not always beautiful to contemplate. Then again frightening whole populations was nothing new to the Bible, either. In the Old Testament, an incorrigible son refuses to mend his ways despite his parents' pleas, and is a glutton and a drunkard besides. So an implacable Moses orders nothing short of the death penalty as a divine deterrent: "all of his fellow citizens shall stone him to death. Thus shall you purge the evil from your midst, and all Israel, on hearing of it, shall fear" (Deut. 22:21).

Martyrdom. Suicide is merely the act of putting oneself to death, whereas martyrdom is suffering death for a cause, usually a religion. Martyrs do not commit suicide, do not seek death, for themselves or anyone else. They do not murder. Both Islam and Christianity condemn suicide but not martyrdom. The New Testament, for example, acknowledges martyrdom ("whoever loses his life for my sake will find it" [Matt. 10:39]), but it does not give it nearly the stress the Koran does. Indeed, after the power of faith in war, the second lesson of Badr was the courage that faith provides—a contempt even of death, much assisted by the promise of Paradise. The Koran specifically mentions both those who leave their homelands to fight and those who protect them as candidates for Paradise, so that the recent Arab terrorist invaders of non-Arab Afghanistan and their Afghan protector, Mullah Omar, could pluck the following lines out of their seventh-century context, then take comfort from them:

> Those who believe,
> And adopt exile,
> And fight for the Faith,
> In the cause of God,
> As well as those
> Who give (them) asylum
> And aid,—these are (all)
> In very truth the Believers:
> For them is the forgiveness
> Of sins and a provision
> Most generous. (8:74)

"It will be a provision which lasts forever and is on the most generous scale," as Yusuf Ali puts it. Later, in the Crusades, the popes, too, would promise Christian warriors "remission of sins" for fighting the "wicked race" of Muslims. This assurance presented a strange scenario in which, by killing each other, both sides went directly to heaven. That "that was then," the seventh and twelfth centuries, and "this is now," the twenty-first, is a difference extremist Muslims do not seem to fathom.

We have recently seen modern Muslim fighters living under this seventh-century code—nurturing a contempt of death and a lust for Paradise—such as those who reported to the terrorist camps in Afghanistan and the World Trade Center hijackers. One of the hijackers' leaders, as we shall find in chapter 11, actually provided his men with a vignette of Paradise's pleasures, in case they forgot. In the house used by the Al Qaeda terrorist organization in Kabul, U.S. troops found a letter from a militant using the name Abu Yasser. It stressed that "hitting the Americans and Jews is a target of great value and has its rewards in this life and, God willing, the afterlife." Countless other examples have come out of Afghanistan, showing how terrorists and torturers think they are applying the Koran and will taste Paradise for murder.

One torture victim was Sayed Abdullah, a studious Muslim who worked for the Red Cross in Afghanistan, the red cross on his ID card suggesting to the Taliban that he was a Christian, as did the fact that his large book collection included two Bibles. Accused of possessing a Bible, which was illegal, and of converting to Christianity, which would be the much worse crime of apostasy and could bring the death penalty, Sayed was arrested, beaten, tortured. "I swear to God," he told the Taliban soldiers holding him. "I swear on the holy Koran. I am not the man you are looking for." "God is blessing us," the soldiers chanted as they beat Sayed while he lay facedown on a table. "God will reward us." Later, according to the *Washington Post*, when Sayed repeated that he had never converted, a soldier pulled his head by the hair, put a knife to this throat, and said, "Give me permission to cut his throat so I may be rewarded by God." Sayed was later freed when his mother bribed a Taliban commander with five thousand dollars, which she raised by selling their house and almost everything in it.[6]

"Why would a prophet study war, even a holy war?" some Christians ask today. But if they will return to their Bible, they will find that Muhammad certainly did not invent the concept of a jihad. In the previous millennium, in Isaiah's "Oracles Against the Pagan Nations," we find God declaring a holy war against Babylon:

I have commanded my dedicated soldiers,
I have summoned my warriors,
eager and bold to carry out my anger.
Listen! the rumble on the mountains:
that of an immense throng!
Listen! the noise of kingdoms,
Nations assembled!
The Lord of hosts is mustering
an army for battle.
They come from a far-off country,
and from the end of the heavens,
The Lord and the instruments of his wrath,
to destroy all the land.   (13:3–5)

Muhammad and Jesus

By contrast, the message of Jesus is entirely different, even if its spirit was violated again and again by later Christians. So how can one ignore, many ask today, the stark distinctions between Gentle Jesus and "General" Muhammad? By allowing himself to be persecuted and finally put to death, did not Jesus set an example for his followers, even when they are under attack? When Jesus was seized and put under arrest, Peter drew his sword and clipped off an ear of one assailant, but Jesus told Peter: "Put your sword back into its sheath, for all who take the sword will perish by the sword" (Matt. 26:51–53). The image of the peaceful Jesus has survived even the massacres of the Crusades and the Spanish Inquisition. In fact, when the crusading churchmen went looking for support in the New Testament, they were hard put to find it. As James Reston Jr. points out, they came up with a few lines in Timothy about being a soldier of Christ, but Timothy was using the phrase merely as a metaphor for a dedicated teacher of the faith: "Bear your share of hardship along with me like a good soldier of Christ Jesus. To satisfy the one who recruited him, a soldier does not become entangled in the business affairs of life" (Tim. 2:3–4).

But some Muslims say the difference between Muhammad and Jesus is not what it seems. Yusuf Ali says of the Battle of Badr: "Destruction and slaughter, however repugnant to a gentle soul like that of Muhammad, were inevitable where evil tried to suppress the good. Even Jesus, whose mission was more limited, had to say, 'Think not that I am come to send peace on earth: I came not to

send peace but a sword' " (Matt. 10:34). "More limited" is putting it mildly. In
Matthew, Jesus was not preaching holy war but rather warning the apostles that
they can expect hostility as they go about proclaiming the gospel. Not only hostility, but even death.

In the end, war was indeed what most clearly separated the lives, the actual
experiences, of Jesus and Muhammad. H. G. Wells's sketch of Jesus hints at the
similarities and differences in the lives of the two:

> [Jesus] was clearly a person . . . of intense personal magnetism. He attracted
> followers and filled them with love and courage. Weak and ailing people were
> heartened and healed by his presence. Yet he was probably of a delicate
> physique, because of the swiftness with which he died under the pains of cruci-
> fixion. . . . When he first appeared as a teacher he was a man of about thirty
> [Muhammad was forty]. He went about the country for three years spreading his
> doctrine, and then he came to Jerusalem and was accused of trying to set up a
> strange kingdom in Judea; he was tried upon this charge, and crucified together
> with two thieves. Long before they were dead, his sufferings were over.[7]

Muhammad, on the other hand, could not have had a frail physique. Whether
he had a choice in the matter or not, he was a warrior—a holy warrior, Muslims
would say, but a jihad is no less a war for being holy. Indeed, it is all-out war, or,
as the Saudi Koran's notes put it, "with full force of numbers and weaponry." We
move to the ninth sura, the second of the Koran's so-called war suras. In the im-
perative mood that recurs throughout the Koran, Allah commands:

> . . . fight and slay
> The Pagans wherever ye find them,
> And seize them, beleaguer them,
> And lie in wait for them
> In every stratagem (of war).   (9:5)

This verse certainly might make readers today think of Bin Laden: kill them
wherever you find them; abduct, harass, ambush them; use every trick or "stratagem." But these tactics were already common in the Middle East long before
Bin Laden showed up in headlines, as in the kidnappings and murders in the
1970s in Beirut, where as it happened both the younger, not yet radicalized Bin
Laden and I were present. (Bin Laden would appear in then cosmopolitan Beirut
as just another rich Saudi playboy—"a drinker and womanizer, which often got
him into bar brawls," according to one biographer—and not known to me, who as

Middle East bureau chief of CBS News had to be more concerned with the kidnappings and murders.)[8] The "abduct-harass-ambush" tactics had also appeared in the vastly more important seizure of the American Embassy in Iran in 1979. Not to mention the seizure of the Russians' embassy in Iran way back in the nineteenth century, for these tactics reach much further back than our times.

Indeed, they make Muhammad a pioneer in guerrilla warfare—in defense of the faith, Muslims would quickly add—and a warrior the Pentagon should start including in its studies, along with American Indians, American Revolutionaries, the Communist Chinese, the Vietcong, and other famous special forces at home and abroad. At the beginning of the war on terrorism, U.S. authorities did actually study new tactics, even torture and the possibility of murdering individual Bin Laden agents in some of the forty countries where he operated. Barton Gellman reported in the *Washington Post:* "[T]he Bush Administration has concluded that executive orders banning assassination do not prevent the president from lawfully singling out a terrorist for death by covert action. . . . [A new directive] broadens the class of potential targets beyond bin Laden and his immediate circle of operational planners and also beyond the present boundaries of Afghanistan. . . . Inside the CIA and elsewhere in government, according to sources, much of the debate turns on the scope of a targeted killing campaign."[9]

Westerners often accuse Muslim warriors of "treachery," just as the Koran warns its own fighters against enemy treachery. Who is better at it? The hadiths quote Muhammad as commenting that whenever he resolved to attack, he gave the opposite indication to the enemy, which sounds like nothing more than common sense. But certainly, Muslim fighters have long been famous for surprise.

• In 1811 the Egyptian nationalist leader Muhammad Ali invited nearly five hundred leaders of the resisting Mamluks, the old slave-soldier regime, to a reception. As they left the party through a narrow street, the gates were closed at both ends, and sharpshooters stationed above opened fire, killing every one of them.

• On September 9, 2001, two Arab TV newsmen were interviewing Northern Alliance leader Ahmed Shah Massoud in Afghanistan, after their agency had promised to send "one of our best journalists." They pointed the camera in his face and began to ask, "How will you deal with the Bin Laden issue when you are in power?" With that question, the bomb in the TV camera exploded. Two days later the World Trade Center and the Pentagon were attacked, and America's allies, the Northern Alliance, found themselves without their leader, mortally wounded by the camera bomb.

• In November 2001 Taliban commanders in northeastern Afghanistan said they were surrendering their city to Northern Alliance troops and were ready to embrace them. The Alliance troops were overjoyed. "Kanduz has been captured!" they roared, and rushed in. They were greeted not with embraces but with Taliban rockets, and they rushed away in ignominious defeat.

"Lie in wait for them in every stratagem of war." Or as God tells us in two other verses of the war suras (Saudi version): "O you believe! When you meet those who disbelieve, in a battlefield, never turn your backs to them . . . unless it be a stratagem of war" (8:15–16).

The Battle of Badr did not end the first jihad. In the second round, a year later, Abu Sufyan defeated the Muslims at a place called Uhud. The Prophet was hit by a stone and fell, breaking a tooth and cutting his lip. His wounds were nursed by Fatima, his daughter by Khadija and now Ali's wife. She was about nineteen at the time. That same year of 625 saw the Muslims still at odds with their Jewish fellow townsmen in Medina. This time they expelled the second Jewish tribe, seizing their houses and date palm gardens. This expulsion would not be the end of this local conflict, but again the larger war—the conclusion of Islam's first jihad—intervened.

Abu Sufyan returned to the front to attack Medina itself in about 627, Year 6 of the *hijra*. By then "General" Muhammad—for that is what he was; indeed, he was one of the greatest generals of his era—was able to field three thousand men. Yet he faced the same terrible odds as at Badr. Abu Sufyan had rounded up a confederacy of ten thousand fighters, among them his own Meccan army, Bedouin mercenaries, black slaves, and, fatefully, a Jewish contingent—an eclectic mix that would give the fight its name in the Koran, "the Battle of the Confederates." But when Abu Sufyan's magnificent cavalry attacked Medina's defenses on six hundred Arabian horses, they ran straight into a Muslim idea. Literally. A trench.

The trench was not a new concept—the Prophet had borrowed the idea from one of his officers, Salman, a Persian who supervised the digging before the Confederates attacked—but it was certainly new to Arabian desert fighters, including Abu Sufyan, or they would not have plunged right into it. It gave the fight its other name, "the Battle of the Trench." As Philip Hitti noted, it even anticipated 1914 with its tanks-versus-trenches, although in 627 it was simply an effective Muslim idea, a Koranic "stratagem." Muhammad's trench turned the Meccans' desert attack into a month's siege, which demoralized the Bedouins, who just wanted their money, and ended with the attackers simply giving up and going home. Besides this lesson of innovation, which often does come from the smaller, more creative force, Islam had now taught the important advantage of a band that is fiercely united by one faith against a much larger army with mixed goals and loyalties. This is one of the advantages (another was home turf) that allowed the recent Arab terrorist invaders of Afghanistan to hold out so long against the American-British-Northern Alliance combination, and to escape into the outside world, each man to himself perhaps for a while but all united by their fanatic version of Islam.

After the Confederates were defeated, the pagans of Mecca would never again mount a serious challenge to the Muslims of Medina. For his part the Prophet-general expanded his base, signing new treaties with desert tribes and welcoming yet more converts from Mecca.

Sultan Ahmet Mosque, Istanbul, by Thomas Allom. *Courtesy of the author.*

6

Separating from
Judaism and Christianity

Now that the first jihad in history was won, the Muslims made a terrifying move that consolidated Muhammad's control of Medina. They moved against the remaining third tribe of local Jews, called the Qurayzah. As mentioned earlier, members of the first tribe had been wiped out or forced north into Syria after a communal fight that broke out three years earlier, and the second tribe was expelled the following year. Now the third Jewish tribe was targeted; they had not only refused to recognize the Muslims' Prophet but actually joined the Muslims' enemies in the Battle of the Confederates.

"Filled with terror and dismay" after the battle, the Medinese Jews "shut themselves up in their castles" outside the city, according to the notes in the Washington Islamic Center's Koran. The Jews "sustained a siege of 25 days, after which they surrendered." It was not Muhammad who chose their punishment; rather, the Jews asked that it be decided by the chief of a tribe with whom they were allied. Once it was carried out, the Prophet described it for all time in a revelation, in which God addresses the Muslims:

> And those of the people
> Of the Book who aided
> Them [the pagans], God did take them
> Down from their strongholds
> And cast terror into
> Their hearts, (so that)

> Some ye slew, and some
> Ye made prisoners.
> (33:26)

Six to seven hundred Jewish men were killed, the women were sold, and their property was divided among the Muslim fighters. As the Koran elsewhere speaks of mercy to any who are captured in war, this massacre of POWs raises many questions among non-Muslims. Anticipating this, the Washington Koran's translator says the tribal chief was less brutal than Jewish law. For a defeated enemy city that was nearby and therefore might still threaten the Jews' religion, Deuteronomy prescribes, as Yusuf Ali points out: "total annihilation: 'thou shalt save alive nothing that breatheth' " (Deut. 20:16). The Washington Koran's notes say, "According to the Jewish standard, then, the Quraiza deserved total extermination—of men, women and children." Instead, for this Muslim massacre, the tribal chief applied the more lenient Jewish treatment for defeated enemies in a "very far off city": "put every male in it to the sword: but the women and children and livestock and all else in it that is worth plundering you may take as your booty."

Karen Armstrong, a former nun who recently taught at the Leo Baeck College for the Study of Judaism, defends the Muslims. "The massacre of the Qurayzah was a horrible incident, but it would be a mistake to judge it by the standards of our own time." She finds several explanations for it: it was a primitive world; "the Muslims themselves had just narrowly escaped extermination"; had the Qurayzah been exiled, they would have returned to attack another day; and Muhammad "was not expected to show mercy to traitors like the Qurayzah." Here Armstrong wades into the broader issue of Muslims, Christians, and anti-Jewish persecution. The massacre did not show any hostility toward Jews in general, she argues. Jews continued to be respected as People of the Book, some continued to live in Medina, "and later Jews, like Christians, enjoyed full religious liberty in the Islamic empire."[1] Even soon after the massacre, the Muslims would work out agreements for coexistence with many Jewish communities, although, as we shall see, under threat of attack on one important occasion.

Armstrong concludes, "Anti-semitism is a Christian vice. Hatred of the Jews became marked in the Muslim world only after the creation of the state of Israel in 1948 and the subsequent loss of Arab Palestine." But that does not mean it should be ignored. As Arieh Stav shows in the illustrated *Peace: The Arabian Caricature,* Nazi-like anti-Semitism was still flourishing in several Arab countries in the 1990s; as the century closed, Osama bin Laden's subsequent terrorist propaganda, openly anti-Jewish, found an audience as well. But Armstrong insists that such hatred cannot be justified by the Koran. "Because of this new hostility towards the Jewish people, some Muslims now quote passages in the Quran that refer to Muhammad's struggle with the three rebellious Jewish tribes to justify their prejudice. By taking these verses out of context, they have distorted both the message of the Quran and the attitude of the Prophet, who himself felt no such hatred of Judaism." The Lebanese American Philip Hitti noted, coldly and without comment, that the third Jewish tribe was "the first but not the last body of Islam's foes to be offered the choice between apostasy"—renunciation of their own faith—"or death."[2]

A year after the Battle of the Trench, in 628, the Prophet targeted Mecca itself. In a bold stroke, he led fifteen hundred of his followers in a pilgrimage there, to convince the Meccans that the their Kaaba could play a central role in Islam. The pagan Quraysh sent two hundred cavalrymen to meet them nine miles north of Mecca, where they probably could have wiped out the Muslim pilgrims in short order. But it was not that simple. It would have been a horrible blow to Mecca's reputation, and economy, to attack pilgrims. In addition, the Quraysh already faced a growing internal challenge from increasing converts to Islam, whereas Mecca desperately needed to maintain the northern trade route to Syria that the Muslims had suddenly rendered deadly. So, in a scene that anticipated Henry Kissinger's peregrinations, "messengers shuttled back and forth," as Philip Hitti wrote, from the battlefield at al-Hudaybiyan to Mecca.

The result was no battle at all, but a nonaggression treaty based on each side's need to remove the other as a threat but that also allowed Muhammad to extend his control over much of Arabia without pagan interference. Later in 628, Muhammad accomplished both this goal and the containment of the exiled Jews who had fought against him. He challenged the fortified Jewish stronghold of Khaybar, an agricultural center one hundred miles north that had become the principal haven for Medinese Jews. After a two-week siege, during which Muslim women came out from Medina to serve as nurses, the Khaybar oasis surrendered, and agreed to supply half its agricultural yield to the growing Muslim state. Others showed less resistance as Muhammad sent armies to reduce various tribes and towns across the desert, especially in the north along the borders of the Byzantine Empire. Additional treaties were signed with the Christians of Aqaba and the Jews of three oasis towns, under which they would be protected in return for payment of a land and head tax. Muslim influence soon extended to the southern edges of Palestine and even to the Dead Sea.

The Prophet moved to strengthen Islam internally as well. He separated it further from Judaism and Christianity by creating a permanent ceremonial structure for it. He made Friday the Sabbath and established the tradition of the call to prayer from the minaret of the mosque, instead of by a trumpet and gong, or bells. He called for fasting throughout the sacred month of Ramadan. He had already established that his followers should make pilgrimages to the Kaaba, kiss the black stone, and perform other rituals. He had already changed the direction toward which Muslims should pray, from Jerusalem to Mecca. But the original requirement to pray toward Mecca three times a day, deemed too easy, or too easy to ignore, would be increased to five. Sanctioned in the Koran itself, these practices that define a good Muslim came to be listed by priority as the Five Pillars of Islam.

The Five Pillars of Islam

There was a beautiful simplicity about the Five Pillars, both in their form and in the way they offered direct access to God. They have the same appeal today to hundreds of millions of Muslims the world over. The five pillars are, in order:

The profession of faith, or declaration of belief that
"There is no god but God, and Muhammad is His Messenger"

By wide agreement, pronouncing this creed alone makes one a Muslim, although many hold to a broader creed that expresses belief in God, his angels, his books, his prophets, and a judgment day.

Prayer, performed at least five times daily, in private and public,
while facing in the direction of the Kaaba in Mecca

It includes a recitation of the profession of faith and readings from the Koran. The ritual positions for prayer are mentioned in the Koran: standing, bowing, kneeling, and prostrating oneself; no single physical act in Christianity or Judaism so expresses an individual's subservience to God. Nothing so distinguishes Islam, and strengthens it, as this requirement, rather than just encouragement, of prayer to be a good Muslim—unless it is the hajj, or pilgrimage, another of the pillars, although the hajj is only a once-in-a-lifetime requirement, if that. Daily prayer ensures the religion's success, guarantees devotion. It is the lesson of regularity. Think of how to get to Carnegie Hall: practice, practice, practice. Think of the daily regimes of the old Western watering places, where the regular schedule was always more curative than the water. Think, if you must, of America's best-selling *Body for Life* diet-and-exercise program: if you agree to have those tiny meals six times a day, when would you find time to do anything else but pray to Bill Phillips? It works.

The scheduling of Muslim prayer is carefully ordered. One performs the five-times-daily prayer in one's home, business, or neighborhood mosque, or in the open air. Nothing will detour a devout Muslim from this program of prayer in the Middle East, although one sees much less outdoor praying by Muslims in the West, so little that it can lead to misunderstanding. A tour guide on the National Mall in Washington was once startled to see a small group of Muslims prostrating themselves in the direction of the Lincoln Memorial (and the far-off Kaaba behind it), doubtless leading unenlightened American bystanders to think, "That's not really necessary."

Every Friday, the Sabbath, the faithful are summoned to prayer at their local mosque, the call from the minaret played over loudspeakers in most Muslim countries, where the chant of the muezzin himself is but a fading memory of grandparents. The Koran itself reminds us of how easy Muhammad wanted this Sabbath meeting to be for busy Muslims. Rather than a day of rest for God and the faithful, as the Sabbath is for Jews and Christians—why would God need to rest?—the Muslim Sabbath is simply a work break for those devout who pray five times daily in any event. Afterward, God said, return to work:

> O ye who believe!
> When the call is proclaimed
> To prayer on Friday
> (The Day of Assembly),
> Hasten earnestly to the Remembrance
> Of God, and leave off
> Business (and traffic):
> That is best for you
> If ye but knew!
>
> And when the Prayer is finished, then may ye
> Disperse through the land,
> And seek the Bounty
> Of God: and celebrate

The Praises of God
Often (and without stint):
That ye may prosper.

(62:9–10)

Like weekly Christian and Jewish services, the Friday meeting includes news and guidance affecting the religious community, conducted by the community's leader, the imam. Its use as a political platform by some imams has been a controversy in the United States and Britain, especially after the World Trade Center attacks, which forced them to tone down their anti-American rhetoric. A larger meeting for the surrounding area is held at least twice a year.

Almsgiving

Charity is not merely encouraged for Muslims but a religious obligation and mark of devotion to God, intended to help the poor, purify oneself, and provide a means to salvation.

Fasting

During the entire month of Ramadan, Muslims refrain from eating, drinking, and sexual intercourse from daybreak to sunset. It is a reminder of Lenten fasting but much more widely practiced among Muslims and rather more difficult, emphasizing Islam's tenet of self-control.

The hajj, or pilgrimage to Mecca in Saudi Arabia

It has been called "the zenith of a Muslim's life." Those who are physically and financially able to should make the hajj at least once before they die, and it is a truly once-in-a-lifetime experience, an extraordinary display of equality and brotherhood. In a spirit of total self-abnegation before God, the men all wear the equalizing *ihram,* two seamless white sheets; the women may wear any dress they choose, but on this one religious occasion they do not wear a veil. For many, there is the joy of belonging to a worldwide *ummah.*

When during his own hajj the African American Muslim leader Malcolm X slept under an open sky one night along with other Muslims, as he later told Alex Haley, "I learned that pilgrims from every land—every color, and class, and rank; high officials and the beggar alike—all snored in the same language." Muhammad captured that spirit in one oration quoted in the early literature: "There is no superiority for an Arab over a non-Arab and for a non-Arab over an Arab; nor for a red-coloured over a black-coloured and for a black-skinned over a red-skinned except in piety. Verily, the noblest among you is he who is the most pious."[3]

All are equal before God as they perform the rituals of the hajj, including walking seven times around the Kaaba, running seven times from Mecca to Marwa to recall Hagar's search for water, standing half a day to pray on the plain of Arafat, stoning three pillars that symbolize Satan's temptations, and sacrificing an animal in memory of Abraham.

Some Muslims consider jihad to be a sixth pillar. It means "struggle," or "holy war," in the context of the Koran's commands to fight against infidels, or "disbelievers," not the People of the Book—the Jews and Christians. Many Muslims believe that Islam is in a state of permanent jihad aimed at converting the entire world, but not necessarily by force. This is the meaning of jihad as enshrined in the crossed-swords insignia of the Kingdom of Saudi Arabia. The notion of "jihad" was not particularly controversial until recent years and the rise of the Saudi-born terrorist Osama bin Laden, who, with no authority to do so, declared a jihad on the United States.

Of course, Muslim leaders in various countries have gone to war in numerous limited jihads through the centuries, and the rallying cry "Jihad!" has also been bandied about almost casually during crises and war by those looking for a holy fight. During the Lebanese civil war starting in the mid-1970s, for example, one group or another might claim to be fighting a jihad, as it sometimes worked as a recruiting strategy, like a finger-pointing poster saying, "Allah Wants You!"

Overused, "Jihad!" was just as likely to be ignored. Who has the authority to declare a jihad? After the attacks on New York and Washington, Saudi officials said that only a government could declare a holy war, but in times of crisis, the real answer seems to be anyone who can get away with it, such as Bin Laden.

In fact, there has been a strong movement among mainstream Muslims in recent years to emphasize a different jihad, the individual's or community's duty to "strive in the way of the Lord," the peaceful but constant struggle to live virtuously, to do good, to avoid bad habits. Many say this was the original meaning of the concept in the Koran. "This is the grand jihad, in here," said the Saudi Embassy spokesman in Washington after that September 11, as he tapped his heart. Wrapped most of the way around the embassy building, however, were those decorative insignia of palm trees and crossed swords. Still more tellingly, the Saudi government's Koran translation, printed before the attacks, says in its notes that jihad is actually one of the pillars of Islam:

> "*Al-Jihad* (holy fighting) in Allah's Cause (with full force of numbers and weaponry) is given the utmost importance in Islam and is one of its pillars (on which it stands). By Jihad, Islam is established. Allah's Word is made superior. . . . By abandoning Jihad (may Allah protect us from that) Islam is destroyed and the Muslims fall into an inferior position; their honor is lost, their lands are stolen, their rule and authority vanish. Jihad is an obligatory duty in Islam on every Muslim." [4]

Capturing Mecca

By 630, it was time for Muhammad to seize Mecca. He did it without a fight. At the head of a thousand followers, the Prophet entered the city in triumph in late January, strode into the Kaaba, and declared, "Truth hath come!" By one account he smashed to pieces the shrine's 360 idols; by another, he touched them with his lance, and they fell to the ground. He ordered pictures of the prophets on the walls erased with water from the Zamzam well, except for one of Jesus (a prophet of Islam, after all) and one of Mary ("above the women of all nations"). Christians might be reminded here of Jesus casting the merchants out of the temple in Jerusalem, or the people greeting his arrival in the city by strewing palm fronds on the streets.

Muhammad treated the prostrate pagans with kindness and forgiveness, even sparing the life of his fierce wartime enemy, Abu Sufyan. He issued a startling, revolutionary proclamation, centuries ahead of the Western Enlightenment: "Every claim of privilege or blood or property is abolished by me except the custody of the temple and the watering of the pilgrims." [5] It was likely during this Meccan visit that Muhammad declared the Kaaba forbidden territory to the polytheistic pagans, a ban later applied to all non-Muslims. A U.S. president might visit with the pope in the Vatican, but if he goes to Saudi Arabia, even if he is very close by in Jedda, as President Nixon was, the most powerful man in the world will not enter the holiest city in Islam—until the day the American president is a Muslim.

By one estimate, in a millennia and a half no more than fifteen "Christian-born Europeans" have succeeded in seeing the two holy cities of Mecca and Medina and getting out alive. Given those percentages, it might be interesting to meet one of them: Sir Richard Burton, the rollicking mid-nineteenth-century Orientalist who among countless other exploits "discovered" Lake Tanganyika (with John Hanning Speke) and translated the *Arabian Nights*. Sailing the Mediterranean on his way to Mecca, the cheeky thirty year old stopped in Alexandria to adopt certain measures "to appear suddenly as an Eastern upon the stage of Oriental life." He shaved his head and grew a beard, and as he plunged into a crowd, he mumbled, *"Alhamdolillah!"* his approximation of "Praise be to Allah, Lord of the (three) worlds," at which the spectators whispered "Muslim!" A little boy stared at him and said, *"Bakshish!"*—a tip that Arabs demanded, as Burton explained, not only for services they rendered to you but for services you rendered to them. Burton earned the crowd's immediate respect, not by giving the child money as some American tourist might do, but by replying, *"Mafish,"* or "'there is none,' equivalent to 'I have left my purse at home.' "[6]

Young Burton decided to pose as a wandering Persian dervish, one of the Muslim sects known for such devotional exercises as whirling dances leading to trances (they came out of hiding in Afghanistan after the defeat of the Taliban). "No character in the Moslem world is so proper for disguise as that of the Darwaysh," he wrote. "The Darwaysh is allowed to ignore ceremony and politeness, as one who ceases to appear upon the stage of life; he may pray or not, marry or remain single as he pleases . . . and no one asks him—the chartered vagabond—Why he comes here? Or Wherefore he comes there? . . . Moreover, the more haughty and offensive he is to the people, the more they respect him, a decided advantage to the traveler of choleric temperature"—a tactic that stood the British well that entire century. In this guise, he obtained a passport as a thirty-year-old Indo-British subject named Abdullah, crossed over to Arabia, and attained access to the holy cities by changing into white clothes, "which the Apostle loved," and riding a donkey. At which aspect some Bedouin bystanders, at the gate of Muhammad's own mosque in Medina, wondered, as Burton recalled it: "By what curse of Allah had they been subjected to ass-riders?"[7]

Back in the seventh century, from his base at Medina, Muhammad now extended his control farther into the desert, winning the allegiance of tribes and often converting them in the so-called nationalization, or Arabization, of Islam. This process reached its height in "the year of delegations," 630–631, during which more pagan tribes, seeing the future, bought into Islam by submitting to a tax—and "God's Will." Some supposedly came from as far as the Oman

region in the far southeast and Yemen in the south. By now, Islam was the law of
the peninsula and Muhammad its chief of state and commander in chief. A measure of his strength at this time was the expedition he personally led in mid-631 to
Tabuk, 350 miles north-by-northwest of Medina. It was in the southern Palestinian region of Syria, the farthest north he ever took his army. His mission was to
confront the rumored threat of an invasion of Arabia by the Byzantine Christians.
It never came off, but a force of thirty thousand fighters had rallied to Muhammad's banner.

In early 632, the Prophet returned to Mecca for his last pilgrimage and made
what many Muslim scholars consider his most important speech, in which he declared: "Know ye that every Muslim is a brother unto every other Muslim, and
that ye are now one brotherhood." In this valedictory at age sixty-two, Muhammad reiterated that brothers should not fight brothers:

> The Believers are but
> A single Brotherhood:
> So make peace and
> Reconciliation between your
> Two (contending) brothers.
> (49:10)

"The enforcement of Muslim Brotherhood is the greatest social idea of Islam,"
says Yusuf Ali. "And Islam cannot be completely realized until this ideal is
achieved."

Ironically, the militant movement that was founded in the 1920s and took its
name from Muhammad's great speech, the Muslim Brotherhood, has devoted itself to fighting other Muslims, the ones in power, across North Africa. Indeed, the
Prophet's great tenet of brotherhood has frequently been violated by modern
Muslims, in the Iranian Revolution, the Iran-Iraq War, the Persian Gulf War between Iraq and American-backed Kuwait, and the Afghanistan war between the
Taliban and the U.S.-backed Northern Alliance.

One of the wonders of Islam is the ability of Muslims in the Middle East to
blame these embarrassing fights entirely on somebody else, this era's chief
scapegoat being the United States. Princeton historian Bernard Lewis pointed
out that when Muslim dissidents actually seized the Kaaba in Mecca in 1979,

touching off a bloody gun battle, a Pakistani Muslim mob reacted by burning the American Embassy in Islamabad, the Pakistani capital. When Iraq moved against Kuwait in 1990, Osama bin Laden ignored that issue and instead attacked the stationing of the U.S. troops in Saudi Arabia.

Muslim brothers may fight brothers, but third parties should watch out.

Racetrack & Sultan Ahmet Mosque, Istanbul, by Thomas Allom.
Courtesy of the author.

7

One Worldwide Religion?

Islam, this vast band of brothers, does seek to convert the world, or, in the case of the terrorists, conquer it. Christians have had similar goals, and still do. "Driven in part by the rise of Islamic fundamentalism," the *Wall Street Journal* reported recently, "a host of Christian churches and missionary groups are engaged in a world-wide campaign to convert Muslims. . . . Religious publishing houses have produced a vast library of how-to books on recruiting Muslims." One of these books is called the *True Furgan*, after the Koran chapter *Furqan* (Criterion) for distinguishing right from wrong. The Christian volume labels its own chapters "suras" and mimics the Koran's sentence structure.[1]

Islam's desire to triumph throughout the world is expressed in three key Koranic verses that are ignored in most of the current analysis of Islam. One Muslim scholar has said two of the verses were prompted by Muhammad's quarrel with the Christians; the Saudis say the first occasion involved both Christians and Jews. In any event, the wording in all three verses is virtually the same. The Saudi translation begins with the charge that the "disbelievers," and the Jews, and the Christians, all "want to extinguish Allah's Light" and concludes with this most important verse in one of the war suras whose mention is so politically incorrect on our campuses: "It is He Who has sent His Messenger (Muhammad) with guidance and the religion of truth (Islam), to make it superior over all religions" (9:33).

Translators do not disagree on this verse, which is repeated as 61:9 and 48:28. Yusuf Ali makes it "to proclaim it over all religion," noting that "Islam will outshine all else," and elsewhere speaks of "the divine disposition of events in the coming of Islam." In the repeated 61:9 verse, the Saudis render it "to make it victorious over all (other) religions," and in a footnote, they offer this vision of

how part of Islam's world triumph will come about: "Isa (Jesus), the son of
Maryam (Mary) will descend as a leader of the Muslims and it is a severe warning
to the Christians who claim to be followers of Isa (Jesus) and he will break the
Cross and kill the pigs, and he will abolish the *Jizyah* (tax); and all mankind will
be required to embrace Islam with no other alternative." [2]

The Koran translator Maulana Muhammad Ali makes the verse read "to prevail over all religions" and calls it "the prophecy of the ultimate triumph of Islam
in the whole world." Then he points out that under Muhammad, Islam had already begun its march to convert the world. "In Arabia itself, Islam became triumphant in the lifetime of the Holy Prophet. Idolatry was wiped out from the face
of the country, while many of the Jews and Christians accepted the Religion of
Truth." And, as indeed we shall see in chapter 8, "The Prophet's death, instead
of putting any check to the advance of Islam was a signal for an unparalleled advance of his religion." [3]

When the Saudi-born Osama bin Laden claimed credit in a videotape for the
attacks on Washington and New York, he used a different source to confirm
Islam's future world triumph. He cited a hadith, a saying of Muhammad as
quoted by the son of his friend Umar, the future caliph: "I was ordered to fight the
people until they say there is no god but Allah." The actual hadith went on to
reaffirm that Muhammad was God's Messenger and that the conquered people
would have to perform Muslim prayers and pay the poor tax. Muhammad did apparently say something rather like this in that speech during his last pilgrimage;
it appears in the Koran as 2:193. But the Koranic reference is to a fight with the
pagans, not with everybody, and apparently refers to a specific, limited defensive
war. Moreover, whereas the Saudi translation version says "fight them until there
is no more *fitnah* (disbelief and worshiping of others along with Allah) and (all
and every kind of) worship is for Allah (Alone)," the Washington Islamic Center's
translation is much milder:

> And fight them on
> Until there is no more
> Tumult or oppression,
> And there prevail
> Justice and faith in God.

Many Muslims today would agree that this Koranic verse about a group of pagans
in Muhammad's day does not foresee any worldwide conversion by force, but the
terrorists who substitute Americans for the pagans, or infidels, are dangerous
dissenters.

How did Muhammad live? "In one of those clay houses," wrote Philip Hitti, "consisting, as do all old-fashioned houses of present-day Arabia and Syria, of a few rooms opening into a courtyard and accessible only from it. He was often seen mending his own clothes and was at all times within the reach of his people." Ever since, countless Muslims around the world have tried to live in the same modest way, in contrast to the "good life" chased, or feverishly dreamed of, in the West and, for that matter, the East. Muhammad's private conduct "has had as long-lasting effect as his public acts," thought the British writer D. G. Hogarth. "Serious or trivial, his daily behaviour has instituted a canon which millions observe at this day with conspicuous mimicry." [4]

Hogarth's *Arabia* appeared in 1922, but the millions have only multiplied. More recently, there was S——, night manager of the CBS News Bureau in Lebanon.[5] Whenever I stopped by late to check on something for the nightly television broadcast, which went on at one-thirty in the morning Beirut time, or when my crew and I returned from shelling in the South, or an Israeli air raid—whatever the event apparently so crucial to millions of Americans, there would be good old S——, unmoved, fixing his supper, darning his socks, or in his bedclothes preparing his cot. He understood the news better than anyone there, had lived through it all, but said little. One is reminded of Bernard Lewis's remark that "there is something in the religious culture of Islam which inspired . . . a dignity and a courtesy toward others never exceeded and rarely equaled in other civilizations."[6] The night manager was like that, noble, exquisitely courteous, yet simplicity itself, sustained by Muhammad's way, a good Muslim.

Close imitation of a spiritual leader was not an Islamic innovation. Four centuries earlier, the Christian monks had begun taking to great lengths the duty to imitate Christ, forsaking everything—family, ambitions, possessions—to follow him, "a powerful testimony to the faith" that actually, as Harry Crocker writes, "would play an enormous role in saving civilization after the fall of Rome." Still, these were monks, not ordinary Christians, imitating Christ. "The conduct of the Founder of Christianity," Hogarth observed, "has not so governed the ordinary life of his followers" as Muhammad has. The reason, however, is fairly obvious. Muhammad was not considered divine but a historic human being who lived and died, whose earthy biography unreels in colorful detail in the Koran, the hadiths, and the early literature. It is a less daunting challenge for Muslims to try to live like the man Muhammad in his everyday, nonspiritual life—mending his clothes, helping Aisha—than for Christians to imitate one they worship as the Son of God.

Moreover, if it is true, as Hogarth writes, that as a spiritual leader "no

Founder of a religion has been left on so solitary an eminence as the Muslim Apostle," he is not really alone in Muslim memories. Many love to recall the countless anecdotes and intrigues in the lives of Muhammad, his friends, his wives, and the early caliphs who built the Islamic empire. It is grand opera, sometimes soap opera, but it also reminds us that many Muslims, largely through their religious education, have an extraordinary awareness of history.

One might find nothing to argue about in Hogarth's conclusion about Muhammad—"No one regarded by any section of the human race as Perfect Man has been imitated so minutely"—except its implications. Could this be one reason so many fundamentalist Muslim societies, culturally, politically, and economically, are so frozen in their grand opera? Hogarth thought that the mass urge to copy Muhammad's everyday conduct has had such a long-lasting impact "chiefly because of the static tendency of Arabian society," but does it not also contribute to the stasis? Nowhere has this backwardness been more evident than among the Arab terrorist leaders, who even as they seek Western technology as a weapon yearn for the "the glory of religion" in the earliest days of Islam. It seems unlikely that much of that yearning went on in Islam's later halcyon days, when it led the world in the arts and sciences, with great contributions coming from non-Arabs as well as Arabs. Extreme Arab fundamentalists and terrorists like Bin Laden and his cohorts have shown themselves publicly to be much less attracted to that extraordinary progressive period. Indeed, for all their concentration on him, the extremists have almost nothing in common with Muhammad, who, to judge from everything we know about him as a creative, flexible, forward-looking leader, would have condemned the terrorists, just as he would have reveled in the intellectual ferment of Islam's golden age.

What Would Muhammad Do Today?

One day in A.H. 11—historians make it June 8, 632, C.E.—Muhammad complained of a bad headache. He died soon afterward, twenty-two years after taking up his calling as the Prophet. He was buried as simply as could be, under the floor of Aisha's home. He left no sons; three years earlier Muhammad had deeply mourned the death in infancy of Ibrahim, the son given to him by Mary, the Christian Copt. His only surviving child was his daughter by Khadija, Fatima, who had married Ali. The Prophet's wives had been ordered not to remarry after his death, and did not.

What was Muhammad's legacy? It was incalculable. Through eight years of

warfare and diplomacy he had created a unified state in western Arabia. He had
founded a new religion, a forward-looking monotheistic faith that would become a
meaningful way of life for the world's Muslims throughout his own millennium, the
next, and now into a third. Its rock would be the Koran—recording "in language of
great force and beauty," to repeat Albert Hourani, "the incursion of a transcendent
God, source of all power and goodness, into the human world He has created."

The Koran's 114 suras, or chapters, contain more than 6,239 verses in the
Washington edition (the enumeration varies slightly in some editions). Inconve-
niently for historians, the suras are not presented chronologically, in the order in
which Muhammad reported the revelations. Instead, by his own command, they
are organized by length, the beginning chapters being the longest, except for a
brief introductory sura, and the final chapters running to only a few verses each
(six in the final one).

In fact, the suras are presented in roughly reverse chronological order. For
the most part, the longer ones that open the Koran give us the revelations that
Muhammad experienced after he left Mecca to establish the first Muslim community in Medina. They are necessarily long because they spell out religious
doctrine and duties, including prayer, fasting, and pilgrimage, and the first Islamic laws. Among the laws are the prohibitions on wine, pork, and gambling,
and ordinances relating to war and holy war, slavery ("the freeing of slaves" as
Hitti noted, "is encouraged as something most pleasing to God and an expiation
for many a sin"), crime, inheritance, marriage, divorce, and adultery. All of these
doctrines, duties, and laws, Muslims believe, were handed down by God.

The thirty-four "Medinese suras" not only are presented first in the Koran
but are the foundation of Islamic law to this day. That Muhammad wanted to introduce the book with them reveals his determination that Islam should thrive as
a strong, ever expanding community. His relegating to "the back of the book" the
sharper, impassioned early revelations experienced during his first twelve years
in Mecca shows he had no doubts about the enduring power of his Message for individual men and women. Scholars disagree on whether Muhammad himself
began writing out the Koran, indeed over whether he could write at all. Orthodox
Muslims insist he could not. They point to a verse that refers to him as "the *ummi*
[illiterate] prophet" to counter arguments that the Koran is not the literal Word of
God, or that God's Word might have been altered in Muhammad's writing it down.
On the other hand, some modern scholars have argued that as an active trader
Muhammad could probably read and write, and that "*ummi*" here means a mem-
ber of a community without a book or scripture.

Although scholars do not agree on the precise date of the Koran, they do generally agree that the recording of the revelations, whether initiated by Muhammad or his followers, was completed in book form within twenty-five years of his death, or by about 657. That makes the Koran more contemporary with the people and events it describes than is the Bible, indeed far more in the case of the Old Testament, whose accounts of events dating back to about 1800 B.C.E. were written over the course of a millennium, from about 1000 B.C.E. to shortly before the birth of Christ. The New Testament was put in writing starting fifty to sixty years after Christ's death and completed in the later years of that first century C.E.

So the Koran was a book entirely of its own time even more than the Bible was. It began reporting God's interventions on earth even as they happened. And today it is more alive than ever, its gigantic daily readership probably exceeding the Bible's because part of it is recited during prayer five times daily—and almost everywhere in the same language. Unlike various translations of the Bible—from the Old Testament's original Hebrew and Aramaic and the New Testament's Greek—translations of the Arabic Koran are not accepted as official, as the Word of God. After all, God spoke to Muhammad, albeit through an angel, in Arabic.

Because the Arabic version has always been the only true Koran, and in part because of the magnificence of its poetry, for which Muslims also give God the credit, the book went untranslated in any language for centuries. At long last, in the midst of the Christian panic called the Crusades, Peter, the abbot of Cluny in France, converted it into Latin in an effort to discredit it. Alexander Ross, the vicar of Carisbrooke, made the first English translation, from the French, in 1649. It was snidely titled *The Alcoran [Al Koran] of Mohamet . . . Newly Englished, for the Satisfaction of All That Desire to Look into the Turkish Vanities.* Such attacks could hardly have troubled Muslims, because only the Arabic version was the God-given Koran; indeed, many considered it "untranslatable," as the English historian Francis Robinson observes in his *Atlas of the Islamic World.* "Muslims still feel so today. Thus many came to affirm their faith in a language they did not understand: there was just the ineffable power of giving voice to the very words of God." [7]

It is true millions of Muslims around the world recite from the Arabic Koran during prayer without understanding the words, though they do have the assistance of translations into some forty languages. Even many Arabs do not understand the book's ancient, classical Arabic. As Muslims often point out, the majority of Roman Catholics never understood the Latin of the mass, either. But that was then: the Latin mass is almost extinct; the true Koran still lives only in

Arabic. How important is it for non-Arabic speakers to have a command of the language, which few do? Not very, obviously. Although many fundamentalists argue that knowing Arabic is essential, a great many Muslims find it is not, just as Catholics never have had to know Latin nor Jews the Hebrew of the Torah to consider themselves faithful.

As we consider now what terrorists have done in Islam's name, we might well ask: What indeed would Muhammad have done? He would have condemned the terrorists immediately, unlike the millions of frightened proterrorist Muslim demonstrators of recent years, who seek to emulate the Prophet but not his courage. In his wars against the pagans, Muhammad himself never resorted to what we now call terrorism. Fanatics still living in the seventh century might hold up the Koranic advice that warriors make ready "to strike terror" into the hearts of their enemies and those

> others besides, whom
> Ye may not know, but whom
> God does know.   (8:60)

But nowhere do we find Muhammad conducting terrorist attacks in response to that and other Koranic commands, such as "fight and slay / The Pagans wherever ye find them" (9:5). Which proves what is merely common sense to most Muslims: it was merely seventh-century battlefield advice. Yet when Osama bin Laden plagiarized the latter verse, giving it a broader reading—Kill the Americans wherever you find them—and when terrorists agents did kill Americans in the attacks on New York and Washington, many thousands of approving Muslims rallied in the streets in some countries.

Muhammad the American

When Muhammad captured pagan Mecca, we did not find him perpetrating the horrors of the future reigns of terror after the French (the word *terror* in this political sense dates to 1795), Russian, Iranian, and Taliban revolutions. Nor, as he fought for the faith, did he engage in anything like classic modern terror as defined by *Webster's*—"violence (as bombing) committed by groups in order to intimidate a population or government into granting their demands"—and as practiced by Bin Laden's Al Qaeda network. Nor, as we have seen, is there any support in Muhammad's book for Bin Laden's war to make all testify that there is no god but Allah. Muhammad was an experienced, up-front general—unlike Bin

Laden, who specialized in torture, sneak attacks on defenseless innocents, and blind "martyr operations" for deeply troubled young Arabs. Had the Prophet wished, he could have attempted what we now call terrorism, attacking random populations, but he never came close to it. He was rarely in hiding, except on the few occasions when he had no choice; he was not even a loner.

In fact, as a civilian in Mecca, he was a respected businessman beloved by his family and friends; a helpful personal counselor; a man centuries ahead of his time on the rights of women, whom he liked, admired, and honored; a tolerant leader who honored the other great faiths. In Medina, he became a statesman and diplomat, an innovative general, a tough Arab chieftain who could have perhaps stopped the massacre of Jewish men after the Battle of the Confederates but a diplomat and negotiator with other Jewish communities. All things considered, if Muhammad were alive today, he might well be an American.

As for what he would, rather than would not, have done, the record of his life and book is clear. Just as he did in the heat of persecution, embattled leadership, and war, he would have stood up today for his principles; debated and negotiated with his rivals; tolerated their ideas until he could win them over; taken care of his family, friends, followers, and community; and fought in the open.

But the question now becomes: After Muhammad, what would Islam do? The religion, after all, is more than Muhammad and the book; the early written code that is its religious, legal, and civil foundation includes two other guides as well: the hadiths (traditions) and the *sharia* (Islamic law). The terrorists claim to abide not only by the Koran but also by the hadiths, the sayings and actions of the Prophet that were not in the Koran but were recounted by his surviving relatives and friends, sometimes by their descendants. Fundamentalists, and for that matter many other Muslims, believe that everything Muhammad said or did was divinely inspired, whether recorded in the Koran or not, so they accept the hadiths as God's Word as well.

Written down or memorized by specialists called "people of the hadith," and gathered from across the Islamic empire over two and a half centuries, the hadiths became a mammoth and highly suspect mass of some two hundred thousand. Before the tenth century, however, they were researched by scholars operating independently and culled to shorter, more convincing collections, most famously that of al-Bukhari, which totals fewer than twenty-eight hundred. A scholar named Muslim was also a highly regarded compiler.

Because the hadiths are said to quote the Prophet himself, only the Koran itself is more revered, even among moderate Muslims. The sayings provide additional guidelines to everyday behavior, which the vast majority of Muslims adapt to twenty-first-century circumstances, as most Christians and Jews do in interpreting the Old and New Testaments. Extremists, however, take this seventh-century advice as literally as they do the Koran and find it a lot more supportive, largely because they can pick the hadiths that they like among the thousands that survive. Bin Laden did just this in the videotape made just before his Kandahar stronghold was taken over by the Afghans and their American allies.

Like the Koran, the hadiths offer counsel on how to live a faithful, righteous life. In view of recent events, however, it might be helpful to cite a few of the hadiths concerning jihad, not in its sense of personal struggle in the right path of Allah but in its equally Islamic sense of holy war. The examples quoted here are from two small compilations sold at the Washington Islamic Center, where President Bush could have picked them up if he had dropped by its bookstore during his visit after the attacks. The first, drawn from al-Bukhari and another compiler of the hadiths, was used by Bin Laden in his last tape from Kandahar, as he faced defeat: "On the authority of the son of Umar [the second caliph], the Prophet said: 'I have been ordered to fight against people until they testify that there is no god but Allah and that Muhammad is the Messenger of Allah.' " To terrorists, that sounded like a fight to convert the world. But the Koran itself famously advocates conversion only by conviction, not conquest—"Let there be no compulsion / In religion" (2:256).

Still another hadith quotes Muhammad as saying, "Islam is a dominant force and is not to be dominated." Of course, one would have no trouble detecting such muscle flexing in other ancient scripture, notably the Old and New Testaments.

Another example is a jihad-related hadith that might be popular among the young Saudis who went to Afghanistan: "I love to be killed in the way of Allah, then to be revived to life again, then to be killed and then to be revived to life and then to be killed and then to be revived to life and then to be killed." That this is taken out of the context of a seventh-century war rarely matters to extremists.

◆ ◆ ◆

Islamic law is called the *sharia*, which originally meant "the path leading to the water," or the source. Developed over the three centuries following Muhammad's death, it is a code of religious, civil, and social rules based on the Koran and the hadiths; Muslim scholars thus consider it divine, God's last Word to man. When legal questions come up, the *sharia* is interpreted by the *ulama*, a group of religious scholars in each country, but they have little room to maneuver, which is not something they want to do anyway. The code is frozen in time, specifically the eleventh century, when it was completed. Any effort to change a *sharia* text is considered a *bida,* or "act of innovation, which is as near as Islam came to the Christian idea of heresy," to quote Francis Robinson, the University of London historian. This leads to an even more important contrast between the West, where "law has grown out of and been molded by society," as Robinson writes, and Islamic states, where law—eleventh-century law—"precedes and molds society."[8]

For the most part, the terrorists and their supporters, however, are actually not trying to live in the eleventh century of the completed *sharia,* which they find too advanced; they are seventh-century men, partisans of the Prophet, they think, and his friends. But they do try to get their hands on the apparatus of the later *sharia* as a weapon, which is possible if they control the country or have great influence in the mosques. For example, the support of the *ulama* can be useful. In Afghanistan, the Taliban presented its decision not to expel Bin Laden to a council of *ulama,* who upheld it. Individually or collectively, the *ulama* can also issue fatwas (legal decisions), and not just on routine questions of law but on great controversies, such as the Ayatollah Khomeini's 1989 fatwa calling on Muslims everywhere to try to kill the British author Salman Rushdie, and his publishers as well, for alleged blasphemy in his novel *The Satanic Verses.*

The Rushdie case will be taken up in chapter 10, but it should be noted here that Khomeini's fatwa, which presumably he issued in his dual role as imam of Iran and one of its *ulama,* was controversial within Islam. Some questioned its presumption in commanding all Muslims, Saudi Arabia's *ulama* actually rejected it, and many Iranian intellectuals were secretly embarrassed by it. A month after it was issued, it was condemned as un-Islamic by all but one of forty-nine member states of the Islamic Conference. But there it was, however isolated: an open invitation to kill, allegedly based on religious law, from the leader of the Islamic Republic of Iran. Bernard Lewis, having written of Islam's great tradition of individual dignity and courtesy, continues: "And yet, in moments of upheaval and disruption, when the deeper passions are stirred, this dignity and courtesy toward others can give way to an explosive rage and hatred which impels even the government of an ancient and civilized country—even the spokesman of a great spiritual and ethical religion—to espouse kidnapping and assassination, and try to find, in the life of their Prophet, approval and indeed precedent for such actions."[9]

This point returns us to one of the Koran's war suras:

>   . . . fight and slay
>   The Pagans wherever ye find them,
>   And seize them. . . .

The violent extremists pluck this command from its battlefield context, and for pagans they substitute modern secular enemies. It was not until 1998 that a moderate Iranian government dissociated itself from the Salman Rushdie fatwa, which is not to say that some individual terrorist is not still out there, thinking he is planning God's work. In fact, extremists have found a way to keep the Rushdie fatwa operational today. In the meantime, the fatwa had set a precedent for Bin Laden's later order to Muslims to kill Americans everywhere, never mind that he had no religious authority to issue it. Here is another example of how the terrorists and their supporters are using this tool of Islamic law. In Bin Laden's last Kandahar tape, an unidentified Arab sheikh speaks of another Saudi sheikh's issuing a fatwa played on a religious radio station: "He said this was jihad, and those people [the World Trade Center and Pentagon victims] were not innocent people."

These fatwas are an extreme exception to the quiet routine of the *ulama* as they interpret the *sharia* in all fields, and oversee the administration of the *madrasas*, or religious schools, at all levels. Of these schools, the most important of all is Al-Azhar in Cairo, founded in 972; the oldest university in the world, it has been prominent in today's Islamic revival.

But how has Islam come to this at the opening of the twenty-first century C.E.—to rigid, joyless societies; violent "brotherhoods"; discontented masses in the Middle East and central and Southeast Asia; and the murderous false religion of the terrorists? Once that question is addressed in the following pages, we can take on the increasingly urgent ones posed by Muslims and non-Muslims alike. Where do Muslims stand today on global expansion? Is there really a "clash of civilizations"? How do Muslims feel about the future of religious government? About the West's most sacred values, such as separation of church and state? Democracy? Freedom of speech? Women's rights? Many Americans are too young to remember that during an American presidential election more than four decades ago some of these same questions were being asked—about the Vatican. Are they valid questions today?

To answer them, we need to review the twelve hundred-year process that has brought us today's Islam, beginning with one of the most startling series of conquests in history.

Mountain Pass, Bulgaria, by Thomas Allom. *Courtesy of the author.*

8

Conquering Half the World

Within a century of Muhammad's death his followers would rule the greatest territorial empire yet, broader than the realms of the Greeks, Romans, Persians, and Byzantine Christians. It reached from the Atlantic shores to central Asia and in a few brief years would slice into the frontier lands of China itself. Amazingly little of this is known in the West, where the teaching of history hopscotches over it, merrily jumping from the Romans to the medieval Europeans, except in America, where history is hardly taught at all. Of course, this is due to the old truth that the winner gets to rewrite the record, editing out what he does not like. Until recently, Westerners have certainly not liked the embarrassing story of their ancient comeuppance, intellectual and military, by a once unstoppable religion from the East. When they were forced to think about it, it scared the bejesus out of them. Now, startled by the apparition of Islam rising, they might want to review what it was that their teachers skipped over so quickly—what it was that Muhammad's men and women achieved in a hundred years.

On the Prophet's death an argument broke out over the succession. A group to be known as the *shiatu ali,* or Party of Ali (later, Shiites), thought that Muhammad should be succeeded by a dynasty of his blood relatives. Cousin Ali should be the first leader, to be followed by the descendants of Ali and his wife, Fatima, the Prophet's own daughter. It would not be long before Ali's partisans would be fighting Islam's first and second civil wars, but they lost this first political contest to a larger group who much later would be called Sunnis. They believed Islam should be based closely on the sunna, or customs and practices of the Prophet. It should be led by the one that the majority of the community's leaders considered most likely to follow in the Prophet's perfect way. So there would be no dynasty, at least not yet.

The new chief of state was called the caliph (*khalifah*), or "representative" of Muhammad. His most important role was military, as commander of the faithful, but he was also the imam, or religious leader of the community. He was not, however, Muhammad's spiritual successor, as once widely believed, because the Prophet could have no successors: he was God's last Messenger, "the seal" of the apostles. To this day the Sunni majority have revered the first four caliphs—all members of the Companions, Muhammad's close friends and advisers—as the "Rightly Guided Ones," the *rashidun*. Their conquests began almost immediately.

Consider how swift the sword of the *rashidun*. The first was the wealthy Abu Bakr, Muhammad's father-in-law and right-hand man ever since those last threatening Meccan days ("We are only two." "No, God is with us."). Now, in two quick years, 632 to 634, he squelched the tribal revolts that erupted after the Prophet's death and brought virtually the whole peninsula under Muslim rule. But further revolt and dissension lay ahead, to put it mildly: Abu Bakr would be the only Rightly Guided Caliph not to be murdered.

Next came the tall, powerful Umar ibn al-Khattab, who was also the Prophet's father-in-law (father of Hafsah) and the first great Islamic conqueror. In one decade his armies pushed north, west, and far to the east. They crushed the Persians, extending Muslim control all the way from Mesopotamia into what today are western Pakistan and Afghanistan. Did the Muslim fighters see the two huge Buddhas at Bamiyan, carved into a cliff of the Hindu Kush mountain range? One towered 114 feet, the other 165 feet. The statues' Greek robes were a reminder of Alexander's subjugation of Afghanistan three hundred years before Christ; the figures themselves recalled the later Kushans, who converted to Buddhism. If any of the villagers or farmers could have told them, Umar's seventh-century conquerors would have been amazed at how old the statues were—one dating back two hundred years, the other four hundred years—far older, probably, than any man-made sculpture back on the Arabian peninsula. For the next thirteen centuries, even as the Buddhas' faces wore away, these two colossi would be venerated by pilgrims from India and China and in our time known and treasured by historians all over the world.

In the spring of 2000, using explosives, the Taliban government under Mullah Muhammad Omar destroyed them as insults to Islam. Was the mullah trying to imitate Muhammad smashing the idols in the Kaaba? Was he reverting to the first commandment of the first monotheism, "You shall not have other gods besides me. You shall not carve idols for yourselves in the shape of anything in the sky above or on the earth below or in the waters beneath the earth; you shall not bow down before them or worship them" (Exod. 20:3–5)? What message can be read in the strange, parallel fates of those towering double symbols of tolerance, the Buddhas of Bamiyan and the Twin Towers of New York City's World Trade Center?

Westward, across the Red Sea, Umar's fighters swept over Christian Egypt. They even snatched Alexandria, though far outnumbered by the fifty thousand-man garrison protecting this home port of the Byzantine navy. Hardly believing it himself, the Muslim commander sent word back to Umar in Medina: "I have captured a city the description of which I shall refrain from giving. Suffice it to say that I have seized 4,000 villas with 4,000 baths, 40,000 poll-tax paying Jews and four hundred places of entertainment for the royalty."[1]

For all that, the towering Umar sought to live like Muhammad. It was said he owned but one shirt and one cloak, both patched, and slept on a mattress of palm leaves. None of that temporal modesty could really rise above the symbolic, however, because he also happened to have a growing empire at his disposal. In the north, the fresh Muslim flame devoured Byzantine Syria, including Damascus, the destination of so many caravan trips by the orphan/merchant and his father. It was only eighteen years after Muhammad's miraculous ascent from Jerusalem on a white horse that his father-in-law's fighters, on no telling how many Arabian horses, reached that city. The Persians had returned it to the Christians as part of a truce. Umar himself accepted Jerusalem's surrender to its latest captors, striding into the rubble near the Wailing Wall, personally helping to clear the rubbish from the Temple Mount, and choosing a site for something entirely new there, a mosque.

Umar's assassination—a Persian Christian slave stabbed him with a poisoned dagger—hardly quenched the Muslims' thirst for empire under the third Rightly Guided Caliph, Uthman bin Affan, a son-in-law of Muhammad. The Muslims grabbed the eastern Mediterranean island of Cyprus and pushed west again, reaching beyond Egypt to annex half of today's Libya. In the midst of those heady moments, however, an unexpected issue surfaced: soldiers' rights and remuneration. Their "working conditions," which forced them into spartan garrisons far from their families, became an open political issue back in Medina.

Finally, a group of discontented soldiers from Egypt murdered Uthman in his home, and the mutineers proclaimed Ali caliph at last, the fourth of the Rightly Guided Ones. Another strong faction, however, recognized Muawiyyah, the Muslim governor of Syria, setting up Islam's first civil war.[2]

It opened with a bloody family affair. Ali, the Prophet's son-in-law, first found himself pitted against no other than Aisha, the Prophet's own widow. Certainly, Ali, who was then based in present-day Iraq, had the credentials to be fourth caliph: he had been the first male convert to Islam, lived in Muhammad's household in the early Meccan days, and was his first cousin, a blood tie that was more important than son-in-law. But he was also identified with the rebelling soldiers; worse, he refused to punish Uthman's assassins. This the stubborn Aisha just wasn't going to take, so she helped lead a rebellion against Ali—literally, riding with the rebels to a showdown near Basra in Iraq, where in grand style she watched the proceeding from a palanquin, an enclosed litter, on her camel, thereby giving it the memorable sobriquet "Battle of the Camel." As well seated as she was, though, the Prophet's widow could hardly have liked what she saw from her famous perch, as Ali's forces won easily, saving his caliphate—if only for a moment.

As Aisha returned to the relative quiet of retirement, the civil war raged on, and it really is hard to underestimate its significance. After all, for the first time the Muslim "brothers" were at full-scale war. The second caliph, Umar, had been murdered by a foreigner and a non-Muslim—a Persian Christian—but it was fellow Muslims who had assassinated Uthman, an unprecedented shock to the Muslim community. Ali now faced the man who wanted to unseat him and become caliph of that entire community, the politically savvy Muawiyyah, although the ostensible cause of the war was the latter's determination to avenge Uthman's murder. As the victim's closest blood relative, Muawiyyah had Arab and Muslim tradition on his side in seeking revenge, but just in case he forgot, Uthman's widow sent him her husband's bloodstained shirt.

In a way it was the Battle of Badr all over again because Muawiyyah was also the son of Abu Sufyan, Muhammad's one-time worst enemy. The two bands of "brothers" battled to a stalemate near the bend of the Euphrates in Iraq until Muawiyyah, one of the political geniuses of early Islam, made an unusual move. As his chances to vanquish Ali started to shrivel, he had his men fasten copies of the Koran on their lances, an invitation to decide on the caliph by third-party arbitration. Ali finally accepted this offer, to the fury and outrage of many of his supporters, who insisted that the Koran required rebels to be crushed:

> If two parties among
> The Believers fall into
> A quarrel, make ye peace
> Between them: but if
> One of them transgresses
> Beyond bounds against the other,
> Then fight ye (all) against
> The one that transgresses
> Until it complies. . . .   (49:9)

One day in 661, with the issue still unsettled after five years of war, stalemate, and arbitration, Ali made the serious mistake of going to the mosque in Kufa, his base in today's Iraq. There a Muslim extremist ran a poisoned saber though the last of the *rashidun*. Ali's followers immediately pushed for his son Hassan to take over, but Hassan declined and threw his support to Muawiyyah, who thus became the fifth caliph of Islam.

Islam on the Move

With the end of the first civil war came nothing less than a sea change that signaled Islam's imperial future, the creation of a vast empire. Islam's capital was moved from the holy but provincial city of Medina in Arabia to the great conquered Syrian capital of Damascus, where Muawiyyah established the first dynasty of caliphs, the Umayyads.

It is true the first male Muslim after Muhammad had not died in spirit. Ali's supporters still believed the Prophet should have been succeeded by his own family—an Alid dynasty, from Ali down through Hassan and Hussein, who were his sons by Fatima and thus the Prophet's own grandsons. Nor had those spiritual ancestors of the modern Shiites sheathed their swords. As a matter of fact, in 680, Hussein, his family, and his followers opened Islam's second civil war by marching out of Medina to battle the hated Umayyads, hoping to pick up support along the way and reclaim the caliphate. It was a disaster. Hussein's seventy-odd fighters were wiped out in a never-forgotten fight near a place called Karbala in Iraq. On the ninth day of the first Islamic month, Muharram, all of Hussein's family save his infant son, Ali, were massacred. On the tenth Hussein himself was killed. Ali, in his arms, was spared.

There would be fierce Shiite rebellions in coming centuries, but it was the massacre of the Prophet's surviving family and their friends that would never be forgotten, leaving the Shiites with a persecution complex and a sense of independence. Karbala and its ritual reenactment every year shed some light on Shiite Iran's monstrous war with Sunni Iraq from 1980 to 1988 and its dismissal, as mere "fanatics," of Bin Laden and his Arab terrorists in Afghanistan.

Sixty years after the Prophet's death, the Umayyads began constructing Islam's first great building—and made sure Christians and Jews noticed. It was the golden Dome of the Rock in Jerusalem, in the area known as the Temple Mount to Jews and as El-Haram esh-Sharif, the Noble Sanctuary, to Muslims. Its wooden cupola wrapped today in a gleaming gilt-aluminum covering, the shrine is dressed in glazed Kashani tiles and encircled by exquisitely chiseled Koranic verses. Although the enclosed rock is said to mark the spot of Abraham's proposed sacrifice of his son, it is the story of Muhammad's ascent from this place that makes Jerusalem the third-holiest city in Islam, after Mecca and Medina.

What few of today's Christian and Jewish visitors to the Dome realize is that its ostentation is calculated. It stands not far from the Christian Church of the Holy Sepulcher over the traditional site of the Crucifixion and Resurrection. Built in 335 at the order of the Byzantine emperor Constantine, the church had been destroyed by the Persians in 614 and rebuilt in 628, just a few years before the Muslims captured the city. According to one of his relatives, the caliph Abd al-Malik, "when he saw the immense and dominating dome of the Church of the Resurrection [Holy Sepulcher], feared that it would dominate the hearts of the Muslims, and he therefore erected the Dome which we see on the Rock." Of course, fear of exposure to other faiths was not new and is hardly dead. Present-day Saudi Arabia is a leader among conservative Muslim countries still protecting their faithful from exposure to Christianity. But even centuries before Islam, Moses counseled Jews at war to wipe out nearby hostile communities, "lest they teach you to make any such abominable offerings as they make to their gods" (Deut. 20:16).

On first encountering this splendid shrine many years ago, I discovered that it was about much more than keeping up with the Holy Sepulcher Joneses. Until then the relics and shrines of the Old City had seemed in harmony even if the people were not; the ancient contentions, the destruction of the temples, and the

Crucifixion had long since become subjects for peaceful study, not passion. Whatever problems there were had nothing to do with this wondrous outdoor museum that was the Temple Mount, with its soothing old art and architecture; the problems were caused by the politicians. But here that dream was interrupted by a voice from the seventh century. Amazingly, the voice was still out there, still fighting, declining to be a mere work of art, or maybe in the act of being a great one. The voice was the Dome's Koranic poetry, loudly commanding Christians, "Say: He is God, / The One and Only," and trying to wrench them from their belief in a Son of God: "He begetteth not, / Nor is He begotten" (112:1, 3).

This shout from the wall produced a funny initial reaction on my part. The voice was rude. What was this shrine doing, trying to start a fight—and at exactly the wrong time, when the human world was already fighting, trying to tear each other apart? Could it not see that the other relics, Jewish and Christian, had long ago fallen into peaceful silence? But then what was I doing, arguing with a building, with its Koranic inscriptions, as if, like any Muslim, I could be in direct communication with God? Of course, it is now clear that what the Dome of the Rock was doing—has been doing since it was built—was broadcasting a warning to its visitors, to the world. Watch out, it says:

> The religion before God
> Is Islam (submission to His Will)
> . . . .
> . . . if any deny the Signs of God,
> God is swift in calling to account.   (3:19)

The poetic voice of Islam's first great shrine, placed in the middle of Jerusalem, added up to nothing less than empire-building, or so thinks historian Bernard Lewis (who admittedly is controversial and seen by some of his critics as too conservative and even hostile to Islam). To Lewis the Koranic inscriptions conveyed this message (in Lewis's words): "Only religion can justify empire. Only empire can sustain religion. . . . God has given a new dispensation and a new order to the world. . . . The new dispensation had come to correct their [the Jews' and Christians'] errors and to supercede them." After the Dome of the Rock, Islam's next architectural masterpiece was the Umayyad Mosque, constructed between 705 and 715. Islam's fourth-holiest site, it is still such a living presence and occupies such a huge chunk of space in Damascus that to an American it almost has the bulk, the heft, of a football stadium or the like, rather than a thirteen-century-old house of God, but then for Muslims a mosque is very much a living presence and always will be.[3]

Islam Explodes

The Prophet had not been dead a century when the Damascus-based Umayyads exploded into far-off western Europe, frightening Christendom to its bones. Crossing the Strait of Gibraltar, their North African armies gave the cape at its far end the name Tarf al-Gharb, or "skirt of the West," Islam's most occidental limit yet. In English, the phrase *Tarf al-Gharb* would become *Trafalgar*, the limit of Napoléon's designs on England, thanks to Nelson's last stand in 1805. It was in 710 or 711 that this mixed bag of Arabs, Berbers, and later Syrians—to be known by the romantic but inaccurate catchwords *Moors* and *Saracens*— began their conquest of Spain by defeating the last of the Visigothic kings, who had implanted Roman culture and Christianity in the peninsula. The conquerors would call this country Al-Andalus, as in today's Andalusia, the former Muslim heartland.

In a mere nine years, Islam's fighting faithful captured most of Spain north to the Pyrenees and prepared to push into a panicking France. There, in a lopsided but historic contest, a small Muslim force was defeated by Charles Martel's Franks. It was this defeat in 732, a century after the Prophet's death, that effectively halted Islam's advance into western Europe. Seven years later, for good measure, the same Charles expelled the Muslims from the Rhone Valley, where they had reached Lyons. These defeats in France still left the Umayyads in charge of nearly all Spain for three centuries, and of the Kingdom of Grenada for four more, during which spectacular span their universities, and their medicine, mathematics, architecture, and literature, became the cultural lighthouses of barely civilized Christian Europe.

Islam seemed well on its way to its worldwide victory. By the centenary of Muhammad's passing, his followers' unprecedented territorial empire stretched from the Atlantic to today's Kazakhstan in the former Soviet Union and to the foothills of the Himalayas. Soon they would be knocking on the door of China. But some historians do not buy the notion that the Muslims had conquered all that territory merely by the faith of its fighters. Some of these scholars have cited a rapidly growing population, poverty, and hunger as among the factors that may have pushed the Arabs out of their homeland.

"Not fanaticism but economic necessity drove the Bedouin hordes (and most of the armies of conquest were recruited from the Bedouins) beyond the confines of their arid abode to the fair lands of the North," the Arab American historian Philip Hitti concluded. He quoted a ninth-century Syrian poet: "No, not for Paradise did thou the nomad life forsake; Rather, I believe, it was thy yearning after bread and dates." More recently, though, scholars have begun to dismiss the "demographic-pressure" argument for Muslim expansion. In any event, once they started advancing on other countries, the Arabs found them ripe for conquest. Among the conditions that invited them in, Hitti mentioned the exhaustion of countries long torn by the Byzantine-Persian wars, heavy taxes, schisms in the Christian church, and pockets of friendly Arab, Semite, and Hamite populations.[4]

Arabian military tactics were another factor in the open country of western Asia and across North Africa, especially "the use of cavalry and camelry— which the Romans never mastered," Hitti said. While the infantry counted on the bow and arrow, along with the sling, shield, and sword, the cavalry used the lance as its principal weapon as it covered the army's wings. An important practice, used in armies ever since, was the preservation within the army of smaller fighting units, at that time the tribes, each one hoisting its own proud banner on a lance. Moreover, the battlefield favored the Arabs. "The Arabs were at home in the desert; their enemies were not," as Bernard Lewis writes. To the Arabs, "the desert was friendly, familiar, and accessible: to their enemies, it was a remote and terrible wilderness, full of hardship and danger. . . . The Arabs could use it as a route of communication to send messages, supplies, and reinforcements, as a retreat in times of emergency, safe from molestation or pursuit—and as a road to victory."

If the Koran's battle cries were not the only explanation for the Muslims' triumphs at arms, Muhammad's book did have a great deal to do with an even greater achievement, their success in holding and building an empire. Here, too, the captured countries were ripe for conversion—peaceful conversion, for the Muslim armies did generally honor Muhammad's dictum: Let there be no coercion in religion. Byzantine Christians paid high taxes and suffered through persecution and internal religious strife, whereas the Jews were treated better by the Muslims than by the Christians and Persians. The modern Koran translator Maulana Muhammad Ali, having shown us that the Koran predicts "the ultimate triumph of Islam in the whole world," adds: "The first century of the Muslim era saw not only vast Christian communities swelling the ranks of Islam, in Egypt, N. Africa, Asia Minor, Persia and Central Asia, but also brought to light the amazing fact that Islam, coming into contact with all the great religions of the world, with Zoroastrianism in Persia, with Buddhism and Hinduism in India and Afghanistan, and with Confucianism in China, conquered the hearts of the followers of every religion . . . so that great Muslim communities sprang up in the whole known world."

It is worth hearing Ali's reasons for Islam's success, not only to get a Muslim view of that spectacular century but also for his insights into how Muslims see their religion today, especially vis-à-vis Christianity and Judaism. To the conquered peoples, he notes,

> [Islam] presented the whole truth and infused a new life into all people who accepted it, while every other religion presented only partial truth. Every religion accepted this or that prophet, while Islam accepted all the prophets of the world, and every religion had obscured the great Truth of Divine Unity by mixing up with it some kind of *shirk* [joining or associating other gods with the one true God], while Islam presented the purest monotheism. Islam . . . appealed to every people, and the truth of the words—*He it is who Sent His Messenger with guidance and the Religion of Truth that he may make it prevail over all religions*—shone out in full resplendence.

But the story has a special twist, which, like the Shiite and other traditions, shows the diversity of beliefs within Islam. After quoting the "prevail over all religions" verse, Ali adds: "Yet we are told in a reliable *hadith* that even a greater manifestation of the fulfillment of these words will be witnessed in the later days when the Messiah of this *ummah* makes his appearance."[5] What Messiah? I am indebted to Bruce Lawrence, professor of Islamic studies at Duke University, for pointing out that Ali belonged to the Ahmadi movement, which believes that its founder, Hadrat Mirza Ghulam Ahmad Qadian, was the "messiah," or "reformer," mentioned in this hadith.

Islam's Golden Age

The next century would see the Islamic empire at its zenith, but not under the Umayyads. A Persian-led, Shiite-backed revolt brought to power a new dynasty, the Abbasids, destined to rule for five centuries. Descended from the Prophet's uncle Abbas, they claimed to rule by divine right and were able to establish Islam's first absolute monarchy. Not particularly attached to the Prophet's ideas about brotherhood, however, the first two Abbasid caliphs proceeded to massacre not only the leading Umayyads but even the

Persian rebel leader who had brought the Abbasids to power, as well as many prominent Shiites. And just as the Syrian-based Umayyads had moved Islam's capital from Medina to Damascus, the new dynasty, introduced by a Persian movement from the east, created a splendid new seat high by the caravan route between the old Persian and Byzantine Christian empires. It would be called Baghdad.

Starting under the legendary caliph Harun al-Rashid (Aaron the Upright, or Rightly Guided), who ruled from 786 to 809, Baghdad would become the capital of one of the most enlightened empires in history, the world's most accomplished civilization for five hundred years. Yet in a remarkable historical coincidence, the West presented Harun with a rival in both power and territory. It was Charlemagne, grandson of the Frank Charles Martel, who had halted the Muslim advance in France. When the pope crowned Charlemagne emperor of the West in 800, it marked the start of another world power, the Holy Roman Empire, which included most of what are modern-day France, Germany, Belgium, the Netherlands, Italy, Austria, and Croatia. Charlemagne had also managed to take back a slice of Spain for the Christians, including Navarre and the Spanish March (borderland) in the northeast.

Harun communicated with Charlemagne. It is not likely the Arab tried to lord it over the Frank, although the Lebanese American historian Philip Hitti suggested he could have. "Arab scholars were studying Aristotle," Hitti wrote, "when Charlemagne and his lords were reportedly learning to write their names." Actually, Charlemagne was quite accomplished for his time. He maintained libraries of Greek and Roman manuscripts and could speak German, Latin, and Greek.

A story is told by one of Charlemagne's modern coreligionists, Torquato Cardilli, the Roman Catholic-born Italian ambassador to Saudi Arabia. The envoy converted to Islam, thus becoming one of Harun's coreligionists. In recent years he proudly displayed a clock in his office in Riyadh, supposedly a replica of one that Harun had sent to Charlemagne. The original was a technical marvel in Europe at the time, and the story goes that whenever it chimed the hour in the Frank's castle, everybody suspected evil spirits. It is a charming story, indeed, but if the ambassador/convert and the *Washington Post*, which reported the story, look at it a little more closely, they may find the tale a little less charming, because mechanical clocks are generally thought to date from six hundred years later, in the fourteenth century. Still, however unlikely the story of the Italian Muslim ambassador, there is certainly no question that Harun's Islamic realm was far in advance of Charlemagne's backward Holy Roman Empire.[6]

A glittering fraction of Harun's world, and of his successors', was captured in those tales collected from all over the Islamic empire—*A Thousand and One Nights* (or *Arabian Nights*)—among them the stories of Aladdin, Sinbad, and Ali Baba. The artistic genius of this world lay in the diversity of its far-flung peoples, which Islam has never lost, and its open-mindedness, which it has never regained. "The conquered peoples met and mingled as never before in the great *Pax Islamica* carved out by Arab arms, and a brilliant civilization was created," writes Francis Robinson. "Trade grew as men and goods moved from China to Egypt, from Spain to western India. . . . Persians, Iraqis, Syrians, Egyptians, all made their contribution to an extraordinary creative achievement in architecture and the arts."

Calligraphy is often called the most important Islamic art because it was ordained in the first revelation, announcing that God "taught by the pen," and also because it blossomed very early in reprintings of the Koran and in the decoration of mosques. Along with it flourished ceramics, ornamentation (on everything, in exquisite detail), painting (Persian miniatures), and literature. Introduced by a Chinese prisoner of war in the late 700s, papermaking got under way in Khurasan, along the Iranian-Afghan border, then spread throughout the empire. This expanded book publishing, of course, but also opened the gates for a twelve hundred-year flood of government "paperwork." Bernard Lewis uncovered an Arab story to the effect that a suspicious Harun al-Rashid made government employees use paper instead of papyrus, parchment, or other material because what was written on paper could not be erased or changed without leaving telltale marks. Paper had pretty much replaced papyrus by the mid-900s.

It was really in the sciences that the Islamic empire shone brightest. This little-appreciated fact provides one answer to that popular question among American handwringers: "Why do they hate us?" The answer is: "You have forgotten something," namely, that the West of today owes much of its glory to the Islam of yesterday, especially in mathematics, astronomy, geography, and medicine. But then Muslims forget that the Islam of yesterday owed much of its glory to the Greece of the day before—to mathematicians, astronomers, and philosophers whose works were first translated by the Muslims. The Greeks' and the Muslims' own works were then passed on to Europe, especially through Muslim Spain, where they were translated in turn from Arabic into Latin and Hebrew.

Thus, the "Islamic Enlightenment" that started in the ninth century led directly to the European Renaissance in the fourteenth. It could be argued that it even contributed to the European Enlightenment of the eighteenth. In the West, the latter is called simply the Enlightenment, as if there had not been one nine hundred years earlier. Whereas the European version rejected religious traditions in favor of rationalism, the Islamic Enlightenment had found a rationalist strain *within* its religion, a green light to science (literally, as green became the color of Muhammad's banner). If only the anti-intellectual Islamic fundamentalists of today, who want to hold back science, knew how un-Islamic that is. Indeed, that first revelation on that Night of Power in the Mount Hira cave was a call to science—for Muslims not only to write, but also to acquire knowledge. To Western ears it sounds almost secular:

> And thy Lord is most bountiful—
> He who taught by the pen,
> Taught man what he knew not.   (96:1–5)

Muslims believe this was a call to seek knowledge as a way of more fully experiencing God. Islam was also one of the few religions that required science to practice it, as science reporter Dennis Overbye wrote in the *New York Times.* From the days of the Three Wise Men, the Arabs and others had to study the stars to find their way across the desert, but Islam took it a step further. Muslims and mosque builders from the Atlantic to China now had to figure out which way to face when praying five times a day. Which way was the Kaaba? Where in a mosque should one locate the *qibla* indicating the direction toward Mecca? In his *Astronomy in the Service of Islam,* David King of Goethe University in Frankfurt points out that the Islamic empire's astronomers were assigned to pinpoint the directions as accurately as possible.[7] Soon much of East and West would be pinpointing problems in the same mathematical language, the system of Arabic numerals that was handed down through Spain, a contribution whose imortance is incalculable (even with Arabic numerals).

Not even palace intrigues and fighting could stop Islam's absorption and dissemination of science in the name of Allah. Having defeated his brother in a civil war, Harun's son Abu al-Abbas al-Mamun established a translation service called the House of Wisdom. It gave the world the Greek astronomer Ptolemy, who argued that the universe revolved around the earth, but the Muslims did not stop there. By the thirteenth century, the Persian astronomer Nasir al-Din al-Tusi clarified Ptolemy's work; he did not reject it, but he adopted a critical approach to science that influenced Europe until Copernicus made the sun the center in the early sixteenth century.

The Iraqi known as Alhazen led the way to modern optics and experimental science. And from the northeastern reaches of the empire came the masterwork of the Uzbek known as *Avicenna,* an encyclopedia that would be the standard medical text in Europe for centuries. Also in the East was Omar Khayyam. More than the familiar tent maker and rebellious poet, he was one of the most famous mathematicians of his day, one of the developers of the Persian calendar.

Culturally and intellectually, then, this was not an Arab empire, and certainly not what anyone today would call "fundamentalist," with the backward-looking orthodoxy that word implies and the hatred of unrestrained art and science. It is not what fundamentalist Muslims want to hear these days, but with its diversity, its tolerance, and its curiosity, that great empire looked less like their vision of Islam and more like some ancient America. It even liked modern gadgetry. In the palace of the caliph Al-Muqtadir was the room of the Tree, which stood in a giant circular tank of clear water. The historian of Baghdad at the time recorded that the tree had eighteen branches, "every branch having numerous twigs, on which sit all sorts of gold and silver birds, both large and small. Most of the branches of this tree are of silver, but some are gold, and they spread into the air carrying leaves of different colors. The leaves of the tree move as the wind blows, while the birds pipe and sing."[8]

Yet the sheer reach of this fantastic empire undermined the Baghdad caliphate that sat on top of it. Stretched thin, its political and military power began to fade, permanently, as did Arabian political influence within. A century after Harun's reign, a rival, Shiite caliphate was set up in North Africa by one Ubaydullah, who claimed he was descended from Ali and Fatima. He established a dynasty called the Fatimids. Based first in Tunisia and fielding a mixed army of Berbers, blacks from Sudan, and Turks, the Fatimids moved to Egypt, then cut deeply into the Islamic heartland, eventually ruling from Palestine and Syria to western Arabia to the Nile Valley.

Until then—for more than three centuries—the first Muslim conquerors had treated Jerusalem's Christians quite well, as People of the Book, but now the Fatimids launched a campaign of persecution that culminated with the destruction of the Church of the Holy Sepulcher in 1009. They destroyed not only the Byzantine basilica but also the sepulcher that was the presumed tomb of Jesus, pretty much obliterating it. The Christian community would start to rebuild the church in 1042 but could not restore the natural state of the cave where Jesus was said to have been buried.

At home, the Fatimids answered the splendor of Baghdad by creating the imperial city of Cairo. On state occasions, writes Albert Hourani, "the caliph would come from behind a curtain, holding his scepter in his hands; he would mount his horses and proceed to the palace gate, where all the trumpets would sound. Preceded and followed by his entourage and soldiers, he would ride through streets adorned by the merchants with brocades and fine linen." The new city's attractions included Al-Azhar (founded in 972), the oldest university in the world and long the most important center of Islamic research and study. The Fatimids did not attempt to convert the Egyptians to Shiism; rather, most remained Sunnis, as Hourani notes, "with large Christian and Jewish populations living on the whole in peaceful symbiosis with them."

The rise of the Fatimids prompted the surviving Umayyads in Andalus to set up a third caliphate in self-defense. They made Cordoba their seat, turning it into the most beautiful city in Europe after Constantinople (now Istanbul). Cordoba was a further embarrassment for the waning Abbasids in Baghdad but a glittering advertisement of Islam's intellectual and artistic superiority over the rest of the world. Today an exquisite surviving wing of a former palace known at the Alcazar is but a faint suggestion of what was once Islam's European capital. Another idea may be had in an enumeration by Arab historians who looked at Muslim Cordoba and counted one million inhabitants, two hundred thousand houses, six hundred mosques, eighty schools and colleges, and a public library with six hundred thousand volumes. Philip Hitti wrote that the inhabitants "enjoyed luxurious baths at a time when washing the body was considered a dangerous custom at the University of Oxford."

Still another picture might be had by considering that the work of one Cordoba resident, the philosopher Ibn-Rushd, known in the West as Averroës, was important not only to Muslim but to Christian thought as well. As H. W. Crocker III notes in *Triumph: The Power and the Glory of the Catholic Church*, it was Averroës who "transmitted a modern Aristotelian approach to Western philosophers," most notably to the church, which with its genius for adaptation then "took Aristotelian reason and made it its own."

Muslim Spain's contribution to Judaism was no less important. The Muslims' poetic tradition enthralled not only young Spanish Christians, who found it worked very well when in love, but also the Spanish Jews, whose own language was Arabic. It led them back to their Hebrew poetic tradition and forward to a revival of Hebrew in their religion. This period was the golden age of the Jews, proposed Maria Rosa Menocal, of Yale University, in a lecture to the Middle East Legal Studies Seminar in Istanbul. It was an age when the Hebrew and Arabic inscriptions on the walls of Toledo's fourteenth-century synagogue included verses from the Koran, "a gesture that makes those walls speak to, and about, a history and a memory we are mostly unwilling or unable to understand." When Jews reflect today that over those earlier centuries they fared better under Muslim than under Christian rule, often the first example they give is Al-Andalus. Only in America, perhaps, have they seen anything like it.

Menocal saw three features at the heart of Muslim Spain: "ethnic pluralism, religious tolerance, and a variety of important forms of what we could call cultural secularism—secular poetry and philosophy—that were not understood, by those who pursued them, to be un- or anti-Islamic." Feared though it may be by fundamentalists, it was this openness that increased Islam's appeal. "The number of Muslims in Iberia grew exponentially during the next several hundred years not because more 'more Arabs' came to live there, but because the original inhabitants of the peninsula converted to the dominant faith in overwhelming numbers." The title of the professor's lecture neatly sums up her point: "Culture in the Time of Tolerance: Al-Andalus As a Model for Our Own Time."[9]

To the east, from the eighth through the eleventh centuries, the Persians, too, announced their political and cultural independence from the Baghdad caliphate as new kingdoms and dynasties were created. Most notably, they nurtured their own magnificent poetic tradition, held aloft by their (to this day) unconquerable Persian language. Folk legends and the history of their pre-Islamic kings were revived by the epic poet Firdawsi, born about 940. He was once dubbed the "Homer of Persia," although his magnus opus, the *Shahnama* (Book of kings), with its sixty thousand couplets, was more than seven times the length of Homer's *Iliad*.

While resurrecting Persia's heroes, the *Shahnama* contains more than an undercurrent of anti-Arab sentiment, as in its tale of the evil Arab Dahhak, who was overthrown and buried in bonds and shame under Persia's proudest peak, Mount Demavend. Under the last shah, the *Book of Kings* was openly celebrated as testimony to a more glorious and romantic empire, the earlier Persians', and a signpost to the future. In one charming throwback, when Tehran inaugurated its ultramodern, Western-style department store, a cathedral for ultramodern, Western-style (read: wealthy) women, it was named, after that tenth-century poet, the Firdawsi Store.

Islam the religion, if not the empire, thrived under all these different guises—stunning proof of its relevance to so many. The arts and sciences that it nourished grew, too, and in North Africa and Spain the Arabic language held all the way west to the Atlantic. But starting in about 1100, the Baghdad caliphate itself was all but doomed. The heartland faced a series of nomadic invasions, first Muslim Turk, then pagan Mongol, which went on relentlessly for five centuries. These were interrupted by quite a different visitation, highly publicized (and wildly misunderstood) ever since in the West: the Crusades.

Church of the Holy Sepulcher, Jerusalem.
Courtesy of the author.

The Crusades

A Christian Jihad

This is a new kind of evil . . . and we understand, and the American people understand, this crusade, this war on terrorism, is going to take a while." [1] So stated the president of the United States five days after the attacks on New York and Washington. As the protests started coming in, he backed off the word *crusade*, which was taken by some Muslims and others as a fully loaded threat. Not to mention that the Crusades would be a sad example to follow for the war on terrorism as they were an outright failure. It would be like the president saying, "The American people understand that this military disaster is going to take a while."

Before the Christian soldiers came to free the Holy Land, Turkish nomads known as the Seljuqs had extended Islam into the eastern half of modern-day Turkey, threatening the Byzantine capital of Constantinople. Other Turks carried it beyond the Buddhas at Bamiyan—then dating back eight hundred years!—into Kashmir (where for the past half century their Muslim descendants have been fighting Indian rule).

The Seljuqs took Baghdad in 1055, preserving the caliphate but diluting its power by establishing the universal sultanate. The sultan—a title that was now used officially for the first time—exercised total military authority at home and abroad, reducing the caliph almost to a figurehead. It was a long way down from the absolute monarchy that the Abbasids had established three centuries earlier. It was also the end of full Arab control of the Islamic empire, which was now in the hands of Seljuq Turkish Muslims in the east and breakaway Arab caliphates in Cairo and Cordoba. By 1071 the Seljuq Turks had won a massive victory over the Byzantine Christians near Lake Van in present-day Armenia, and they had captured Jerusalem from the Fatimids.

With that triumph, the Muslims were on the eve of their first major confrontation with the Christians in the Holy Land since back in the first Islamic century, when Umar the Conqueror walked through the war rubble of Jerusalem to pick a site for a mosque. It was a combination of threats to the Christians—the Fatimids' destruction of the Church of the Holy Sepulcher, their ban on Christian pilgrimages, the Seljuqs' continued mistreatment of the Christians in Jerusalem, their immediate threat to Constantinople—that brought the long-delayed response: a 175-year Christian jihad. Some six hundred years later, in the early 1700s, it would be dubbed the "Crusades"—in Middle French *croisades,* in Spanish *cruzadas,* literally actions for the cross, after the Latin *crux.*

It took nearly a quarter century after the Seljuq capture of Jerusalem for a pope, Urban II, to preach the First Crusade, at the Council of Clermont in France. Urban came through with "probably the most effective speech in all history," thought the Arab Christian writer Philip Hitti. The pope exhorted all Christendom to reconquer Jerusalem, to "enter upon the road to the Holy Sepulcher" and "wrest it from the wicked race." In the process, the pope said, they would rescue the threatened Byzantine Christians, who might one day be brought back into the Roman fold. Christianity at that time might have been deeply riven between the western and eastern churches, but the prestige of the former was at a high point. As historian H. W. Crocker III writes, the immediate response to Urban's appeal demonstrated "the papacy's undisputed leadership of Christendom."[2]

The Christian fighters for their one God had a lot in common with the Muslim fighters for their one God. If Urban's charge—"wrest it from the wicked"— had something of an impassioned Muslim plea about it, so did the rallying cry of his soldiers: "God wills it!" Of the Frankish nobility who commanded the Crusaders, Robert Harrison writes: "To the medieval nobleman piety meant a familiar, almost intimate relationship to the human natures of Jesus, Mary and the saints of the church, and included not only what we think of as religious devotion, but also an unswerving loyalty, national pride, chivalric honor, and a fierce sense of personal dignity. . . . As a Christian symbol the sword acquired even more than ordinary significance. Its shape made it inevitably a makeshift crucifix."[3] Which makes one remember the Muslims' stories about Muhammad's Companions, the Muslims' sense of pride and honor, and their devotion to the sword of Allah.

The hot and heavy recruiting by the nobles and the church was very much in the spirit of a jihad. The pope promised the individual Crusader remission of sins, or "credit" in Heaven, for having been to the Holy Land. Like the Muslims' earlier breakout from Arabia, however, this and the later Crusades were brought on by more than religious fervor. As also in the case of the jihads, a major factor was economic hardship among French and German nobles, who now saw a way to open new markets and established foreign realms. In addition, the Byzantine emperor, Alexius I, had asked for help, and as mentioned above, the pope still prayed for reunification. As for the feudal peasantry, they might have hoped for, if not salvation, at least an escape from famine and plague.

Little heavenly credit was earned in the opening act of the First Crusade— an armed pilgrimage by thousands of men, women, and children across Europe, from France to Constantinople. On the contrary, this Christian "peasants' crusade" was a disaster for all concerned. Organized by the fighting monk Peter the Hermit and the knight Walter the Penniless, it was accompanied in France and en route by murders, pillaging, and persecution of Jews, a foreboding of much worse to come. Of the Christian attacks on the Jews, the Cambridge lecturer and rabbi Nicholas de Lange writes in his *Atlas of the Jewish World:* "During the crusades there were assaults on Jewish communities of the Rhineland. . . . Such attacks continued at intervals for centuries, and the total loss of life is appalling. The Jews, generally forbidden to carry arms, were unable to defend themselves, and relied entirely on the protection of their rulers and neighbors. Too often help was not forthcoming. In several places Jews killed themselves and their families rather than fall into the hands of the Christian mobs."[4]

Many in the Christian "peasants' crusade" were themselves murdered by outraged residents of the countries they were tramping across for God, or at least for their local monks and impoverished nobles. Many others, who made it all the way, were killed by Turks in the environs of Constantinople. Nor did the organized Christian armies get off to a good start later in that year of 1096. After bitter arguments with Alexius, the westerners agreed to return all reconquered lands to him. Though later partially renounced, this agreement set a pattern of distrust between the Romans and Byzantines, damaging the prestige of Christendom. Two years later it was scarred again in one of the most horrifying events of the Crusades.

It is a story that explains why Muslims find the Christians just as "treacherous" as they in war. Keeping in mind the Muslims' long memory, one might wonder whether the story does not also shed light on the murders of the Soviet troops near Kandahar, where, as described in chapter 2, the victims' bodies were cut up and boiled. In this case, the Frankish commander promised to spare the residents of the Syrian-Turkish town of Maara if they would stop fighting. As the modern historian Amin Maalouf tells the story, the Syrians agreed, but three days later the Crusaders returned, massacring the townspeople. A Frankish writer, Radulph of Caen, gave more details: "In Maara our troops boiled pagan adults in cooking-pots; they impaled children on spits and devoured them grilled."

The Christians investigated, which produced an explanatory letter to the pope: "A terrible famine racked the army in Maara, and placed it in the cruel necessity of feeding itself upon the bodies of the Saracens." But Maalouf says such atrocities were not always committed out of desperate hunger. On the contrary, one group of fanatic Crusaders that winter would "roam through the countryside openly proclaiming that they would chew the flesh of the Saracens and gathering around their nocturnal camp-fires to devour their prey." The Crusader Albert of Aix, who was at Maara and who had a highly developed set of priorities, testified: "Not only did our troops not shrink from eating dead Turks and Saracens; they also ate dogs!" Maalouf says that the Turks never forgot, and for centuries later their writers described the Franks as anthropophagi.[5]

Massacre in Jerusalem

The combined Christian armies of this First Crusade, about one hundred thousand strong, were victorious beyond a doubt, but at an enormous cost. In 1099 they attacked the walls of Jerusalem with two mobile towers. One of them was wiped out, but the other survived a counterattack by jugs of "Greek fire"— the ancient equivalent of Molotov cocktails—launched by catapult. In *The Crusades Through Arab Eyes*, Maalouf (who is from a Lebanese Catholic family) cites two ancient Arab sources on the horrifying capture of Jerusalem. First, Ibn al-Athir writes, "The population of the holy city was put to the sword, and the Franj [Frankish Crusaders] spent a week massacring Muslims. They killed more than seventy thousand in al-Aqsa Mosque." Then, the chronicler Ibn al-Qalanisi: "Many people were killed. The Jews had gathered in the synagogue and the Franj burned them alive. They also destroyed monuments of saints and the tomb of Abraham, may peace be upon him!"

The Crusaders sacked the Dome of the Rock, once and sometimes still called the Mosque of Umar, after the caliph who had conquered Jerusalem four and one-half centuries earlier. Maalouf compares that entry into Jerusalem with this one. Back then, inside the Church of the Holy Sepulcher, the patriarch invited Umar to unroll his prayer mat where they stood, but Umar declined, saying, "If I do, the Muslims will want to appropriate this site, saying, 'Umar prayed here.' Then, carrying his prayer mat, he went and knelt outside. He was right, for it was on that very spot that the mosque that bore his name was constructed. The Frankish commanders, alas, lacked Umar's magnanimity. They celebrated their triumph with an ineffable orgy of killing, and then savagely ravaged the city they claimed to venerate."[6]

By the time the Crusaders got there, there was not much left of the Holy Sepulcher to wrest away, as Urban II had requested, the Fatimids having destroyed the church a half century earlier. It would take another half century for the Christians to rebuild it in the Romanesque style that survives to this day, though with no semblance of the natural cave that was said to have been the original tomb of Jesus.

The Christian conquerors elected the foremost of their commanders as baron and defender of the Holy Sepulcher. This was Godfrey of Bouillon, the duke of Lower Lorraine, to be celebrated for centuries in European songs and legends, especially in the medieval French *chansons de geste*. Godfrey thus became the first ruler of the Latin Kingdom of Jerusalem, as it was renamed upon his death the following year. His brother Baldwin succeeded him and took the title of king. This new and greater, this Christian, realm of Jerusalem comprised other parts of Palestine plus parts of Syria and present-day Lebanon—new Christian states in the Holy Land, with a total of some 250,000 souls. The Latin Kingdom of Jerusalem would survive in toto for eighty-eight years, then in truncated form (without Jerusalem itself) for one more century. The Crusaders would thus be a power in the Holy Land for nearly two hundred years. Their kingdom would exist on paper for several centuries beyond that time.

The Second Crusade

The failed Second Crusade, from 1147 to 1149, had nothing to do with Jerusalem or the Holy Sepulcher. It was prompted by the Muslim reconquest of the Armenian city of Edessa in Turkey, the capital of one of the Frankish states in the Holy Land. The only way to avoid recording this expedition as an outright failure would be to count such peripheral developments as the taking of Lisbon by English Crusaders and the Germans' colonizing of Slavs to their east.

Like Muslim fighters expecting Paradise, those soldiers in the Second Crusade were promised remission of sins and cancellation of debts, the latter for the nobles as the peasants could only dream of having debts. Among the unforgettable pictures from this and the other expeditions was the sight of kings and queens and wives riding off to war at great distances. Of course, it had long been common (remember Aisha at the Battle of the Camel), but today it would be rather like the American president and the first lady leading their troops through the Hindu Kush mountains into Kashmir.

In the Second Crusade, led by King Conrad III of Germany and King Louis VII of France, the latter was accompanied by his twenty-five-year-old queen, the temptress Eleanor of Aquitaine. As James Reston Jr. notes, Eleanor allegedly slept with her uncle at Antioch, prompting Louis to keep her under wraps for the rest of the campaign (to continue the comparative-religions theme, Reston suggests the French court of the day may have borrowed its sensuality from the Muslims in Spain). In any event, they were never able to pay their respects at the Holy Sepulcher in the new Latin Kingdom of Jerusalem. Albeit sin-free and debt-free, the Germans were decimated in Turkey, while their French coreligionists were mauled by the Seljuqs at Damascus.[7]

The Third Crusade

The Third Crusade, from 1189 to 1192, is the most storied because of the colorful figures involved, especially Richard I, king of England; Philip II, king of France; and their enemy, Salah al-Din, known in the West as Saladin. Like Muhammad and Harun, Saladin was yet another venerated Muslim chieftain who was quite the opposite of extremist Islamic leaders today.

Given his huge reputation in the West as well as the East, one might have thought Saladin to be a physically commanding figure, but he was quite small and somewhat feeble, with an insignificant beard. His personality more than made up for it. Celebrated for his courtesy and gallantry, he was more chivalrous than the chevaliers he was fighting, mixing courtesy, diplomacy, and wisdom. These qualities shine through in a letter quoted by Reston in his *Warriors of God: Richard the Lionheart and Saladin in the Third Crusade*. King Richard had asked Saladin for a face-to-face meeting before the Battle of Acre: "It is not customary for Kings to meet," Saladin replied, "unless they have previously laid the foundations of a treaty. For, after they have spoken together and given one another tokens of mutual confidence, it is not seemly for them to return to making war upon one another." The principle of prearranged summit meetings is still practiced today. Protocol for summit meetings between the two Christian kings, old friends, was quite different. Reston, having discussed the Lionheart's homosexuality, says Richard and Louis generally managed to get over their own squabbling, "perhaps with a wink and a flirtatious glance."

Though remembered in much of the Arab world today as the greatest of Arab heroes, Saladin was not an Arab but a Kurd. He rose to power in the service of the Turks who controlled the Abbasid caliphate, then was sent to represent Syria at the Fatimid court in Cairo. Some representative. He abolished that Shiite caliphate in 1171, returned Egypt to the Abbasid caliphate, and seized control of Syria itself.

Saladin's résumé also included more than one attempt on his life by assassins, or rather the Assassins, the Muslim sect whose name was said to derive from their frequent diet of hashish. Early in Saladin's 1175 campaign in Syria, an Assassin rushed into his tent and stabbed him in the head. But having survived a previous attack, as Amin Maalouf tells it, Saladin was wearing a headdress of mail under his fez. Then the Assassin stabbed him in the neck, only to hit the mail inserted into his high tunic collar. A soldier arrived and took out the Assassin, but then two more attacked Saladin. Finally, more soldiers appeared and killed all the Assassins, and Saladin became the first sultan of Egypt and Syria. Some have suggested this gave birth to the Arab dream of Egyptian-Syrian unification, but Umar the Conqueror had achieved that five centuries earlier.

But there was more to Saladin's civilization than Assassins. One can get another idea of this great Kurdish soldier and his realm by considering one of his subjects. For if the Egyptian Jews had for the most part thrived under the Fatimids, Saladin went his predecessors one better by patronizing the "second Moses." Or so they would label Moses ben Maimon, or Maimonides, because of his many contributions to Jewish law. Writing in both Hebrew and Arabic, he was one of the leading philosophers of his time, reconciling Judaism with Aristotle (as translated into Arabic) and influencing the Christian philosopher Saint Thomas Aquinas. A child of the "Islamic Enlightenment," Maimonides was born in Cordoba in the midst of its combined Muslim and Jewish glory. He sits there today, holding a book, in a statue inscribed "Cordoba to Maimonides." In fact, though, he left Cordoba as a thirteen year old after the Christians recaptured the city in 1148. His family settled in Cairo, where in the spirit of that Islamic era's scientific and philosophical genius Maimonides became a celebrated doctor, mathematician, astronomer, philosopher, and eventually chief rabbi. He owed at least one of his jobs to Saladin, who made him court physician.

Here, too, Saladin can be contrasted with Richard, whom Reston presents as ardently anti-Jewish. Richard's coronation, we are told, had been marked by beatings of the Jewish elders who came to pay him tribute and by the burning of Jewish homes in London. "Richard's rank anti-Semitism," Reston writes, "grew into overt sadism. To him a good joke was to extract the teeth of Jews in a lingering process." As the call to fight for the cross spread across England, Richard made a few efforts to contain the persecution of Jews, but after he left for the Third Crusade, it only got worse, one historian noting, "Many of those who were hastening to go to Jerusalem determined first to rise against the Jews." In a parallel to the Jewish suicides in the Rhineland, Jews who were driven into the tower at York also opted for mass suicide.

Saladin finally marched against the Christian forces in Palestine in 1187. First he grabbed Tiberias, on the western shore of beautiful Lake Tiberias, the biblical Sea of Galilee. Through the first millennium C.E., Tiberias had been a center of Jewish learning, and it is there that the tomb of Maimonides can be found. Next Saladin captured the port of Acre, one of the oldest communities in the world, on the Bay of Haifa in present-day Israel. Finally, he recaptured Jerusalem itself for the Muslims, and in response Pope Gregory VIII summoned the Third Crusade.

Besides Richard and Louis, the Christian counteroffensive against Saladin also brought out Frederick I, the Holy Roman emperor, but he died on the way to the Holy Land. The remaining two kings of Occident racked up only one real military success: the recapture of Acre, and even here Saladin's forces seemed more driven than the Crusaders.

If today anyone doubts the usefulness of the Koranic verses as marching orders, let them consider how the holy book affected the fight for Acre five hundred years after Muhammad's death. Saladin anticipated defeat and so burned the port at Haifa to deny it to the Christians, as Reston tells it. Then a swimmer brought him news. These Muslim swimmers, ancestors of the United States Navy Seals, would sometimes get messages or gold through blockades by diving under the enemy ships and carrying them to the opposite shore. One Muslim swimmer was killed, but his body washed up later on the opposite shore, the messages and gold still attached to his body—a rare case, as Saladin's personal secretary noted, of a man accomplishing his mission while dead.[8] From this Bay of Haifa swimmer, Saladin received a letter scrawled by his desperate commander at Acre, the grand emir Mashtub. "We have sworn to die together," the emir wrote his sultan. "We will fight until we fall and will not yield the city while there is breath in our bodies. . . . Since we are resolved, be sure that you do not humble yourselves before the enemy or show yourselves faint-hearted." Reston adds, "With their pact of mass suicide, the defenders were already wrapping themselves in the green mantel of martyrdom." The Muslims' refusal to surrender does perhaps sound to non-Muslims today like suicide—and like the terrorists at Kandahar eight centuries later. But maybe there is another way to look at it.

Was "Give me liberty or give me death!" a suicide note? Was Churchill asking the defenders of Singapore to commit suicide when he told their commander: "There must be no thought at this stage of saving the troops or sparing the population. The battle must be fought to the bitter end at all costs. The 18th Division has a chance to make its name in history. Commanders and senior officers should die with their troops. The honour of the British Empire and the British Army is at stake"?[9] The Japanese might wrongly have thought the British were acting like kamikazes, but one person's suicide is sometimes another's act of honor or "martyrdom operation."

The Koran is enlightening again when during the assault on the Muslims at Acre they were frightened by what seemed like an earthquake, until, in Reston's account "a soldier stepped forward with an explanation. He had seen a thousand cavalrymen appear suddenly, shaking the earth, and they were all dressed in the green of martyrdom. And thus the martyrs of yore were joining the Muslim host." To the Koran reader it conjures the Battle of Badr, when God said:

> I will assist you
> With a thousand of the angels,
> Ranks on ranks. (8:9)

Yet Saladin found the Christians holier than he, or so he claimed in order to whip up his troops. "Regard the Franj! Behold with what obstinacy they fight for their religion, while we, the Muslims, show no enthusiasm for waging holy war." But the reputation of Richard Coeur de Lion was tarnished by the execution after Acre of some twenty-seven hundred Muslim prisoners of war, and much more by his failure to take Jerusalem, although he and Saladin did conclude a truce granting the Christians access to the Holy Sepulcher and other privileges.

The Later Crusades

The next five Crusades were no more successful for the Christians. In the Fourth, they specialized in attacking other Christians. Instead of seeking to free the Holy Land and unite the Roman and Byzantine churches, as Pope Innocent III wanted them to, they sailed out of Venice, whose treasury was financing the expedition, and attacked one of Venice's rival ports in Yugoslavia, the Christian city of Zadar. Later they attacked and sacked Constantinople itself in a scandal that ruined any chances of uniting the western and eastern churches.

The Fifth Crusade included a hopeless Palestinian expedition by Andrew II of Hungary and failed efforts by papal forces and the titular king of Jerusalem, John of Brienne, to conquer Cairo.

The Roman church's determination to retake the Holy Land was reflected in its excommunication of several Crusade leaders, notably Philip, the Holy Roman emperor, and others for the sacking of Zadar (they were later reinstated in the church), and Frederick II, also a Holy Roman emperor, for failing to reach Jerusalem in the Sixth Crusade. Frederick kept at it, though, and the next year, 1228, actually negotiated a truce that gave the Christians Jerusalem, Bethlehem, and Nazareth.

They held on to Jerusalem until, sixteen years later, it again fell under Muslim control, which led to the Seventh Crusade. That expedition began and ended ignominiously in Egypt, where Louis IX of France surrendered, then wound up spending four years adrift in Syria.

In the Eighth and final Crusade, in 1270, the same Louis IX got as far as North Africa, where he died; his cocommander, Edward I of England, was victorious in Acre and Haifa across the bay and signed a truce with the Muslims. After the two centuries of the Crusades, the Muslims had a stronger grip on the Holy Land than when Urban II had called upon Christians to "enter upon the road to the Holy Sepulcher."

If one considers the reconquest of Spain as part of the Crusades, as some historians do, that expulsion of the Muslims from Europe could be placed on the positive side of the balance sheet for the Christians (though not necessarily for Spain, for it wiped out a stunning civilization). Andalus had already begun to falter within. Early in the eleventh century, the Umayyad caliphate that had reigned from Cordoba ended with the death of Hisham III and split into rival Muslim kingdoms. Christian kings in northern Spain began to move south, taking Cordoba in 1148, defeating the Muslims at Toledo in 1212, and containing the Muslims in the ports around Cadiz and in Grenada. Jewish exiles from Cordoba settled on the hill that was Grenada. One was Ismail Ibn Nagrila. He became the leader of Grenada's army in its battles with rival Muslim cities and also wrote poems. In one, he revealed how comfortable he was as a Jew in Andalus: "I am the David of my age." [10]

In the following century, after the Castilians seized the rest of Andalusia, Grenada became increasingly isolated. "After 1248," writes Maria Rosa Menocal, "standing by itself in its splendid and snow-capped mountain stronghold, lonely and surrounded, was Grenada. For the next two hundred and fifty years, under the rule of a single dynasty called the Nasrids, Grenada was in crucial ways a very different place from what al-Andalus had been. Among other things, there were no *dhimmi* (the Peoples of the Book), no Jewish or Christian populations, in that cornered place."

Looking back, we can see what sometimes still happens today when Muslim communities are cut off from the rest of the world, from the outside contact that once produced such brilliant results for Islamic communities in the arts and sciences. The Muslims in Grenada "turned ever more inward, becoming progressively more purely Islamicized," Menocal notes. It was during this sad state that they built the exquisitely ornamented but "fittingly sepulchral monument now known as the Alhambra, from the Arabic 'The Red Fort.' " But their isolation was hardly of their own doing. Time was closing in on non-Christians. The Crusades had accelerated anti-Jewish hatred and pogroms in Europe, and the Roman Inquisition, a system of church tribunals for heretics, was just getting under way. The Spanish Inquisition would not be established until about 1480 under King Ferdinand and Queen Isabella.

One can imagine, or perhaps one cannot imagine, the horror of the Muslims as Jews and heretics were burned at the stake in the Catholic Church's autos-da-fé. Eleven years later Grenada was finally subdued. Isabella and Ferdinand climbed the hill on the following New Year's Day to sign the surrender in the Alhambra. Later in that year of 1492, in the midst of the Spanish holocaust, the Jews were ordered to get out of the country. Their deadline happened to be the day on which Columbus sailed for America.

This Cristóbal Colón may have been a secret Jew himself. A number of authorities, including the Spanish biographer Salvador de Madariaga and the *Encyclopedia Britannica*, as well as such impassioned amateur historians as Simon Wiesenthal, have supported this claim. One theory is that he was descended from Catalans who fled a pogrom and settled in Genoa, Italy, where he was born Cristoforo Colombo. The American historian Samuel Eliot Morison writes movingly about what Columbus must have felt as he came across the expelled Jews on their way to the port of Palos, where the *Niña*, *Pinta*, and *Santa María* were docked, but Morison and Nicholas de Lange in the *Atlas of the Jewish World*, among others, beg to disagree that Columbus himself was Jewish. I once reported on the elaborate arguments both sides have fashioned, only to conclude they are all inconclusive. But Professor Menocal has added a fascinating postscript: when Columbus landed in the New World, his translator was a Jew. And this Jewish translator spoke to the Indians of Cuba in Arabic.

The Crusades rank with the Inquisition as one of Christianity's disasters. They were accompanied by unthinkable cruelty and bloodshed. They intensified the massive European persecution of non-Christians, especially Jews, that led directly to the Inquisition. By sacking Constantinople, the Christians made permanent the schism between the western and eastern churches and set up the Byzantine Empire for its overthrow by the Muslim Turks. At the same time, the Crusades shut off the invigorating flow to Europe of Islamic scholarship and science through Sicily and Spain. And for all that, the Christians failed to accomplish their goal of recapturing and (obviously) holding Jerusalem and the Holy Land, leaving the Muslims more in control than they were before.

◆◆◆

In the year 2000, as he prepared to visit the Holy Land, Pope John Paul II included the Crusades when he marked the millennium by apologizing for his church's past sins. Also mentioned were the church's treatment of Jews, Muslims, women, and ethnic groups. He did not satisfy everybody. The grand mufti of Jerusalem was upset that this first pope to pray in a mosque did not expound on his apology for the Crusades when he came to Jerusalem. On the other hand, not all of the Catholic faithful are pleased that John Paul II got into a habit of apologizing. "If his repeated apologies for any conceivable Catholic historical offense grate on those who wish the Sack of Byzantium to be a feast day of the Church," writes H. W. Crocker III in his history of the Roman Catholic Church, "it would seem churlish to deny the benign intent that motivates them—or the strength that lies behind the apologetic words." As Crocker reminds us, the pope did not suffer from what Freud called "the narcissism of small differences."[11]

The Crusades Today

But if the Crusades were a disastrous failure, why do Arab terrorists seek revenge for them? For it is not the West or the American president who bandy about the scare word *Crusades* but the terrorists. Nor are the terrorists the only modern Arabs preoccupied with the Crusades. "The Arab world—simultaneously fascinated and terrified by these Franj, whom they encountered as barbarians and defeated, but who subsequently managed to dominate the earth—cannot bring itself to consider the Crusades a mere episode in the bygone past," writes Amin Maalouf. "It is often surprising to discover the extent to which the attitude of the Arabs (and of Muslims in general) towards the West is still influenced, even today, by events that supposedly ended some seven centuries ago."

To some modern Arabs, the 1956 Suez expedition was simply an English-French Crusade and Israel is a new Crusader state, whereas John Paul II was more than willing simply to forget his would-be assassin of more than two decades ago. The latter was Mehmet Ali Agca, a Turk, who had written, "I have decided to kill John Paul II, supreme commander of the Crusades." In dismissing the Turk from his mind, the pope was truly enjoying freedom from "the narcissism of small differences." It upset the Arabs all the more that the West, which lost the war, went on to power and glory. Although the Crusaders covered themselves in blood, it is true that they registered a few direct gains from the Crusades. Their holy wars bolstered the stature of the papacy and Europe's courts while increasing trade and the wealth of the Italian ports. The Renaissance arrived even without the fabulous Islamic university that was Andalus.

As has been noted earlier, modern Arab envy of the West's good fortune, which still runs deep, was perhaps prefigured at the beginning of Islam, when the Prophet lacked a book and saw how well the Christians and Jews were doing with theirs. But the Prophet himself was a learner, a progressive, unlike his extreme fundamentalist followers. It is often politically incorrect to discuss the failures of victims, but one of the few historians who does just that was himself an Arab, the Lebanese Catholic Maalouf, who surveys the consequences of the Crusades for the Muslim world in an excellent epilogue to his book *The Crusades Through Arab Eyes.*

Maalouf points out that the Muslims may have wound up with a stronger hold on the Holy Land after the Crusades, but they failed to profit from it; indeed, they had proved incapable of learning from the Crusaders. In retrospect it is not surprising. They had been weakened as a people during the long decline of Arab influence within the Islamic empire. Many of the empire's greatest thinkers had been non-Arabs, as were many of its leaders after the Seljuq Turks took Baghdad in 1055; Maalouf points out that a few generations after the fall of Baghdad, the sultan could not even speak Arabic and needed an interpreter to talk to the caliph. "Dominated, oppressed, and derided, aliens in their own land, the Arabs were unable to continue to cultivate the cultural blossoms that had begun to flower in the seventh century." [12]

Besides having lost their power, the Muslims could not build stable institutions, whereas the Crusaders created "genuine state structures as soon as they arrived," setting up legislative councils with certain powers over the monarchs and a clearly defined role for the clergy. "Nothing of the sort existed in the Muslim states," Maalouf writes. "Every monarchy was threatened by the death of its monarch, and every transmission of power provoked civil war." Maalouf finds plenty of support for his views in the writings of a famous Arab traveler, Ibn Jubayr, who told of passing by farms and villages under Crusader control in Syria. The inhabitants were all Muslims, and they were much better off than Muslims in Muslim territory. Their farms were "efficiently cultivated," wrote Ibn Jubayr, "their dwellings belong to them and all their property is unmolested. All the regions controlled by the Franj in Syria are subject to the same system: the landed domains, villages and farms have remained in the hands of the Muslims." [13]

But did this small community of Muslims learn from this? Were they comfortable with their prosperity, success, and good, albeit foreign, government? No. They feared it might contradict their religion. As a matter of fact, even Ibn Jubayr had his worries: "May God preserve us from temptation!" Thus, those baffled by the retrogressive, antiscientific, anti-intellectual masochism of today's Islamic fundamentalists should note that it is not new, although Muhammad himself would have been shocked by it.

"Doubt invests the heart of a great number" of the successful Syrian villagers and farmers, as Ibn Jubayr put it, "when they compare their lot to that of their brothers living in Muslim territory" and see that "the latter suffer from the injustice of their coreligionists, whereas the Franj act with equity." We certainly would not want to copy the foreigners' good habits, would we? God might not approve. Maalouf says even Ibn Jubayr himself, who admired what he considered the fair and sound administration of the Crusaders, believed that it also "constituted a mortal danger to the Muslims. . . . Might not the latter turn their backs on their own coreligionists—and on their religion" if they lived well under the Crusaders? "Throughout the Crusades," Maalouf points out, "the Arabs refused to open their own society to ideas from the West." [14]

Islamic fundamentalists have exactly the same fear of the West today. But Maalouf finally takes a middle road. Although he calls the Muslims' closed minds "a malady," he blames it on the aggression of the Crusades. And he has found a psychological explanation for why many Crusaders learned Arabic while the locals, except for some Christians, "remained impervious to the languages of the Occidentals." It made sense for the conqueror to learn the language of the conquered, but for the latter to learn the enemy's language "seems a surrender of principle, even a betrayal." This analysis fails to explain why throughout the colonial period the English and other Europeans were famous for not learning the local languages (insisting that the locals really understood, or would if one just spoke louder), or why vast numbers of the colonized had no trouble learning English, French, or other European languages.

In any event, in the end this Arab Catholic writer did not agree that the Crusades were a dismal failure for the Europeans or that the Muslims wound up better off. The Crusades "ignited a genuine economic and cultural revolution in Western Europe; in the Orient these holy wars led to long centuries of decadence and obscurantism. Assaulted from all quarters, the Muslim world turned in on itself. It became over-sensitive, defensive, intolerant, sterile." In fact, however, the Islamic arts and sciences had already contributed far more to Europe's surge toward civilization than did the Crusades, which actually hindered it by cutting off the flow of Islamic contributions.

Maalouf has enjoyed a bit of a revival on American campuses since September 11, 2001, but one prominent professor commented privately to me, "Maalouf's Arab nationalist self-pity doesn't deserve to be repeated here by you." Indeed, Maalouf's conclusions are seriously damaged by his use of the term *Arabs*. As the professor pointed out, the Muslims in Crusader days "did not yet think of themselves as 'Arabs,' a concept that only took root in the late nineteenth century; they thought of themselves as Muslims (or Christians), presumably, and then as members of specific clans, families, or tribes. 'Arab' was a quasi pejorative meaning 'nomad-bedouin' until the modern usage kicks in, which it was slow to do." Thus, when some of the locals failed to learn from Crusader governments, they were operating not as members of some Arab civil system whose people were just stubbornly dense but as isolated Muslim clans, families, or tribes bound to tradition. And Maalouf was clearly writing as a modern Arab nationalist, even equating all Muslims with Arabs when he said that after the Crusades the Muslim world immediately turned in on itself. Long before that, Islam would expand again, albeit not under Arab control and no longer as a political empire.

Death of the Islamic Empire

Meanwhile, the other "assaults from all quarters" on the Muslim world were far worse than what Francis Robinson calls "the pinpricks" of the Crusades and the loss of Spain and Sicily. The first were the Mongol invasions of Genghis Khan, who conquered the Caucasus and pushed into Persia even before the Crusades were over. Perhaps it was only by a diplomatic misunderstanding that Genghis Khan declined an invitation from the Franks to join them in wiping out the Muslims. His grandson Hulagu went on to sack Baghdad itself, the capital of the already fading Islamic empire, in 1258. It was the first time since Muhammad that pagans had conquered the Muslim heartland. While burning Baghdad's buildings, the Mongols killed nearly eighty thousand inhabitants, including the last of the Abbasid dynasty. Accounts differ on whether Al-Mustasim, the thirty-seventh caliph in that line, and his family were put to the sword or trampled to death under carpets.

But as of that day, 626 years after the election of Abu Bakr as the successor to the Prophet, the original Arab caliphate and with it the original Islamic empire were dead, never to be revived—except in the dreams of today's extremists, who in any case disembark from Islam's train of progress after the seventh century. Founded by the four Rightly Guided Caliphs who succeeded the Prophet, the empire had spread from the Atlantic to the mountains of China in little more than a century, then reached its height under Harun the Rightly Guided. But its political and military authority had been stretched far too thin, and the Turk and Mongol invasions finally knocked it off, with no help from Crusaders needed (indeed, as mentioned above, it was actually rejected). Buried along with the empire and its Arab caliphate were the general political power and influence of the Arabs, whose role had begun to weaken long before under the early Abbasids.

But—and this fact is especially worth remembering today—Islam the religion would go on to breathtaking achievements. It would expand well beyond its original political and military empire, taking root around the coasts of Africa, into Southeast Asia, and far into eastern Europe. Nor was Islam dead in the homelands. In Egypt it survived in something close to its original form, first under the Mamluks, the oligarchy of mainly Turkish and Circassian slave troops who overthrew the Ayyubid dynasty founded by Saladin, and then under the Ottoman Turks who would follow them in 1517. Syria, Arabia, and North Africa escaped the Mongols through the mid-fourteenth century, partly because that empire, too, was overextended militarily.

The fierce, all-destroying Mongols did return in a final assault on the Islamic heartland by Timur Lang, the lame, or Tamerlane, who even forced Cairo into temporary subservience. What is remarkable, though, is that the Muslims in Iraq, Turkey, Iran, and areas eastward actually converted their pagan rulers— "which must be accounted one of the greatest of Muslim achievements," says Robinson, "as it ensured that Central Asia to the Altaic mountains would continue to be Muslim." Along with religion, the arts and sciences would flourish in this seemingly unstoppable Muslim world, especially in Persia and the future Afghanistan.

The Mongols might have attempted to conquer Egypt as well had it not been for the discouraging strength of the Mamluks. This military oligarchy gave the world another of the Middle East's famous femmes fatales by doing something altogether unprecedented: they put a woman, a wife of the previous sultan, in charge of the world's strongest Muslim power at the moment, and called her a sultana. Her name was Shajar al-Durr. After they raised her to sultana, or queen, she married Aybeg, one of the Mamluks, and made him sultan, and they ruled for seven years, partly from their bathroom.

One day, as Maalouf tells the story from the dusty archives, Shajar al-Durr was giving her husband a bath as she liked to do, and decided to scold him "for having taken a pretty 14-year-old girl slave as his concubine. 'Do I no longer please you?' she murmured. . . . Aybeg answered sharply: 'She is young, while you are not.' " With that, the sultana grabbed a dagger, stabbed him, and tried to run away, but fell, fatally slamming her head against a marble slab.

The Mongols would give way to the Turkish tribesmen who supplied the bulk of their military strength. Of the three major Muslim empires that eventually succeeded the Mongols—the Mughals farthest east, where among many other wonders they gave the world the Taj Mahal; the Safavids, whose poetic civilization flowered in Persia, especially in their wondrous capital of Isfahan; and the Ottomans—it was the latter that would last the longest by far.[15]

The Ottoman Empire

Starting out as a small community of holy warriors on the edge of the Byzantine Christian empire, the Ottomans broke into northwestern Turkey and captured Constantinople in 1453, two and a half centuries after the Roman Crusaders had sacked it. Just as in Spain, where the conquering Castilian Peter the Cruel had walked into the Great Mosque of Seville and started praying there, then ordered it turned into a cathedral, Sultan Mehmet the Conqueror performed his first Sabbath prayers in the Church of St. Sophia, then ordered it converted into a mosque. He must have been amazed at this already nine hundred-year-old church, with its enormous dome.

Standing in it today, one is awed by the idea that such a space could be covered by a man-made sky. In the conquering Ottomans, the St. Sophia dome instilled that envy we might have seen in Muhammad's fascination with the

Christian and Jewish books. Indeed, when the Ottoman architect Sinan built his mosques for the former Christian capital, including the Sulaimaniye Mosque that lures the world arriving by way of the Golden Horn, he was intentionally trying to outshine the Church of St. Sophia. He said so, just as in Jerusalem the builder of the Dome of the Rock had plainly declared that he was trying to outdo the Church of the Holy Sepulcher. "Christians," wrote Sinan of his masterpiece at Edirne, Turkey, "say they have defeated the Muslims because no dome has been built in the Islamic world which can rival the dome of St. Sophia. It greatly grieved my heart. . . . I determined to erect such a mosque, and with the help of God, in the reign of Sultan Selim Khan, I made the dome of this mosque six cubits wider and four cubits deeper than the dome of St. Sophia." [16]

The capture of the city of Constantine (the name was not officially changed to Istanbul until 1930) opened the way across the Bosporus to Europe. The Ottomans next took Greece and expanded northward, annexing Herzegovina and controlling Bosnia. In 1517, when they seized Egypt, the Ottoman sultans assumed the title of caliph, claiming that an Abbasid descendant had passed it on to them. They were certainly not Quraysh by ancestral background, as the previous caliphs had been, nor were they even Arabs. But they united the religious and temporal leadership in one person for the first time since the Seljuqs had separated them by creating the universal sultanate five hundred years before.

By the seventeenth century, under the Ottomans, Muslims were in control of even more of the planet than they had ruled under the Islamic empire. The sultan ruled from Georgia, Azerbaijan, and western Iran into the Muslim heartland, including the holy cities of Mecca and Medina. His realm reached across North Africa to Morocco and far into eastern Europe, from southern Russia and Bulgaria west to Hungary and the gates of Vienna. Even as it inherited large Christian populations, the empire retained the zeal of its holy warrior founders. The Ottoman ruling class had to be Muslim, the state worked hand in hand with the *ulama,* and the *sharia* was for the most part the law of the empire, except in the state administration, where it was inadequate. At the same time the state converted great masses of its subjects and conquered peoples. Although absolute power resided in the sultanate, the highly structured bureaucracy, the equally organized army, and the loyal and respected *ulama* all combined to create an efficient, premodern state. [17]

The Ottoman Empire remained a world power for four hundred years, into the mid-nineteenth century. But it declined rapidly with the rise of European colonialism and was brought to a close by World War I. European Christian states overthrew the Ottomans, and the British and French pushed them out of the Holy

Land and back into Anatolia. After the Ottomans were defeated in 1918 and Constantinople occupied, the postwar Turks rose again, but under a modern, secular regime led by the nationalist Mustafa Kemal, better known as Kemal Atatürk, or simply Atatürk, meaning "Father Turk." He had little patience for the backwardness of the Ottomans and the rules of Islam, such as the covering of women when they went out, which rule he simply abolished. Confirming a fait accompli, Atatürk formally abolished the sultanate in 1922 and the caliphate in 1924. These events are what the terrorist Osama bin Laden referred to when he said in a videotape, as American bombers bore down on his camps, that Islam had suffered "humiliation and disgrace" for more than eighty years. To understand the enormity of Islam's defeat under the reformer Atatürk, consider Francis Robinson's summary: "The last ruler of the august house of Osman [was] packed unceremoniously into the Orient Express for Paris. Religious schools and religious courts were swept away; the last vestiges of the *Sharia* were replaced by the Swiss legal code; state training of *ulama* ceased . . . and the Turks were compelled to abandon their multifarious headgear in favor of the hat, which had long been a symbol of Europeanization and in which it was impossible to perform the Muslim prayer."[18]

There were a few weak attempts to revive the Arab caliphate, including one in 1916 by Hussein, a Hashemite descendant of the Prophet's family who was sharif of Mecca and king of the Hijaz, but his claim to the caliphate was widely ignored even in the Arab world. His descendants did go on to rule Iraq (they are no relation to the recent Iraqi ruler, Saddam Hussein Al-Tikriti) and still occupy the throne of Jordan.

Much of the Arab Muslim world had indeed turned in on itself under the European colonial yoke through the mid-twentieth century. As Amin Maalouf notes, this inversion worsened as the rest of the world evolved until finally, for many Muslims, "modernism became alien." They were at a fork in the road. "Should cultural and religious identity be affirmed by rejecting this modernism, which the West symbolized? Or, on the contrary, should the road of modernization be embarked upon. . . ?Even today we can observe a lurching alternation between phases of forced Westernization and phases of extremist, strong xenophobic traditionalism." Sadly, they are still at that fork in the road.

Return of the Crusades?

A more urgent question has arisen for Muslims and non-Muslims in the midst of recent terrorism. The Crusades may have been just a blip in Islamic history, but they bulk large in both Muslim and Western minds. Will they return? Could there be another major conflict between the Muslim world and the West? The old religious hatreds have not died. I witnessed at close hand the beginning of the Iranian Shiites' struggle against the shah, the Christian-Muslim war on the eastern Mediterranean island of Cyprus, the resulting standoff between Greece and Turkey, and the Lebanese civil war, and the old embers continue to flare in the Middle East and far beyond. In Africa thousands of Nigerians were killed when Muslims and Christians battled in the city of Kaduna in 2001 after Islam's *sharia* law was imposed. In 2002 riots broke out in the same city as Nigeria prepared to host the Miss World competition. A local journalist, a Christian woman in her twenties, defended the contest against Muslim protesters by writing that Muhammad himself would have been happy to marry one of the contestants. The resulting riots killed more than two hundred people. One Nigerian state issued a fatwa calling for the reporter's death; Nigeria's supreme Islamic body said the state had no right to issue a fatwa, and the reporter fled to the United States.

When these local fires break out, it is dangerous to make conventional military assumptions, and it remains so when the fires erupt into wars, revolutions, or major campaigns of terror—as Americans did on September 11, 2001. Americans were surprised that Bin Laden's fanatics in backward Afghanistan could turn the West's technological genius—computers, airplanes, skyscrapers—into an attack on the West itself. But there should be no cause for surprise in the future, for it is not the West's technological genius anymore but the world's.

As it happens, I have witnessed many moments over the years when military assumptions were not only wrong but also perilous.

• It was fatally wrong to assume that Shiite Muslims, banging primitively on their bare chests with chains in the 1960s to share in the seventh-century suffering of Ali and Hussein, would be no match for their fellow Muslim the modern shah and his sponsor, the most powerful country in the world.

• It was wrong when Greek Cypriot Christians fought Turkish Cypriot Muslims in 1974 to assume that the Muslims were the weaker because they were— well, Muslims. In fact, when an airborne missile crashed into a Christian-held hotel a few feet from me, it was the very model of a modern Muslim missile, Western-made but courtesy of the Turkish Air Force, whose intervention may have helped keep Greece out of the war.

• It was wrong to assume, as CBS producers on West Fifty-seventh Street had been taught by the long Soviet-American "cold war," that you could identify a guerrilla force by its weapons. Russian weapons meant leftist, revolutionary, anti-American. American weapons meant conservative, antirevolutionary, pro-American. So when my CBS crew in Lebanon photographed right-wing Christians training in secret, which revealed that a hot war might be about to break out, the producers apparently killed the story in part because we had said the Christians were using Russian or Czech AK-47 rifles. No way, said the deskbound producers. They would be using American M16s. Lefties use AK-47s. Of course, the New Yorkers were blithely unaware of the open-air arms market that was the port of Beirut, where everybody took what they could get.

Subglobal wars do not follow a script anymore. When civil war did break out in Lebanon, it was not the Palestinian or Lebanese Muslims who were wearing their religion on their sleeves, as Westerners would have expected. It was the young Christians, whose rifle butts glowed with decals of the Virgin Mary and sent my mind whirling back to the Crusades. It was indeed getting hard to follow a war without a program. In many ways, in the Middle East's multiple, dizzying little wars, all sides are the same. Like the vast noncombatant majority of the citizens, the journalists just had to survive.

The panicking, red-faced young Christians who had taken a bunch of us hostage on Cyprus, attacking my crew at one point for fear they might photograph one of their buddies, whose blood-soaked body they were dragging along the floor, were replaced soon enough by Palestinians in Beirut—probably Muslims, but possibly Christians—who kidnapped us and held us at their headquarters one very long day. But what was most unsettling was that all sides in the region—Cypriot Christians and Muslims, Greek Christians, Turkish Muslims, Palestinian Muslims and Christians, Lebanese Muslims and Christians—all seemed itchy to go to war. Could they be contained?

"Events in Lebanon during the civil war could easily become a paradigm for the entire region," Bernard Lewis warned in 1995. The peoples and governments of the Middle East "may unite—perhaps as some are urging, for a holy war, a new *jihad* which, again as in the past, might well evoke the response of a new Crusade."[19]

It was wise of the president to decide he did not mean it.

Edward R. Murrow *(right)* and Ed Hotaling, Teheran.
Courtesy of the author.

10

A (Personal) Persian Interlude

On the morning of November 4, 1979, Moorhead C. Kennedy, the man in charge, looked out the second-floor window of the American Embassy and wondered to himself what it would be like to die. Below him in the street, a seething crowd some four hundred strong shouted: "Death to the Shah!" "Death to Carter!" "Death to America!" Sometime between ten-fifteen and ten-thirty, the screaming protestors, armed with sticks, lead pipes, and baseball bats, invaded the embassy. "To put it bluntly," said a young marine guard named James Lopez, "all hell broke loose and we couldn't stop it." The Iranians held fifty-six Americans for 444 days.[1]

Thus awoke militant Islam after a four hundred-year sleep. During its long slide from the Ottoman empire-building in the mid-1500s, the Muslim flame had flared in the late 1600s, when that empire's armies again reached the gates of Vienna, and in the early 1800s, when the viceroy of Egypt, Muhammad Ali, conquered Sudan, Syria, and part of Anatolia. But not since Suleiman the Magnificent, who extended the Ottoman realm far into eastern Europe, had militant Islam laid down such a challenge to the world at large.

Shiite fundamentalists had kicked out the American-backed shah, ended the Persian Empire's twenty-five hundred-year run (give or take a few intermissions), and humiliated the strongest power in the world. Nor was this first modern Islamic revolution limited to the overthrow of Mohammad Reza Pahlavi and the later seizure of the embassy staff. It also taught five important lessons to terrorists.

Given that this was from the beginning a religious revolution, an observer looking down from Mars might be astounded to note that the American news media virtually ignored the religious issues. They would do the same a little more

133

than two decades later when many commentators would initially assume that the World Trade Center attacks had nothing to do with religion, despite the attackers' insistence that it was all about religion. This strange behavior was due in part to the fact that the Western media knew little about the religion in question and in part to the general Western agreement that religions are good, especially now that they have been tamed by the secular authorities, and should not be criticized. Religions are peaceful. Religions are nonviolent.

But when the air cleared in Tehran, it was obvious the revolutionaries meant what they had said: like it or not, this was a religious revolution, something Westerners had not seen in their lifetimes. An *Islamic* revolution. There had been modern political revolutions in Muslim countries, most notably in Algeria in the late 1950s, but this uprising in Iran and the terrorist lessons that it taught had the force of religion behind them in the person of the Ayatollah Ruholla ("Spirit of God") Khomeini, spiritual leader of a major Muslim nation.

To startled Westerners, it happened in a flash. But in fact the revolution had the force of history behind it as well. As we saw in chapter 8, Iran—Persia—had gone its own way politically after the Islamic conquests, creating a natural tension between mosque and state. The Safavid dynasty had sought to minimize this tension by making Shiism the official religion, but in so doing they introduced a major challenge to the state. English historian Francis Robinson almost seems to be writing about the last shah when he says of earlier Muslim empires, "Should dynasties even at the height of their power pay too scant a respect to the holy law, or should they weaken and lose some of the legitimacy which seemed to come to them through power alone, there were always some among the pious who would use the opportunity to attempt to carve out a wider role for God's law." [2]

Robinson mentions just such a leader who rose to power after four rulers in one Safavid century—1629–1722—flouted the holy law, and were drunkards to boot. He sounds like an early Ayatollah Khomeini-in-the-making. "The leading *mujtahid* [Islamic legal scholar] at the time, Muhammad Baqir Majlisi, was able greatly to influence government policy . . . and to impose his vision of orthodox Shiism on the power of the state to the extent of having the tens of thousands of bottles of wine in the royal cellars publicly smashed." [3]

The Shiite establishment that came to power in the Iranian Revolution had actually played a major role itself in creating the regime it destroyed. The late shah's father, Reza Khan, an army commander, overthrew the last of the Qajar dynasty shahs in 1925, set up a new government, and expelled the Soviet troops who controlled part of the country. Iran's *ulama*, furious at republican Turkey's abolition of the caliphate, opposed any idea of a republican government to succeed the Qajars. "I visited Qom," Reza Khan declared on the eve of his coronation, "and spoke with the divines of that holy city. . . . [W]e came to the decision to recommend to our fellow countrymen that they should cease all talk of a republic." Upon assuming the throne, Reza Khan renamed himself Reza Shah Pahlavi. In 1935 he formally changed the official name of the country as well—from Persia, as Westerners always called it, to Iran, as Iranians always called it.[4]

The founder of this new Pahlavi dynasty preferred Iran's legendary pre-Islamic days of the Kings Cyrus, Darius, Xerxes, and their successors. Though a Muslim himself, he considered Iran's Islamic period a disaster, a long violation of the Prophet's real teachings. As he tried to be Iran's version of Kemal Atatürk (with both egged on by *Time* magazine: "'At a Turk!'"), Reza Shah said he saw no conflict between religion and modernity. "If the Great Lawgiver of Islam were alive today, he would confirm the complete harmony of his true teachings with . . . the civilization of today." But after Muhammad, "for thirteen centuries, in each of which the country ought to have taken a great leap forward, it has remained motionless and backward."[5]

This new dynasty lost no time in abolishing Islamic law and customs. Reza Shah shut down Islamic courts and replaced religious elementary schools with public ones. He called for an end to the religious sacrificing of sheep and the annual Shiite mourning rites marking the massacre of Hussein and his family at Karbala. None of his moves was more noticeable, or less successful, than his effort to give the royal heave-ho to the chador, as the Iranians call the head-to-toe veil that makes women in public disappear (and is the Farsi origin of our word *shadow*). And no chador story was told more often than the one of *Now Ruz* (literally New Day, or New Year's Day) 1928.

The Queen Mother was visiting the shrine at Qom but had chosen to don a light-colored chador instead of the traditional black one. For this—or, according to another account, because her face was uncovered—her royal highness was actually criticized by an *alim*, one of the *ulama*, at Qom. When he heard about it, the furious king rushed to Qom, strode into Islam's holiest Iranian shrine without even removing his boots, and beat the offender with his riding crop. A mere king beating an *alim*! It is hard to imagine the horror Iran's clerics must have felt. As it happened, one of the religious teachers in Qom at the time was twenty-six-year-old Ruholla Khomeini, who one-half century later would put an end to this upstart Pahlavi dynasty.[6]

There were many such shocks to the *ulama* and the mullahs, or religious teachers, as the modern world was forced on them. After Reza Shah abdicated in 1941, driven into South African exile by the British and Soviets because of his pro-German leanings, shah *fils* took a pro-Allied stance and pursued his father's modernization campaign. The chador was actually banned in public places under penalty of fine. As it turned out, it was not the law that survived, it was the chador. Although many middle-class women dispensed with the veil under the second Pahlavi, especially in the glittery stores, restaurants, and clubs that began to decorate that era, many more women continued to don the chador in public. There was a Grand Canyon between the few rich and the millions of poor, and certainly one can see here, besides the strength of religion, the particular class-destroying power of the chador-as-uniform. Those who would make the head-to-toe *burkas* and *abayas* disappear throughout Afghanistan and Saudi Arabia today are not likely to have much more luck. Republican senator Bob Smith of New Hampshire actually said that "we are waging war in Afghanistan to remove these *abayas*," although it seems that, however much the senator might try, many Muslim women probably cannot be bombed into taking off their veils.[7] In fact, they were not bombed into it in Afghanistan, as the senator thought the allies were doing: many women, especially in rural areas, went right on wearing their *burkas*.

Few of the analysts writing brilliantly about the revolution today saw anything coming in the shah's early years. Instead, it seemed very clear back then that Iran really was much more than Islam. As noted in chapter 8, many of the glories of ancient Persia survived the arrival of Islam and adapted it in ways it would have been unnecessary to point out before the uprising of 1979. To glimpse this lost Iran, this tolerant Islam beneath the shah's dictatorship, one might imagine a series of Persian miniatures.

Paint your Iranians on the ancient holiday of *Now Ruz*, which as noted above was the start of the Persian (not the Islamic) New Year, at a festive family table bearing the *haftseen*, or seven *s*s (*seeb*, apple; *seer*, garlic; *sumac*, sumac; *samanou*, like halva; *sairke*, vinegar; *sabsi*, vegetables; and *senget*, like dates), plus other blessed items, such as a holy book, most likely the Koran, though it could also be the Avesta, the sacred writings of Zoroastrianism. Or picture them pouring themselves wine (as in old Sufi miniatures, albeit forbidden by the Koran) from an innocent-looking teapot in the garden of the Hotel Naderi. Draw them on another joyous holiday, at a *pique-nique* spread across a Persian carpet. Or at a wrestling match where competitors tumble down carpets sloping from the ring, imitating Iran's real heroes of that day, neither the ayatollahs nor the shah but the freestyle wrestlers who first brought home Olympic gold, with still treasured names such as Habibi, Takhti, Saifpour.[8]

As the world will see again soon, one of Iran's public achievements, a mixture of the royal and the Islamic, is so stunning it seems an illusion itself: the magical city of Isfahan. On a long-ago visit, two other Americans and I made straight for the bazaar, which easily beat the Tehran bazaar and even Istanbul's and the Arab souks, too, even those of Manama and Damascus. Beat them how? somebody asked. Beat them for mystery and intrigue and wonderment. In the early seventeenth century, when Isfahan was known as Nesf-e-Jahan, or Half the World, British and Dutch merchants haggled in the bazaar over Isfahani carpets, Persian silver, Indian spices, Chinese pottery, and goods brought by camel from Samarkand and Bukhara. However, our first mission was not to explore the bazaar's alluring domed passages but to find the rumored out-of-the-way stairs to a room on the second floor of the bazaar's two-story entrance. From a window there, we gazed out upon a huge square that was Shah Abbas I's masterpiece of urban design and that helped make Isfahan, as Francis Robinson says, one of the most beautiful cities of all time.

Laid out like a busily designed Persian rug, the Maidan-e-Shah, or Square of the Shah (later the Maidan-e-Khomeini), was the center of Safavid Isfahan when it was crowded with Muslims, Christians, and Jews. Rimming the square were the Ali Qapu Palace, where kings watched lions fight bulls and courtiers played the Persian game called polo; the Chehel Sotun, or Forty-Column Palace, whose real twenty columns were reflected in a glistening pool; and the Sheikh Lutfollah Palace, once a ladies' mosque, with its colored dome and masterful tile work. Down by the river, we could snack on grilled corn at the Khaju Bridge, then investigate its booths, or, from the top of the bridge, watch the ancient art of Persian carpet-washing (which Khomeini's successors would rename "Islamic carpet-washing").

For those who still wonder whether Islam conquers all, another non-Islamic survivor was Farsi, once spoken across central Asia and still the language of much of Afghanistan. Islam imposed its magnificent Arabic script on Iran but could not sell it the Arabic language. Equally serviceable, and at least equally esteemed, Farsi survived, giving us some of our tastier words: *aubergine, orange, punch, spinach, sumac, sugar,* not to mention *azure, babouche* (the Turkish slipper), *divan, kiosk, lilac, taffeta,* and more. One source adds *candy* and *peach* to the sweet list, but no less an authority than Professor Fred Donner, outgoing chair of Near Eastern Languages and Civilizations at the University of Chicago, pointed out to me that it was really Arabic that gave us *candy (qandi),* although Sanskrit has a strong claim as well *(khanda).* To prolong this tasty interval another second, Donner noted, too, that the word *peach* did not come from Farsi (which calls it *sheftali* or *holu*) but that in ancient times the fruit itself came from

Persia, so in Latin it became *"persicum,"* or fruit from Persia, whence the Italian *"pesca"* and the French *"peche."* And now, after that typically mouth-watering interlude in a Persian orchard, which also gives us a somewhat better idea of Paradise, back to work.

To conclude, Farsi did absorb a great many Arabic words, but not enough to make an Arab understand the language, and with no guarantee on usage: in the old Arabic-named *qavehkhounehs* (coffeehouses) of Iran, they drank tea. And while Iranians learn to recite the Koran in Arabic, almost as many do not understand the words.

A brief revolution against the shah was pulled off in the early 1950s, but it was not Islamic. It was led by the wily Iranian nationalist Mohammad Mosaddeq, who was actually educated at the chic Sciences Po, the Ecole des Sciences Politiques in Paris, and who had read his law in Switzerland, but would hide this foreign polish by throwing public weeping and temper tantrums and living, whenever possible, in his pajamas. This was quite a contrast with the shah, who like many royals was born without a personality, although he was much assisted by the beautiful, famously green-eyed Queen Soraya, an international celebrity. The world's media loved Mosaddeq's radical-in-pajamas act. The Iranians loved it, too, and when the charismatic prime minister upped and nationalized the Anglo-Iranian Oil Company, he was wildly hailed by anti-Western crowds. This episode so frightened Washington that, after trying to stage a countercoup, the United States helped the shah and Soraya escape to Italy. But that was not that. Fearing not so much the nationalization of oil but rather that Iran would fall under Communist and Soviet control, the CIA helped the Iranian military yank the thirty-four-year-old shah out of Rome and stuck him back on the Peacock Throne (not literally: only the throne's jewels survived, to be stashed in the Bank Melli).

A Tehran politician, Ebrahim Yazdi, told the visiting American historian and journalist Milton Viorst that Mosaddeq's revolution manqué was the turning point in modern Iranian history. "It killed our experiment with popular government. It also blackened the image of America which, having never been involved in colonialism here, has been our ideal in freedom and democracy. I think there was a good chance for our democracy had Mosaddeq survived. Instead, the Shah came back, and in the eyes of all Iranians, he was an American agent. The Shah never overcame that, and neither did the Americans."[9]

Now the shah cracked down, "never allowing the internal situation in the country to slip again from his control," as one of his supporters put it. While continuing to be staunchly backed by the United States as a bulwark against the Soviet Union, the shah through his secret police, known as SAVAK, arrested, jailed, and tortured political and religious opponents without trial. Among the victims of a death squad was the Ayatollah Khomeini's son Mustafa. The shah eventually suspended the parliament to put his reforms into effect and denied such basic human rights as freedom of speech. He also decided Iran needed a return to grandeur and empire.

Here the emperor went too fast for his American Embassy handlers to throw some clothes on him. He styled himself *shahinshah* (kingofkings) and outdid even his late father as he based his regime on the notion that he was the latest expression of Cyrus the Great. It amused the older generation, who knew that this dynasty dated back not to Cyrus and 550 B.C.E but to 1925. Whereas the *ulama* dreamed of returning Iran to the seventh century C.E., the shah preferred the seventh century B.C.E.

Then again, if *Iran* was not a synonym for *Islam*, it was not ancient Persia, either, wherein lay the shah's fatal error. He dismissed Islam, choosing not to wear his Shiism on his epaulet. He was inevitably photographed completing the hajj at Mecca, the emperor now literally without any clothes except for the pilgrim's white *ihram*, but he evinced little interest in Islam at home, when he was not being blatantly hostile. It seems almost unthinkable today that the shah, and the Americans telling him how to act, could have disregarded Islam, ignoring the fact that more than 90 percent of the Iranian population is Muslim, that the mullahs even then watched over life in every corner of the nation.

Never was the mullahs' power so evident as on Tassua va Ashoura, the "Ninth and Tenth," of Muharram, the first month on the Islamic calendar—the days of mourning processions that shah *pere* had tried to abolish throughout the country. On those two days, when and where they could get away with it, thousands of red-faced men and boys would snake through the streets, using ceremonial chains and knives as they lashed and cut their bare chests and backs until they bled generously. By this public penance, they shared in the sufferings of the Prophet's grandson, family, and fighters, massacred in 680—by Muslims.

In a compromise under the last shah the grim processions were permitted while the flagellation was technically banned. The mourners still wound through the streets screaming, "Ya Ali! Ya Hussein!" and the embassy advised the few Americans around to stay indoors, but the mourners were waving less lethal, more symbolic little flagella. They were also bleeding and hurting a lot less for Ali and Hussein, which doubtless upset the mullahs, whom the shah had rendered sadly out of fashion. Indeed, by this time the contempt of the shah and the rich for the traditions of Islam was so taken for granted that the English-language *Tehran Journal* catered to it with a regular feature called "Once the Mullah. . ." It was taken from a collection of stories in which the old mullah, in turban, cape, and gown, was always the goat.

◆　◆　◆

> We will kill them on the special day.
> Kill who?
> Kill the shah and his ministers. Kill the Americans at the embassy.

This was the quiet comment of a student as he strolled through town talking politics with me, his English teacher. It was extremely dangerous in the shah's police state for Ali, as we may call him, to be talking this way to anybody. Nor was it his habit. Like most students then, he kept his religion private; he was interested in technology and worried about finding a job. His warning that "they," meaning, one supposes, the people, would kill the shah and the Americans was obviously a burst of desperate anger. But it was made the more real by his comment that it would happen "on the special day," a reminder of the importance of dates to Muslims. Maybe Ali was trying to get the word out about his country's travails. (I did offer this revolutionary warning to an editor back in the United States, who thought it rather the same old thing from foreign students. The world had little interest in prophecies from the likes of Ali until they came true, as this one did, minus the specific killings that Ali mentioned but with thousands of others.)

John F. Kennedy's vice president dropped by to put in a good word for the shah's reforms, as did USIA director and news legend Edward R. Murrow, as did Jackie, all of them underlining U.S. support for the regime. Lyndon Johnson's comments back then are being repeated today by those urging Iran to modernize with the help of the West. Also reporting for a Tehran newspaper at the time, I quoted Johnson as he called for a balance between defense and "internal modernization. . . . Both are indispensable to a twentieth-century nation." The problem was that it was also a seventh-century nation, whose mullahs were fiercely opposed to modernization. LBJ might have learned something from Ali, but it was probably too late. A year later, Kennedy was dead, Johnson was president, and the Mourning Days became bloody-minded again.[10]

This time, in the Tehran bazaar and in the holy cities of Qom and Mashhad, the Tassua va Ashoura mourners directed their hatred not at their own bare chests but against the shah. The black corteges of 1963 exploded into riots against his programs for land reform, which threatened to weaken the mullahs, and women's rights. Government tanks and troops finally stopped the rioting at a cost of several dead and wounded. Having lived there earlier but then residing in France, I could report in the Paris edition of the *New York Herald-Tribune* that "the spell has not been broken," that a Shiite high priest unknown to the outside world had just been jailed, that his name was Ruholla Khomeini—and that "the old mullah may have the last laugh yet."[11]

Those riots were really the beginning of the Iranian Revolution, though it remained underground: they proved that the mullahs had the power to challenge the shah. Khomeini himself was released, but in 1964, after a sermon at Qom in which he called Iran "a prisoner of America," he was arrested again and exiled to Turkey. After a year there, he went to Iraq for thirteen years, then moved to the Paris suburbs four months before the revolution, and prepared to pounce.

It seemed clear to me, when I went back to Iran and attended the twenty-fifth-hundredth birthday party for his "empire" in 1971, that the shah had by then lost all touch with his subjects, not that he ever had been much in touch in the first place. Prince Philip, Haile Selassie, and such commoners as Vice President Spiro Agnew dutifully reported to the spectacular ruins of ancient Persepolis, where they dined in elegant little tents spread across the south-central Iranian desert. The shah had maximum news coverage for his accession to glory, assisted by American television. The biggest potentate at the bash may have been Barbara Walters, who by the time I boarded the press bus at Persepolis was already on her throne, the right front seat of the bus. The best seat was certainly her due as she was anchoring the thing live, all the way from the Persian desert to Rockefeller Center and the *Today* show. American TV thus joined the American government in conferring legitimacy on the shah's rule. In the process, of course, it rendered the other American reporters there all but unnecessary, which may have been one reason Charlotte Curtis seemed on edge. In our desert press room Charlotte loudly demanded to know whether the twenty-one-gun salute actually had twenty-one guns going off (she worked for the *New York Times*). When the shah in his reedy voice read the words of Cyrus over the loudspeaker, he sounded to my ears as though he really did believe he was descended from him. Afterward, my visit with a television crew to a tiny farm village, where we cooled off with pomegranates and chatted with some poor residents in Farsi, indicated that the shah was certainly not reaching anybody in Iran's mud homes.

Only two years later the kingofkings' image of himself seemed confirmed

again by an explosion in oil prices. The "petrodollar" gusher, tripling and quad-
rupling prices, transformed Iran, thrusting it to the brink of the future. The boom
"grew" the middle class exponentially, as the new money class doubtless learned
to say, and many of the liberal professionals became enthusiastically pro-shah.
The biggest problem was really not how to grow the economy but how to rein it in;
Iran did not really have the talent to manage the growth. As a new decade (and
the unseen revolution) approached, the shah's statisticians said Iran had a supply of 20,000 engineers and needed 36,000 more, 21,000 medical personnel and
a demand for 44,000, and 75,000 technicians and a demand for 117,000 more.
One wonders if Ali found a job and still hoped to kill people.

Which way would the shah go politically? Could Iran be steered toward a
middle-class-inspired democratic republic with new prospects for broad prosperity and political freedom? Not, it seemed, if the shah could help it. By now a
representative of SAVAK was assigned to sit in the offices of the *Tehran Journal*,
a milestone in that little newspaper's history. A democratic republic with political
freedom? Not if Islam's ayatollahs and mullahs—who controlled millions of
young anti-shah, anti-American Shiites—could help it. And they could. From his
Iraqi exile Khomeini had begun recording speeches on cassettes that would be
played in the mosques of Iran's poor neighborhoods, where Americans, the shah,
and apparently even his secret police, SAVAK, rarely set foot. For the ayatollah,
this stratagem was even more effective than being in country, where he would not
only be arrested himself but also lead SAVAK to his supporters. It was an early
example of Islamic extremists using low Western technology against the West.
Later, from Afghanistan, the exiled terrorist Bin Laden would do the same,
recording cassettes for young Saudis back home, where they were a big hit. Also
later, at the other end of the spectrum, the last shah's son, ensconced in Maryland,
would ship cassettes aimed at the Iranian revolutionaries' sons and daughters.

American intelligence was not able to monitor extremist Islam's revolution-
in-the-making, and still cannot do so today. Satellite technology does not pick up
what they say and believe in the mosques of working-class neighborhoods, nor do
visiting Americans frequent them much, except to pick up a great copper tray in
the bazaar.

Finally, after the progovernment newspaper *Ettelaat* ran an attack on
Khomeini in 1978, the shah's forces attacked religious students who turned out to
protest, causing heavy casualties. It was soon clear the shah was over his head,
and he fled to the United States in January 1979, ostensibly for medical treatment.
Two weeks later Khomeini flew in from Paris in triumph. Eleven months after-

ward, Moorhead Kennedy, from his window in the embassy, saw the raging crowd out front.

Since then, some of the hostage takers have said they originally intended to hold the Americans for only five to seven days to protest the admission of the shah into the United States. In fact, they were not the only ones angry at America's harboring the shah. Even before the shah was admitted, the embassy staff itself had sent messages back to the State Department protesting it. "It was killing us," Barry Rosen, the press attaché, said later. "We were eating ourselves alive. Why? Why?"[12]

The hostage takers have given various reasons for changing their minds and holding on to the hostages, one citing Washington's refusal to make concessions and the value of the embassy as a rallying point, others Washington's indications that it would take no serious action against them. And some have said they were relieved when the hostages were freed.[13]

As it turned out, it was not only the revolution but the embassy takeover in particular that taught five important lessons to extremists around the world. Many Westerners are just learning these five lessons now, a quarter century later, but they were picked up quickly by terrorists.

Islam could fight.

The revolutionary Shiites of Iran had suddenly provided fledgling *Islamic* guerrilla bands, as opposed to nationalist or other political units, with a strange new clout. Religiously inspired guerrillas would become prominent in the Palestinians' war with Israel and in the Lebanese civil war. Until now the latter had been a political contest between the Christian and Muslim communities, with only a few minor crusading units flaunting their faith by sticking Virgin Mary decals on their rifle butts.

Islam could fight all right. Some Western writers trying to put Islam in the best light possible choose to ignore the embarrassing Iran-Iraq War, which began within a year of the embassy seizure, lasted eight years, and demonstrated to the world the two Muslim countries' capacity for monstrous bloodletting. Iraq started it, Saddam Hussein claiming he had to protect Sunnis from Shiism, even though many of Iraq's own troops were Shiites (who showed little interest in crossing over to the ayatollah). It ended in a UN cease-fire, Iraq the bloodied de facto winner. With a death toll that must have topped one-half million altogether, the war finally sowed doubt among Iranians about the wisdom of the clerics' absolute power. Iranian political science professor Hadi Semati told Milton Viorst, "Hav-

ing accepted huge sacrifices—a million casualties, including 400,000 dead—
for what we were told was a holy *jihad,* the people suddenly discovered that God
did not defeat Satan, who was Saddam Hussein." [14]

Islamic terrorism is justified.

Westerners who still have trouble accepting that there could be such a thing
as religious terror ("it's not about religion") might note that the group responsible
for the kidnapping, imprisonment, and mental and occasional physical torture of
the embassy staff called itself "Muslim Students Following the Line of Ayatollah
Khomeini." But as that crisis dragged on, terrorism was no longer a very serious
matter for the students, despite the television close-ups of the wilder demonstrators. The future Nobel Prize winner V. S. Naipaul visited the scene some weeks
after the takeover. "It was like a fair, tents, stalls, books, food, hot drinks. [The
students] were in guerrilla garb; they had pitched low khaki tents. . . . They were
only playing at war." [15] It is perhaps understandable that the embassy takeover
should have been dismissed shortly afterward, as it still is today, as a minor affair
by a society willing to deliver four hundred thousand of its poorest young men to
Paradise. In any event, the embassy terrorists' original message had already
been sent.

The message that terrorism in the name of Islam was acceptable traveled
fast. It may well have inspired the Muslim extremists who, a year after the embassy attack in Tehran, assassinated Egyptian president Anwar Sadat. They
were, after all, thanked by the Iranians, who named a Tehran street after a
leader of the Egyptian assassins. The abduction and imprisonment of the embassy staff led to more Shiite kidnappings in Lebanon's civil war. And ten years
into the revolution, the Ayatollah Khomeini put out a hit on the British Muslim
novelist Salman Rushdie, his fatwa charging that Rushdie's novel *The Satanic
Verses* had blasphemed the Prophet. "I would like to inform all the intrepid
Muslims in the world," Khomeini declared, in what would turn out to be an important contribution to the future strategies of Osama bin Laden, "that the author of the book entitled *The Satanic Verses* . . . published in opposition to
Islam, the Prophet and the Koran, as well as those publishers who were aware of
its contents, have been sentenced to death. . . . I call on all zealous Muslims to
execute them quickly, wherever they find them. . . . Anyone killed in doing this
will be regarded as a martyr." [16] Osama bin Laden would order his agents to do
the same to all Americans, wherever they could be found. Fortunately, the vast
peaceful Muslim majority had no intention of doing anything of the sort, al-

though eventually it took only nineteen hijackers to get started on Bin Laden's mission.

Besides Khomeini's presumption in deciding who was a martyr, the hit on the non-Muslim publishers might also be noted, as it removes apostasy as a motive for the ayatollah. Much would be made of the fact that a month later all but one of the forty-nine member states of the Islamic Conference condemned the ayatollah's advertised hit as un-Islamic and that many Iranians privately opposed it. But none dared criticize it publicly, and the Iranian government did not dissociate itself from it for another nine years.

As a matter of fact, the fatwa survives to this day in the minds of those fanatics who use it to describe Muslims with the courage to defy the terrorists as "Rushdies," thus threatening their lives, too. Rushdie himself objected to this sloganizing of his name at first, but then changed his mind. "For the most part," he said, "I'm comfortable with, and often even proud of, the company I'm in." Extremists again renewed the fatwa to mark its fourteenth anniversary on February 14, 2003. Rushdie, in New York, noted, "If you look at every February 14th, some voice from Iran has piped up to send me a little Valentine card."[17] The Rushdie fatwa, addressed to Muslims everywhere, had made it clear that Khomeini's ambitions for Islam were not limited to Iran. The ayatollah himself, Viorst notes, used the phrase "exporting the Revolution" and called Iran "the starting point" for a worldwide Islamic revolution.

Meanwhile, at home, the Khomeini regime embarked on an internal reign of terror. Revolutionary tribunals executed not only the shah's supporters but eventually other anti-shah opponents of the regime. At one point, Viorst writes,

> pro-Communist elements launched a small vicious civil war, which claimed victims from as high as the top ranks of the clerical hierarchy. Khomeini, however, proved he could be equally violent, as violent as the shah had ever been. Tens of thousands of Iranians died before the resistance was stanched. . . . Khomeini also reshaped the armed forces and the security services, which had remained faithful to the shah to the end. He had hundreds of security agents executed, and thousands purged from the ranks. In rebuilding the security organizations, he imparted to them a character as ruthless as that of the Shah's agencies.[18]

One lucky survivor of the internal terror told Naipaul in Tehran, "After 1982 all the good leaders began to be assassinated. The top people. The assassinations were by different groups. Then comparative second-grade people began to come

up. Only Beheshti [a one-time presidential candidate] was left. And then he was
killed. . . . He wanted relations with all countries except Israel and South Africa.
And he wanted to end the war." After some other deaths, the survivor said, the
regime started to "wipe out" the opposition. It was the sort of Islamic dictatorship
that Mullah Muhammad Omar, the future leader of Afghanistan, might admire.
And it was perhaps the only way that terrorists could achieve the pure world
ummah they sought.

One would-be America-lover was targeted by the terrorists: Jaffrey, a copy
editor on the *Tehran Journal* before it became a complete tool of the shah. A
handsome, inspiring presence in his sharp blue suit, Jaf would light up the little
newsroom as he dished out a good word for everyone, reeled off jokes, and never
let anybody's else jokes go unrewarded with a huge laugh. He loved hearing anything that would give him an idea of what America was really like. Naipaul met
him much later, just briefly, before the embassy takeover, and was equally
charmed: "Mr. Jaffrey was a middle-aged man with flashing eyes and a wide, mobile mouth. He radiated energy." But if it was the same old Jaf, he also put something over on the famous writer, who, of course, had no way of knowing about the
prerevolution Jaf.

"Mr. Jaffrey" told his distinguished visitor that his dream was to live in a
pure *jame towhidi* (society of believers), just as in the days "when the Prophet
ruled, and the spiritual and secular were one, and everything that was done by the
as yet small community could be said to be serving the faith." This was true as far
as it went. After all, it was months before the Americans were seized, and nobody
knew where things were going. It is easy to see Jaf getting swept up in the religious
fervor that boiled over in Tehran at the very beginning of the revolution. But
Naipaul noted that his interviewee was also starting to feel conflicted about the
idea of government and faith being all wrapped together in the society of believers.
"It was just at this point that Mr. Jaffrey's Indian-British education [he was a trans-
planted native of Lucknow in northern India] and experience came into play,
ideas of democracy and law and institutions, the separation of church and state,
ideas that made him sit at his typewriter in the reporters' room and rap out peppery
calls for the mullahs to get back to the mosques and the ayatollahs to get back to
Qom."

What Jaf could not have told Naipaul in those dangerous times was that they
were also ideas that made him love America. They were part of what had made him
hope to see not Britain or India or even the pure *jame towhidi* right away, but
America. Jaf had even called me in New York once to inquire about the possibility.

He could not safely tell Naipaul this, of course. Even if he had, the future Nobel laureate's tale about Mr. Jaffrey's conflicted Islamic ideal would have lost something. As it was, though, Naipaul got the latest on what finally happened to Jaf.

After the takeover of the embassy, the terrorists found a receipt there for payments made to Jaf as a *Voice of America* stringer, three hundred dollars a month. It was dangerous information, and one of them came looking for Jaf. By luck, he was not there, and when he heard about it, Jaf slipped out of his house in the middle of the night, got into his big old Chevrolet, and drove all the way to Pakistan, paying off the guards on both sides of the border. Then he called the office back in Tehran and announced, "I am here with my Chevrolet." The embassy terrorists went through his house and took some things. Jaf died in 1990. It was the end of his dream of the pure society of believers, Naipaul wrote quite accurately. What he could not write was that it was also the end of this gentlemanly, infectiously enthusiastic, devout Muslim's other dream, to come to America.

America is the real target.

Not its protégés, or as one Middle East commentator put it, its "deputy sheriffs"—namely, the shah back then and those strange fellows sharing the American foreign policy bed, Israel and Saudi Arabia. In case Muslims did not get the message, the Iranians spelled out the enemy's name in Koranic terms: "the Great Satan." To some Americans, unaware of Satan's role in the Koran as a living threat, it was merely akin to the childish name-calling of World War II: "Yankee Pig." But many Muslims got the message immediately. As noted earlier, in that same month of November 1979, Muslim dissidents attacked and seized the Great Mosque in Mecca, charging that the Saudi royal family had strayed from Islam—seemingly another strange example of "brotherhood" and one in which the United States had no overt involvement. And how did Muslim demonstrators in Pakistan vent their fury? As Bernard Lewis sarcastically pointed out, they burned the U.S. Embassy, of course. What Lewis missed, though, is that the demonstrators could easily identify the Saudi regime and royal family with their powerful American supporters.

Over the course of more than fifteen years, Iran would proclaim its hatred to the world (including terrorists) by posting signs like the one over Passport Control at Tehran's Mehrabad Airport, "Death to America," or the hotel poster reading, "We Will Inflict on American a Severe Defeat." So in 1998 it would come as terrible news, but not such a surprise, when two U.S. embassies in East Africa were bombed, the dead including twelve Americans and more than two hundred

Africans, many of them Muslims. The lessons of Khomeini were being applied by
Bin Laden.

Here, too, hangs another saga of terrorism at an embassy. Ali Tabatabai was
the former press attaché of the shah's embassy in Washington and an active oppo-
nent of the Khomeini regime, and must have acquired the odd notion that America was a safe place to engage in world politics. One day soon after the revolution,
Ali walked along sedate Massachusetts Avenue, past the shut-down embassy
with its incongruously bright tile work and dome, and defiantly told me and a television camera, "We will take that building back!" It seemed a very dangerous
thing for an Iranian to shout in those days, but there is no way to know whether it
helped bring a postman to a door in suburban Bethesda shortly afterward. Ali
opened the door. The postman's gun rang out three times. The suspect in the
killing was alleged to be a former Howard University student, one David Belfield,
who had converted, taken the name Daoud Salahuddin, and worked as a guard at
the Iranian Interests Section of the Algerian Embassy. When I went there looking
for him in the wake of the killing, this exchange occurred on videotape:

> Is Mr. Salahuddin here?
> Why don't you go do something important?
> Well, a man has been killed. I think that's important.
> People get killed every day.

That state of affairs was indeed the everyday condition that terrorists could live
with, now brought to America. After the shooting, Salahuddin drove immediately
to Montreal, where he boarded a flight to Geneva, then flew to Iran. It happened
twenty years ago, but the next thing one heard of him was quite recent. He was a
movie star. In late 2001, Montgomery County, Maryland, prosecutors identified
him as the actor Hassan Tantai, who played an African American in Afghanistan
in the widely acclaimed Iranian film *Kandahar*. Unmasked, Salahuddin admitted from his Iranian exile that he had killed Ali Tabatabai. "He's an assassin, he's
a terrorist, and he's a fugitive from justice," Montgomery County prosecutor Douglas F. Gansler charged. But he also noted that the United States has no extradi-
tion treaty with Iran.[19]

America is vulnerable.

The Iranian Shiites provided both terrorists and Americans with a strange
new sense of American impotence. Bin Laden told John Miller of ABC News in
1998 that the American government had declined and the American soldier had

become weak and unprepared to fight long wars: "This was proven in Beirut when the Marines fled after the two explosions. It also proves they can run in less than twenty-four hours, and this was also repeated in Somalia. . . . The youth were surprised at the low morale of the American soldiers. . . . After a few hours, they ran in defeat. . . . They forgot about being the world leader and the leader of the new world order. [They] left, dragging their corpses and their shameful defeat, and stopped using such titles."[20]

Television is a terrorist weapon.

It magnified their triumph in Iran and demoralized Americans. In the ABC News headline for its daily television coverage of the embassy takeover—"America Held Hostage"—that word *America* no longer sounded bold and proud but helpless and ashamed. Osama bin Laden sought the same effect two decades later in his bragging, sneering videotapes for Muslim and American audiences. In more ways than one, the endlessly repeated TV slogan "America Held Hostage" (for 444 days) helped prepare us, and the terrorists, and the rest of the world, for the headline "U.S. Attacked" on September 11, 2001.

New York Times, September 12, 2001.
Copyright © 2003 by The New York Times Co. Reprinted by permission.

11

The Terrorists' Handbook

Eight months, ten days, and less than nine hours into the millennium—twenty-two years after Iran replaced the shah's dictatorship with a reign of religious terror—a second terrorist outburst shook the entire world.

Today, as all governments and average citizens still try to come to grips with the September 11, 2001, attacks on the World Trade Center in New York and the Pentagon (for governments and citizens alike, it will take years to absorb the shock), a couple of extraordinary discoveries will help them understand not only the terrorists' operations but also their minds: two documents prepared by the terrorists themselves. The first, which authorities attribute to the Al Qaeda network, is a handbook of plans and tactics for terrorist attacks. The second, a letter carried by the hijackers on September 11, exposes their innermost thoughts as they prepared to board four airliners.

The two documents also reveal the terrorists' religious faith, however much it distorted the peaceful religion as practiced by the vast majority of Muslims—intentional distortion on the part of the terrorist leaders, perhaps ignorant distortion on the part of some of their operatives. The terrorists were "hijacking the religion," as the president and others put it. Within a month of the attacks, the president told the nation: "The United States of America is an enemy of those who aid terrorists and of the barbaric criminals who profane a great religion by committing murder in its name."

But is Islam altogether too hijackable, not in its ancient form, which met the needs of its early centuries, but in its modern form, as actually practiced, with its many variations, its divided leaders, and their frequent reluctance to counterattack Islam's "hijackers"? It is true that within a month of the attacks, as the pres-

151

ident of the United States announced, "Fifty-six Islamic nations issued a state-
ment strongly condemning the savage acts of terror and emphasizing that those
acts contradict the peaceful teaching of Islam." But that denunciation came *after*
September 11. The Islamic Conference and the individual governments of Muslim countries saw no need to be stronger earlier in confronting the terrorists.

With a full year between them, two prominent voices asked exactly the same
question. Two days after the attacks, Thomas L. Friedman wrote in the *New York
Times* of Muslim leaders' failure to condemn suicide attacks before September
11: "Where are the Muslim leaders who will tell their sons to resist the Israelis—
but not to kill themselves or innocent non-combatants? . . . Surely Islam, a grand
religion that never perpetrated the sort of Holocaust against the Jews in its midst
that Europe did, is being distorted when it is treated as a guidebook for suicide
bombing. How is it that not a single Muslim leader will say that?" Sadly, a year
later Salman Rushdie could still ask exactly the same question as he commented
on continuing terrorist attacks on those other "Rushdies," the few moderate
Muslims around the world who defied the extremists: "Where, after all, is the
Muslim outrage at these events? As their ancient, deeply civilized culture of
love, art and philosophical reflection is hijacked by paranoiacs, racists, liars,
male supremacists, tyrants, fanatics and violence junkies, why are they not
screaming? . . . Muslims in the West, too, seem unnaturally silent on these top-
ics. If you're yelling, we can't hear you." [1]

Of course, there's a very simple answer that the Western commentators ignore: many Muslims don't want to be killed by one of the crazy Muslims with
guns. Some try to explain away the silence of the majority by pointing out that
Muslims are discouraged by their religion from fighting or criticizing other Muslims—a useful injunction whenever they want to forget their long history of in-
ternecine warfare. And many Muslims doubtless do recognize a certain piety,
however misguided, in the terrorists. Jane I. Smith, a professor at Hartford Sem-
inary in Connecticut, calls published excerpts of the September 11 hijackers'
last written communication "truly pious." She adds: "Apparently, one can assume what was done was done by people out of a genuine and sincere belief that
they were helping bring about the will of God. . . . And that, in turn, may be the
most frightening thing about it." [2]

In the meantime, the terrorists themselves continue to teach their own violent and, they hope, world-conquering brand of religion. To be answered, it must
be exposed, as it is in the two terrorist documents illuminating the black morning
of September 11, 2001. The first is a manual that investigators found in May 2000
in the home of a suspected Bin Laden agent in Manchester, England. Titled *Mil-*

itary Studies in the Jihad Against the Tyrants, it is a 180-page volume that investigators suspect was used as a handbook by Osama bin Laden's Al Qaeda organization. Prosecutors introduced it as evidence against four alleged conspirators in the 1998 bombings of the two U.S. embassies in East Africa. There is no evidence that the nineteen September 11 terrorists had this manual, but as the *New York Times* pointed out, "much of their conduct reflects its lessons."[3]

Missions and Code of Conduct

Here are some excerpts that suggest how the terrorists viewed the teachings of Islam, starting with their goals and objectives (and keeping in mind that neither the Koran nor any other Muslim teaching gave Bin Laden or Al Qaeda the right to conduct a jihad, or holy war, in the first place):

Missions required: The main mission for which the Military Organization is responsible is: the overthrow of the godless regimes and their replacement with an Islamic regime. Other missions consist of the following:

1. Gathering information about the enemy, the land, the installations and the neighbors.

2. Kidnapping enemy personnel, documents, secrets and arms.

3. Assassinating enemy personnel as well as foreign tourists.

4. Freeing the brothers who are captured by the enemy.

5. Spreading rumors and writing statements that instigate people against the enemy.

6. Blasting and destroying the places of amusement, immorality, and sin; not a vital target.

7. Blasting and destroying the embassies and attacking vital economic centers.

8. Blasting and destroying bridges leading into and out of the cities.

The fact that the main mission—"the overthrow of the godless regimes and their replacement with an Islamic regime"—violates the Koranic injunction "No coercion in religion" hardly troubles the terrorists. They would find justification for their worldwide goal in a hadith, a saying of the Prophet as quoted by a son of his friend Umar the Conqueror: "I have been commanded to fight against the people till they testify that there is no God but Allah." This hadith is a favorite of Osama bin Laden. The fact that Muhammad himself never presented this as God's word in the Koran, but was merely quoted after his death (by a third-hand source) as having said it, carries no weight among terrorists or, for that matter, among many other Muslims who accept the hadiths as divinely inspired.

The Koran and Islam's other teachings do not condone the slaughter ordered above. But in an attempt to justify their recommended mass murder, assassinations, kidnappings, and destruction, the terrorists might also quote the Koran's seventh-century battlefield advice:

> . . . fight and slay
> The Pagans wherever ye find them,
> And seize them, beleaguer them,
> And lie in wait for them
> In every stratagem (of war).   (9:5)

It is interesting that the terrorist handbook considered the places of amusement, immorality, and sin "not a vital target." Of course, in one sense this was putting it mildly, since the frustrated terrorists liked to hang out in these neon palaces of the pagan civilization they loved/hated, which seemed to underline the apparently uncontrollable lust of the Arabian desert that the Saudi translators of the holy book tried hard to control. More important, the policy assigning a low priority to "places of amusement" as targets had been thrown out by October 2002, a month that saw two attacks that were later praised in an audiotape attributed to Bin Laden. The first was a bombing that killed some 200 people at a nightclub on the Indonesian island of Bali, a fashionable international resort—the worst casualty toll from a terrorist attack since September 11, 2001; the second terrorist attack on "a place of amusement" was a massive hostage-taking by Chechen rebels of a Moscow theater, where 117 were killed, all but one of them as a result of a gas attack by Russian government forces trying to end the ordeal. Nor was that the end of it. In late November terrorists in Africa bombed an Israeli-owned resort complex in Mombasa, Kenya—it was called the Paradise Hotel, no less—killing twelve Israelis. They also fired two missiles nearby that narrowly missed downing a planeload of Israeli tourists.

Terrorism analyst Peter Bergen said the Bali nightclub bombing, where most of the victims were Australians, and earlier attacks on German and French citizens, indicated a major shift of Al Qaeda policies toward economic warfare against multinational targets. Indeed, Bergen noted that since Al Qaeda lost its Afghan base after September 11, 2001, and went on the run, it had "morphed into something at once less centralized, more widely spread and more virtual than its previous incarnation."[4]

In a section on operations, the terrorist manual said:

Cell or cluster methods should be adopted by the Organization. It should be composed of many cells whose members do not know one another, so that if a cell member is caught the other cells would not be affected. . . .

Security measures that should be observed in public transportation: The brothers traveling on a "special mission" should not get involved in religious issues (advocating good and denouncing evil) or day-to-day matters (seat reservation . . .) . . . .

It is necessary for any party that adopts Jihad work and has many members to subdivide its members into three groups, each of which has its own security measures. The three groups are: 1. The overt member. 2. The covert member. 3. The commander.

In its general advice for operatives, the manual says a member should:

1. Not reveal his true name to the Organization's members who are working with him. . . .

2. Have a general appearance that does not indicate Islamic orientation (beard, toothpick, book, long shirt, small Koran).

3. Be careful not to mention the brothers' common expressions or show their behavior (special praying appearance, "may Allah reward you," "peace be on you" while arriving and departing etc.)

4. Avoid visiting famous Islamic places (mosques, libraries, Islamic fairs, etc.). . . .

14. Converse on the telephone using special code so that he does not attract attention.

18. Not park in no-parking zones and not take photographs where it is forbidden.

Important note: married brothers should observe the following: Not talking with their wives about Jihad work.

The operations section also details what captured terrorists should do during interrogations—such as yielding the name of a fictitious brother who "conceived, planned, trained and executed the operation" but has since been "sent away on a journey" outside the country. Qualifications include "combat fitness (jumping, climbing, running, etc.), good training on the weapon of assassination, assault, kidnapping, and bombing (special operations)," and a calm personality to allow "coping with psychological traumas such as those of the operation of bloodshed, mass murder."

In a "code of ethics" section on how to maintain good Muslim behavior, the manual says the terrorists do not have to dress like Muslims when among "the polytheists." But it warns that some behavior is still forbidden, "such as drinking wine or fornicating. There is nothing that permits those." The manual continues: "Guidelines for beating and killing hostages—religious scholars have permitted beating. . . . The religious scholars have also permitted the killing of a hostage if he insists on withholding information from Moslems."

The manual has this note on "Prisons and Detention Centers: If an indictment is issued and the trial begins, the brother has to pay attention to the following: Complain to the court of mistreatment while in prison."

◆ ◆ ◆

The second major terrorist document—a letter of instructions that the September 11 hijackers carried—was drenched in the terrorists' version of Islam, but in strange, personal language they could understand, a mixture of general Islamic expressions and their own sometimes childish variations on them. The letter contains, in effect, the "orders of the day" for the nineteen who attacked New York and Washington. Mohamed Atta abandoned it with his luggage at Boston's Logan International Airport. Then he boarded American Airlines Flight 11, the first plane to hit its target, the North Tower of the World Trade Center. Although the orders left in Atta's rental car were the original version, it is not known whether it was Atta himself, the presumed hijack commander, who wrote them. Hijackers of two of the three other planes had apparent photocopies of what became known as "the Atta letter." One was found in a car parked at Dulles International Airport outside Washington, where the hijackers boarded American Airlines Flight 77 and crashed it into the Pentagon. The other photocopy was discovered in the wreckage of United Airlines Flight 93, which crashed in rural Pennsylvania. No copy was traced to American Flight 175 out of Logan, which hit the South Tower of the Trade Center.[5]

The FBI released the Atta letter in the original Arabic in order to avoid complaints about the accuracy and authenticity of a government translation.

The Hijackers' Instructions

"In the name of God, the most merciful, the most compassionate," the *Washington Post* translation of the letter began. "In the name of God, of myself and of my family . . . I pray to you God to forgive me from all my sins, to allow me to glorify you in every possible way. . . . Remember the battle of the prophet . . . against the infidels, as he went on building the Islamic state." The letter thus immediately departed from Muslim tradition, where nobody prays in his own name and his family's. To do so would put the supplicant on a par with Allah. It might have been done in this case out of ignorance or in a deliberate attempt to assuage the individual terrorists as they thought of themselves and their families. As for remembering the battle of the Prophet as he built the Islamic state, this is a reminder of the terrorists' permanent imperialism, their determination to continue building a worldwide *ummah*.

Under the heading "The Last Night" in the upper right-hand corner of the letter's third page—which night Atta and fellow terrorist Abdulaziz Alomari spent in room 232 of a Comfort Inn in South Portland, Maine—the terrorists' fifteen duties for the next morning were numbered and listed. For these, I will use the *New York Times* translation by Capital Communications Group of Washington, with explanatory comments of my own in brackets:

> 1. Making an oath to die and renew your intentions. Shave excess hair from the body and wear cologne. Shower. [This is a confused combination of several Muslim rituals. Washing, which symbolically cleanses the inner self as well, is one of the preparations for attending prayer at the mosque. After death the body is washed. During the pilgrimage to Mecca, after the sacrifice of an animal, the pilgrim shaves. The cologne was perhaps in preparation for entering Paradise.]
> 2. Make sure you know all aspects of the plan well, and expect the response, or a reaction, from the enemy.
> 3. Read *Al-Tawba* and *Anfal* and reflect on their meanings and remember all of the things that God has promised for the martyrs. [*Al-Tawba* and *Anfal* are the "war suras" from the Koran widely ignored by Western scholars and "experts" as outdated. *Al-Tawba*, or Repentance, is the ninth sura, and *Anfal*, or Spoils of War, is the eighth.]
> 4. Remind your soul to listen and obey and remember that you will face decisive situations that might prevent you from 100 percent obedience, so tame your soul, purify it, convince it, make it understand, and incite it. God said: "Obey God and his messenger, and do not fight amongst yourselves or else you will fail. And be patient, for God is with the patient." [It is useful here to note the official Saudi translation of the Koran, with its own emphases, as fifteen of the nineteen hijackers were Saudis: "O you believe! Seek help in patience and *As Salat* (the prayer). Truly! Allah is with *As-Sabirun* (the patient)."]
> 5. Pray during the night and be persistent in asking God to give you victory, control and conquest, and that He may make your task easier and not expose us.
> 6. Remember God frequently, and the best way to do it is to read the Holy Koran, according to all scholars, as far as I know. It is enough for us that it [the Koran] are the words of the Creator of the Earth and the plants, the One that you will meet [on the Day of Judgment]. [The "I" could well be Atta, but again the author is unknown].

7. Purify your soul from all unclean things. Completely forget something called "this world." The time for play is over, and the serious time is upon us. How much time have we wasted in our lives? Shouldn't we take advantage of these last hours to offer good deeds and obedience?

8. You should feel complete tranquility, because the time between you and your marriage in heaven is very short. Afterwards begins the happy life, where God is satisfied with you, and eternal bliss "in the company of the prophets, the companions, the martyrs and the good people, who are all good company. . ." [Note the *Washington Post* translation: "From there you begin to live the happy life, the infinite paradise." Marriage was doubtless of urgent interest to these terrorists in training. As discussed in chapter 2 on Paradise, the Koran repeatedly promises to join the ones who get there with agreeable companions. As for the hurry, Francis Robinson points out that after a Muslim's death, "the bier is borne quickly to the grave; the Prophet said it was good that the righteous should arrive soon at happiness."]

9. Keep in mind that, if you fall into hardship, how will you act [*sic*] and how will you remain steadfast and remember that you will return to God and remember that anything that happens to you could never be avoided, and what did not happen to you could never have happened to you. This test from Almighty God is to raise your level and erase your sins. And be sure that it is a matter of moments, which will then pass, God willing, so blessed are those who win the great reward of God. Almighty God said: "Did you think you could go to heaven before God knows whom amongst you have fought for Him and are patient?" [The *Post* translation of the above section includes orders to read specific verses of the Koran, gives the reason to seek one's own death, and discusses Paradise again: "Always remember the verses that you would wish death before you meet it if you only know what the reward after death will be. . . . Everybody hates death, fears death. But only those, the believers who know the life after death and the reward after death, would be the one who will be seeking death." This order, making clear that the terrorist should be prepared to die, raises the question of whether the lesser operatives were aware they were facing death. Both U.S. authorities and Bin Laden himself have said they were not, in which case the Atta letter might have been directed only at the mission's leaders. In any event, Jonathan Brockopp, assistant professor of Islamic studies at Bard College, has said that mainstream Muslim tradition includes "an important distinction between suicide and martyrdom in that martyrs don't seek death. A martyr seeks to glorify God and be God's instrument . . . and is not necessarily seeking death." But he added that extremists have arrived at their own interpretation of Muslim teachings.][6]

10. Remember the words of Almighty God: "You were looking to the battle before you engaged in it, and now you see it with your two eyes." Remember:

"How many small groups beat big groups by the will of God." And His words: "If God gives you victory, no one can beat you. And if He betrays you, who can give you victory without Him? So the faithful put their trust in God."

11. Remind yourself of the supplications and of your brethren and ponder their meanings. . . . [*Post* translation: "Keep a very open mind, keep a very open heart of what you are to face. You will be entering paradise. You will be entering the happiest life, everlasting life. Keep in mind that if you are plagued with a problem and how to get out of it [*sic*]. A believer is always plagued with problems. . . . You will never enter paradise without a major problem."]

12. Bless your body with some verses of the Koran, the luggage, clothes, the Knife, your personal effects, your ID, your passport, and all of your papers. [The *Post* translation made it "knives" and added: "Make sure that nobody is following you. . . . Make sure that you are clean, your clothes are clean, including your shoes."]

13. Check your weapon before you leave and long before you leave. You must make your knife sharp and you must not discomfort your animal during the slaughter.

14. Tighten your clothes, since this is the way of the pious generations after the Prophet. They would tighten their clothes before battle. Tighten your shoes well, wear socks so that your feet will be solidly in your shoes. All of these are worldly things and the rest is left to God, the best one to depend on.

15. Pray the morning prayer in a group and ponder the great rewards of that prayer. Make supplications afterwards, and do not leave your apartment unless you have performed ablution [washed] before leaving. . . .

THE THIRD PHASE

Before your foot steps in it [the airplane], and before you enter it, you make a prayer and supplications. Remember that this is a battle for the sake of God. . . . [*Post:* "When you enter the plane: Oh God, open all doors for me. Oh God who answers prayers and answers those who ask you, I am asking you for your help."]

Then it takes off. This is the moment that both groups come together. So remember God, as He said in His book: "Oh Lord, pour patience upon us and make our feet steadfast and give us victory over the infidels." And His words: "And the only thing they said Lord, forgive our sins and excesses and make our feet steadfast and give us victory over the enemy, conquer them and give us victory over them." Give us victory and make the ground shake under their feet. Pray for yourself and all of your brothers that they may be victorious and hit their targets and ask God to grant you martyrdom facing the enemy, not running away from it, and for Him to grant you patience and the feeling that anything that happens to you is for Him. [Compare the above with the ninth sura, still in reference to seventh-century battlefield tactics: "If you march not forth, He will punish you with a painful torment." The eighth sura: "When you meet those who disbelieve, in a battlefield, never turn your backs to them. And whoever turns his back to them on such a day—unless it be a stratagem of war, or to retreat to a troop (of his own)—he indeed has drawn upon himself wrath from Allah. And his abode is Hell." God's insistence to seventh-century fighters that they should not retreat was echoed, perhaps, in the fierce resistance of the "Afghan Arabs" during the American offensive in Afghanistan.]

Then every one of you should prepare to carry out his role in a way that would satisfy God. You should clench your teeth, as the pious early generations did.

When the confrontation begins, strike like champions who do not want to go back to this world. Shout, "Allahu Akbar," because this strikes fear into the hearts of the nonbelievers. God said: "Strike above the neck, and strike at all of their extremities." Know that the gardens of paradise are waiting for you in all their beauty, and the women of paradise are calling out, "Come hither, friend of God." They have dressed in their most beautiful clothing. . . .

If you slaughter, do not cause the discomfort of those you are killing, because this is one of the practices of the prophet, peace be upon him. [The references to the smiting above the neck and slaughter are among the cruelest utterances of terrorists anywhere, and reveal the depth of their indoctrination. The smiting advice was originally directed to fighters in the first jihad, the Battle of Badr. The Saudi translation from verse 12 of the eighth sura is: "I will cast terror into the hearts of those who have disbelieved, so strike them over the necks and smite over all their fingers and toes." As Abdullah Yusuf Ali points out in his notes to the Washington Center's Koran, these military tactics for seventh-century fighters using swords and lances recognize that "the vulnerable parts of an armed man are above the neck. A blow on the neck, face, or head, finishes him off. If his hands are put out of action, he is unable to wield his sword or lance or other weapon, and easily becomes a prisoner." Nowhere does the Koran justify the killing of innocents, but it may be on the basis of the above verse that they would attempt to justify slitting the throat of a captive. The *Post* version concludes, "There is no God but God. There is no God who is the God of the highest throne [sic], there is no God but God, the God of all earth and skies. There is no God but God, I being a sinner. We are of God, and to God we return." This declaration is similar to a Muslim's traditional confession of faith before death, which in Arabic should end in "God." Francis Robinson writes, "Just as God was the first word he heard, so it should be the last he utters."]

An American's Response

One tonic for the mind and heart after wallowing in the sickness of the terrorists while trying to understand them was the words of an American. Four days
after the attacks, he was the pilot for United Airlines Flight 564 from Denver to
Washington Dulles. The story of what he told the passengers over the intercom
was circulated around the country by E-mail. Other pilots reportedly made similar announcements. One of his passengers from Virginia, Kathy Rockel, a medical transcriber, passed along what he said, which other passengers confirmed.
David Remnick, writing in the *New Yorker*, called it "a moment of eloquence in
an unspeakable time":

> First, I want to thank you for being brave enough to fly today . . . The doors are
> now closed and we have no help from the outside for any problems that might
> occur inside this plane. As you could tell when you checked in, the government
> has made some changes to increase security in the airports. They have not,
> however, made any rules about what happens after those doors close. Until they
> do that, we have made our own rules and I want to share them with you. . . .
>
> Here is our plan and our rules. If someone or several people stand up and
> say they are hijacking this plane, I want you all to stand up together. Then take
> whatever you have available to you and throw it at them. Throw it at their faces
> and heads so they will have to raise their hands to protect themselves. The very
> best protection you have against knives are the pillows and blankets. Whoever
> is close to these people should then try to get a blanket over their heads. They
> won't be able to see. Once that is done, get them down and keep them there. Do
> not let them up. I will then land the plane at the closest place and we *will* take
> care of them. After all, there are usually only a few of them and we are two-
> hundred-plus strong. We will not allow them to take over this plane. I find it in-
> teresting that the U.S. Constitution begins with the words "We, the people."
> That's who we are, the people, and we will not be defeated.

Remnick said the passengers were then asked to introduce themselves and tell
each other "something about themselves and their families. 'For today, we consider you family,' they were told. 'We will treat you as such and ask that you do
the same with us.' " [7]

St. Sophia Mosque (formerly Church), Istanbul, by Thomas Allom.
Courtesy of the author.

12

A "Clash of Civilizations"?

If a non-Muslim American tore the veil from the "Islam" of his mind, he would find another veil, then another, and another, until he discovered that his Islam is a mannequin of veils, of illusions he creates for his comfort. Here are the principal illusions about Islam in the American mind today.

First is the illusion that the war the terrorists declared on the United States—by calling for the murder of Americans and by the attacks in New York and Washington—is not a war about religion. For Americans, it certainly is not about religion, but as Bernard Lewis summed it up after the attacks, "For bin Laden and those who follow him, this is a religious war, a war for Islam and against infidels, and therefore, inevitably, against the United States, the greatest power in the world of the infidels."[1] The terrorists' greatest hope is that their hysteria catches on in the West—just as the spirit of the jihad infected the Crusaders—and touches off a crazed counterassault on the Muslim world. This hysteria, if it ever came, would feed on another illusion: that there is only one Islam, if we could only get all the veils off it.

In fact, there are many interpretations of Islam and its teachings. Dropping by the bookstore at the Washington Islamic Center, I hesitated between An Nawawi's *Forty Hadith* and Abdul Mamid Siddique's *Selection from Hadith*. Get this one, the bookseller said, the other one is Indian. Indeed, the notion of one Islam is indeed an illusion, or as the Pakistani nuclear physicist Pervez Amir Ali Hoodbhoy observes, "Islam is an abstraction." He points out that in his own family "hugely different kinds of Islam are practiced." As another example, he cites the differences between one Muslim, Pakistani social worker Maulana Abdus Sattar Edhi, "overdue for a Nobel Peace Prize," and another, the recent Taliban

163

leader Mohammad Omar, "an ignorant, psychotic fiend. . . . The religion is as heterogeneous as those who believe and follow it. There is no 'true Islam.' "[2]

Thus, one should ask not, "Where does Islam stand today?" but "Where do Muslims stand today?" That said, when the last veil is stripped from our apparition, there remains the abstracted Islam, the elements of the religion that most Muslims share: the four core beliefs, the five required practices, or "pillars" of the faith, and other key teachings of the Koran. The latter include what some have called the "Sixth Pillar," jihad, leading to a third illusion: that Islam is a religion of war.

The last quarter of the twentieth century saw the birth of modern, large-scale terrorism in the name of Islam, beginning with the Iranian Revolution and its subsequent reign of terror and extending through the September 11, 2001, attacks. This reality has injected new life into the notion that Islam is in a permanent state of war, an ancient Islamic concept whereby the world was divided between the House of Islam, which meant an Islamic state, or states, and the House of War, the rest of the world, where war would continue until the entire world was under Muslim rule. But the Iranian Shiite leaders' reign of terror at home and abroad did not represent all Islam, nor did Al Qaeda and its far-flung supporters, certainly not to an extent that would justify labeling their terrorism, as a headline writer for one national publication did, "The Revolt of Islam." As a friend who is also a leading Islamic scholar at a top university put it, to suggest that war rather than peace, strategy rather than revelation, hatred rather than tolerance are the defining elements of Muhammad and the Muslim community is a ridiculous distortion that could be made only with one's head underground. And on the everyday, practical level, which is where the vast majority of Muslims live, no one would suggest that charming old S——, who doodled about making coffee in his pajamas while tending the CBS office in Beirut, was in a permanent state of war.

And if terrorists find an audience among some—sometimes among millions—of the Muslim poor, it is not because of Muhammad's experience at war or because of the Koran, as one reader of this work pointed out, "but rather because of the oppression, illiteracy, dictatorships, poverty, human rights abuses and hopelessness into which millions of Muslims are born."

Still, it would be treacherous to ignore the fact that the terrorists openly intend to bring about not merely a revolt but a global war that would end in a worldwide House of Islam. Nor does the fact that they are a tiny minority hinder their ability to do so. It does not appear that the attacks on the World Trade Center and the Pentagon were really the opening shots in such a world war, but it certainly felt like it at the time. And the failure of prominent Muslim leaders to speak out against the attacks suggests the number of *passive* Muslim supporters of terrorism is far greater than Westerners want to contemplate. Writing from Jerusalem two days after the attacks, the American columnist Thomas Friedman wondered: "Does my country really understand that this is World War III?" And this time the headline writer, who is often the more important writer, boiled it down to "World War III," without a question mark. A year later, in late 2002, Friedman still saw the ghost of the unthinkable on the horizon. In a mock letter from the president of the United States to "Leaders of the Muslim world," Friedman had the president saying, "I am increasingly worried that we are heading into a civilizational war." [3] In the meantime, we labor under a fourth illusion.

This is the belief that Islam is a religion of peace just like the other major religions and, thus defined, could have no relation to the war with the terrorists. This approach was actually helpful in the laudable nationwide efforts to ward off retaliation against American Muslims after the attacks in New York and Washington. But at the end of 2001, the Pakistani scholar Pervez Amir Ali Hoodbhoy wrote in the *Washington Post:* "For nearly four months now, leaders of the Muslim community in the United States, and even President Bush, have routinely asserted that Islam is a religion of peace that was hijacked by fanatics on Sept. 11. These two assertions are simply untrue. First, Islam—like Christianity, Judaism, Hinduism or any other religion—is not about peace. Nor is it about war." [4]

His next point might seem colored by a Muslim bias, but it still presents the thoughts of a moderate's survey of nonpeaceful religion in near and central Asia, with an off-the-wall U.S. reference thrown in: "In medieval times, both the Crusaders and the Jihads were soaked in blood. Today, there are Christian fundamentalists who attack abortion clinics in the United States and kill doctors; Muslim fundamentalists who wage their sectarian wars against each other; Jewish settlers who, holding the Old Testament in one hand and Uzis in the other, burn olive orchards and drive Palestinians off their ancestral land; and Hindus in India who demolish ancient mosques and burn down churches." [5] Although this survey of regional religious violence that we need to be monitoring is useful, its author certainly gave short shrift to the Muslim extremists' bloody record, one that is hardly comparable in scope to America's few deadly abortion protestors.

The religion-is-peace position also revived the idea that *Islam* actually means *peace,* which happy but erroneous thought was promulgated from the White House down to the local school board, according to one national publication, which promulgated it as well. *Islam* does not mean *peace* at all but *submission* to God's will. The error faded from view after a month or two, although one major publication retreated to the dubious midway position that *Islam* "implies" *peace.* Again, this escape attempt may be based on the Arabic word's etymological link with *"salam,"* which does mean peace.

At first the definition would seem a minor issue. However, the problem with both the definition and the peacemakers' well-meaning suggestion that Islam has no role in the current "war" is that they discourage understanding of the religion. As we have discussed, prior to the attacks feel-good Western students of Islam tended to ignore, or downplay, the importance of the war suras in the Koran, the impact of its calls to jihad and martyrdom, the more bellicose hadiths, and the political implications of the *ummah.* It will be interesting to see how Muslims themselves continue to confront these issues, as they have been doing quietly in many communities, but a more pressing question emerges when we unveil a fifth illusion: that Islam itself has been hijacked by fanatics.

What was really hijacked was our superficial understanding of Islam. Al Qaeda—with its multimillionaire, ex-playboy leader; phony jihads and fatwas; choruses of ignorant, thuggish clerics; and troubled operatives—and other terrorists operating criminal enterprises today certainly do not represent Islam. But as we discussed earlier, the religion as it is widely practiced today has proved ridiculously hijackable, in large part because of the weakness of moderate leaders, their hesitancy in the face of terrorists, and the escalating Palestinian-Israeli war. Hoodbhoy argues that if any hijacking of Islam took place, it went back much further than 2001—in fact, more than seven centuries back, apparently a reference to a fundamentalist takeover that started in the twelfth century and ended Islam's golden age: "No longer would Muslim, Christian and Jewish scholars gather and work together in the royal courts. It was the end of tolerance, intellect and science in the Muslim world."

Terrorist organizations go even further back. Bin Laden and Al Qaeda resemble nothing in the past quite so much as the Assassins, a secret Muslim sect that originated in Iran and Syria. It apparently derived its name from its hashish habit, specialized in terror and assassinations, most notably during the Crusades, and was last spotted in chapter 9, trying to kill the great Saladin. This link to the Assassins suggests another phenomenon that probably hampers our response to the recent terrorism as much as our tendency to cast veils over its sources. It has to do with the strange charms of terrorists. Even the Assassins had their allure (poison, we are told, was for them too cowardly a weapon), or so it seems at this safe remove from their daggers. Having been introduced to a bit of hashish while living in Iran myself, in a teahouse that the Islamic conquest had renamed a coffeehouse, and perhaps while lolling by Isfahan's ancient Khajou Bridge, I am well aware of the region's charms, but would not recommend bending too far in their direction to pacify terrorists—a syndrome that became known as the Stockholm Syndrome.

The Stockholm Syndrome

In the days and weeks after September 11, 2001, America came down with a clear trace of the Stockholm Syndrome. And what exactly is the Stockholm Syndrome? A survival mechanism, by which captives or victims sympathize with their captors or attackers. It originally described in psychological terms how four Swedish bank employees, three women and a man, reacted to being taken hostage by two ex-convicts for six days in 1973. Not only did they defend their captors and resist efforts to be rescued, but two of the women actually became engaged to the ex-cons.

Nor was their case unique. Other hostages, prisoners, and hijack victims have sometimes developed warm feelings toward their captors. One psychologist has suggested it exists on a societal level, even arguing that many women tend to suffer from it in a male-dominated world. The most famous American case that the label was slapped on was the kidnapping of the newspaper heiress Patricia Hearst. And when twenty-year-old John Walker Lindh left wealthy Marin County, California, to move to a Muslim country and wound up joining the Taliban, his parents likened it to Patty Hearst's joining her captors and becoming a bank robber. The four conditions for being a target of the Stockholm Syndrome are said to be:

- A perceived threat to survival while being held.
- Kindnesses from the captors or terrorists.
- Isolation.
- A perceived inability to escape.[6]

Can a large segment of a nation under attack suffer from the Stockholm Syndrome? All that lacked among the above requirements were any small kindnesses from the terrorists. There was a perceived threat to survival. There was the isolation of feeling targeted with no idea where the next attack might come from, of being the only country in the world that was targeted, and of finding something less than the all-out support one would want from friends. There was the perceived inability to escape, the hallmark of terrorist attacks on innocent civilians. But if we did experience a faint strain of a national Stockholm Syndrome, what were the symptoms?

Terrorists hijack four airliners, kill some three thousand people in attacks on the World Trade Center and the Pentagon, and one of the first reactions of many Americans is, "Why do they hate us?" It was startling to hear President Bush refer to the terrorists as "folks," but that could be chalked up to Bushspeak or shell shock, whereas the weak "Why do they hate us?" reaction was not temporary or limited to a few. As the president prepared for his address to the nation nine days after the attack, he met with his counselor, Karen P. Hughes, according to the *New York Times*. "She jotted down some notes: Who are they? Why they hate us?"[7] Fortunately, that weak question turned out not to be the theme of one of the strongest presidential speeches in years.

The answer to "Why do they hate us?" holds the cure. To put it bluntly, if politically incorrectly, the terrorists and their supporters in the Muslim world are jealous. They are victims of a huge case of what has been called culture envy, which, as we pointed out in chapter 1, some have traced to the beginning of Islam. We can talk all night and all day about America's supposed lack of values, its grating triumphalism, and its recent frequent disregard for international law and opinion, but other people have complained about these failings of ours without dissolving into hatred. The difference is that the latter are living far better than those in most of the Muslim countries under the yoke, or heavy influence, of fundamentalism. This envy is all the more rabid because once, in the Middle Ages, Muslims led the world, a fact the fundamentalists sometimes boast about, even though it was mainly they who destroyed that lead and kept pushing them back toward the ever beckoning seventh century.

Through the twentieth century, "compared with its millennial rival, Christendom, the world of Islam had become poor, weak and ignorant," as Lewis notes in *What Went Wrong?* It failed at modernization, and some of its countries wound up in constant need of foreign aid while others depended on a single resource, fossil fuels. "Even these were discovered, extracted, and put to use by Western ingenuity and industry, and doomed, sooner or later, to be exhausted or superceded. . . . Worst of all is the political result . . . a string of shabby tyrannies . . . modern only in their apparatus of repression and indoctrination."[8]

The last half of the twentieth century "brought further humiliations—the awareness that [the Muslim countries] were no longer even the first of the followers [of the West], but were falling ever further back in the lengthening line of eager and more successful Westernizers, notably in East Asia." First, the Muslim countries had to hire Western firms to do their technical work. "Now they found themselves inviting contractors and technicians from Korea—only recently emerged from Japanese colonial rule—to perform these tasks. Following is bad enough, limping in the rear is far worse."[9]

Still, the notion of "culture envy" is controversial among American scholars. A Princeton social scientist, Clifford Geertz, suggests that Westerners' views on Islam depend mainly on how they approach it. He notes that some take a sociological approach, studying the religion's impact on Muslim societies, which until now has given their conclusions an Islamic bias, though he calls it an "Islamic accent."[10] Others, including conservative Christians and journalists in a hurry, look at the faith itself, then use a comparative-religions approach, which usually produces a Christian bias.

Since September 11, the sociologists have been accused of being blind to contradictions in the religion, whereas the comparative-religions crowd, it is charged, has been trying to belittle Muhammad as a victim of envy—envy of the rich, of the powerful, of his scripturally blessed Jewish and Christian neighbors—and do the same with Muhammad's religion. They see Islam, as Bruce Lawrence of Duke University put it to me, "as a kind of Christianity manqué; it wants to be, but cannot be, a victor in the latest round of Crusades."[11] Indeed, the accusation of "culture envy," like most catch phrases, really is overblown. Envy, after all, is one of the prime engines of the Christians' own secular world, and almost everyone else's; obviously, what is finally important is the health and happiness of different societies, not whether one is jealous of another.

And there is no getting around the fact that the scholars' fight has also been about Bernard Lewis, whom some Arabists and Islamists have even accused of being anti-Islamic. Two leading scholars jumped all over me for paying so much heed to him. He became even more of a lightning rod among academicians after September 11 because that cataclysm turned him into a darling of the media, which discovered the clarity and power of his writing. We will take up Lewis again later in the chapter.

To return to the health and happiness of Muslim societies today, however much they share the envy of the terrorists, their sad state is to a large degree self-induced, even after accounting for their long periods under colonialism. Their lack of material, educational, and scientific progress is in good part the product

of a determined anti-intellectualism by the fundamentalists. No matter that this
effort is in direct opposition to the spirit of the revolutionary Muhammad and the
mind-opening Koran, as the great Muslim thinkers and artists of the Middle Ages
knew.

There is something else about Islam and the Koran itself: a poetic, mystic
force that for some can be so overwhelming it leaves little room for mere
mankind's science and art. In an autobiographical novel, *Heirs to the Past*, Driss
Chraibi wrote of the hero's experience, after sixteen years in Paris, of attending
his father's funeral and hearing the Koran. His account helps explain why some
Muslims consider the West's intellectual preoccupations a burden or a threat,
and how he was liberated from them by hearing the Koran. As the reciter read the
verses,

> I was in his voice despite the vast legacy of incredulity that I had received from
> the West. When he reached the end of a verse, he paused, and so it came
> about—an outburst of fervor. And while he chanted, it was like a man in the
> wilderness chanting his faith. And the voice rose and swelled, changed in tone,
> became tragic, soared and then floated down on our heads like a seagull gliding
> gently and softly, little more than a whisper. And so—never again will I go in
> search of intellectuals, of written truths, of collections of hybrid ideas which are
> nothing but ideas. Never again will I travel the world in search of a shadow of
> justice, fairness, progress, or schemes calculated to change mankind.[12]

The Ayatollah Khomeini put it more crudely to his fellow Iranians in 1979
(and also revealed the fundamentalists' familiar obsession with sex): "When de-
mocrats talk about freedom they are inspired by the superpowers. They want to
lead our youth to places of corruption. . . . If that is what they want, then yes, we
are reactionaries. You who want prostitutes and freedom in every matter are intellectuals. You consider corrupt morality as freedom, prostitution as freedom.
. . . Those who want freedom want the freedom to have bars, brothels, casinos,
opium. But we want our youth to carve out a new period in history. We do not want
intellectuals."

Nor democracy, as the ayatollah proudly announced, nor freedom. Lewis
notes that of the more than fifty countries that make up the Islamic Conference,
"only one, the Turkish Republic, has operated democratic institutions over a
long period of time and, despite difficult and ongoing problems, has made
progress in establishing a liberal economy and a free society and political order."
Hoodbhoy, who teaches nuclear physics at Quaid-e-Azam University in Islam-

abad, is very familiar with fundamentalist anti-intellectualism in Pakistan. "Of the 48 countries with a full or near Muslim majority," he writes, none has "a viable educational system or a university of international stature. You will seldom see a Muslim name as you flip through scientific journals."

He told of an exception, the Pakistani Abdus Salam, who shared the Nobel Prize for physics with Americans Steven Weinberg and Sheldon Glashow in 1979. "He was a remarkable man, terribly in love with his country and his religion," Hoodbhoy said. But he was a member of the disfavored Ahmadi sect, which was harshly persecuted, and had been declared a non-Muslim by the Pakistani Parliament in 1974. This Nobel Prize winner died "deeply unhappy," but another Pakistani intellectual's death was worse. It was that of Hoodbhoy's next-door neighbor, another Ahmadi physicist, who in 1994 "was shot in the neck and heart and died in my car as I drove him to the hospital. . . . His only fault was to have been born into the wrong sect."

Hoodbhoy recounts how official Muslim science was marching on in Pakistan during the late twentieth century. One former chairman of his university department, much in favor with the regime, said he took the Koranic verse that states worship on the night of the first revelation is worth a thousand other nights, then somehow combined it with the formula of Einstein's relativity theory, and was thus able to calculate the speed of Heaven. And just what is that speed? Heaven is receding from Earth at one centimeter per second less than the speed of light. Another favored scientist, a nuclear engineer, proposed to solve Pakistan's energy problem by harnessing the power of genies; more recently, he was arrested on suspicion of passing nuclear secrets to Afghanistan's recent Taliban government, which did not speak well of the Taliban nuclear capability.

The jealous extremists not only do not want intellectuals, but do not want free, accomplished women, and today the West's feminist movement is producing the healthiest, most productive kind of envy in the Muslim world. It will be a major cause of that world's inevitable and enormously transforming liberation of women. As Lewis points out, "Muslim sexism, and the relegation of women to an inferior status in society," deprives "the Islamic world of the talents and energies of half its people" while at the same time "entrusting the crucial early years of the upbringing of the other half to illiterate and downtrodden mothers."

If Muslim extremists are sick with envy, the West, and especially America, has its own little personality flaw that it needs to work on. It comes out in that popular American question, "Why do they hate us?" Setting aside the widely unreported facts that most of the world does not hate us—although there are wild swings in the polls from time to time—and that American prestige, or American likability if you prefer, has generally been extraordinarily high in almost all but the depressed Muslim world (and is even high among many there), we are left with a real question: Why would a large segment of a strong people, immediately upon being attacked, assume that it is their fault, so that the first words out of their mouths are, "Why do they hate us?"

Why do we react this way? Could it be the Stockholm Syndrome, a desire to sympathize with our enemy's attack on us? Or is it our magnanimous, forgiving quality as a nation? Which suggests yet another example of the Stockholm Syndrome, as we hear: "Christianity is just as bad. Don't forget the Crusades and the Spanish Inquisition. And remember, Europe, not the Middle East, was the scene of the Holocaust." These comparisons are another exercise in excessive self-criticism.

America suffers a historic terrorist attack, and many Americans respond by saying, "Our ancestors were once just as bad," never mind that was then, this is now. Or they cite isolated modern cases in no way comparable in scope to the organized, worldwide campaign of the Al Qaeda terrorists: murderous violence in Northern Ireland, abortion bombings in the United States, a Jewish fanatic's assassination of Israeli prime minister Yitzhak Rabin—again none of it comparable to the organized, permanent, worldwide terrorist campaign that drew support, sympathy, and money from part of the larger Muslim world.

A good example of a false Muslim-Christian comparison is the use of the word *martyr*. "I cringe when I hear some apply the word 'martyrs' to terrorists who hijacked planes and used them to kill themselves and thousands of innocent human beings," writes the Rt. Rev. Monsignor Thomas Duffy, pastor of the Shrine of the Most Blessed Sacrament Church in Washington. Consider the difference between one of the extremist Muslim "martyrs" and a real martyr. The latter does not seek death; he is not a suicide. But let us hear a dramatic example of the difference from Duffy. He cites the case of Brother Christian, the prior of a monastery in Algiers, who in 1994 wrote in an open letter: "If it should happen one day—and it could be today—that I become a victim of the terrorism which now seems ready to engulf all the foreigners living in Algeria, I would like my community, my Church, my family, to remember that my life was given to God and to this country [Algeria]." Brother Christian refused to identify the terrorists with mainstream Islam, saying that in his life there in Algiers, the capital, and in his study of Islam, he had often found "that true strand of the Gospel and (have) been inspired with respect for Muslim believers." In a sentence that separates true martyrs from extremist Islam's murderers (who rarely die without taking someone else with them), the monk added, "I should like, when my time comes, to have the moment of lucidity which would allow me to beg forgiveness of God and of all my fellow human beings, and at the same time to forgive with all my heart the one who would strike me down." In conclusion, he offered his "lost life" for the Algerian people and again asked forgiveness for the "friend of my final moment," who would not be aware of what he was doing.[13]

"Little more than two years later," Monsignor Duffy had to write to his parishioners: "Brother Christian and six of his brother monks were abducted and assassinated. . . . The Church of Algiers and the world beyond rightly calls these monks 'martyrs,' witnesses of the love taught and personified by Jesus, who likewise suffered assassination." Noting his revulsion when he heard those who killed thousands of innocent people being called "martyrs," Duffy writes, "True, these terrorists lost their lives for a cause, as did the monks; but that is the end of the similarity. The terrorists were embarked on an enterprise of death and destruction; the monks were engaged in a ministry of service and loving care. The terrorists were driven by hate; the monks, by a consuming love for God and for the people they served, most of whom were Moslems. The terrorists were examples of extraordinary hate; the monks examples of extraordinary love."[14]

"A Clash of Civilizations"?

It was Princeton's Lewis who warned more than a decade ago as he considered the rise of fundamentalist violence in Iran and elsewhere: "[W]e are facing a mood and a movement far transcending the level of issues and policies and the governments that pursue them. This is no less than a clash of civilizations—the perhaps irrational but surely historic reaction of an ancient rival against our Judeo-Christian heritage, our secular present, and the worldwide expansion of both."[15]

Three years later Harvard's Samuel P. Huntington published an article, "The Clash of Civilizations?" in *Foreign Affairs,* then, in 1996, an influential book, *The Clash of Civilizations [minus the question mark] and the Remaking of the World Order.* Ever since, Huntington has been given credit for coining "clash of civilizations," even through Lewis used the phrase earlier. Huntington's book proposed a "civilizational" approach to the study of global politics, with the theoretical "clash" as a paradigm for discussion. It did lead to an immediate worldwide debate—*Is there, or will there be, a clash of civilizations?*—which suddenly revived on the morning of September 11, 2001.[16]

"In the emerging era," Huntington had warned, "clashes of civilizations are the greatest threat to world peace." Facing that future, "Europe and America will hang together or hang separately." And "In the greater clash, the global 'real clash,' between Civilization and barbarism, the world's great civilizations, with their rich accomplishments in religion, art, literature, philosophy, science, technology, morality, and compassion, will also hang together or hang separately."

But is a clash of civilizations under way today between the Muslim world and the secular West? Yes, said the Ayatollah Khomeini in 1979, eight months after the Iranian Revolution. His clash was not only with the West: "The governments of the world should know that Islam cannot be defeated. Islam will be victorious in all the countries of the world, and Islam and the teachings of the Koran will prevail in all the countries of the world."

No, the moderate Iranian president Mohammad Khatami told the *New York Times* in November 2001. In his first interview with an American publication since assuming the presidency in 1997, he dismissed Bin Laden and Al Qaeda as "fanatics" and blamed "dirty hands" for trying to "stir negative feelings against the West in the Muslim world and against Muslims in the West." Then Khatami added: "So we must strongly prevent a clash among civilizations and religions and the spread of hatred." [17]

Again, is a clash of civilizations under way? Yes, said Osama bin Laden in the videotape in which he claimed to have planned the attacks on the World Trade Center and the Pentagon. As discussed earlier, Bin Laden quoted a third-hand hadith, from a son of Umar, in which Muhammad supposedly said, "I was ordered to fight the people until they say there is no god but Allah."

No, said Israeli foreign minister Shimon Peres, quoted indirectly in the *New York Times* by Thomas Friedman, who agreed with him. Three days after the September attacks, Friedman wrote: "As Mr. Peres himself notes, this is not a clash of civilizations—the Muslim world versus the Christian, Hindu, Buddhist and Jewish worlds. The real clash today is actually not between civilizations, but within them—between those Muslims, Christians, Hindus, Buddhists and Jews with a modern and progressive outlook and those with a medieval one." [18]

Whether the recent terrorism actually represents the first stage of a clash between the West and Islam—the horrific possibilities of which are hard to imagine—Samuel Huntington saw real potential for such a clash developing, not necessarily on the battlefield, but in the demographic tables, the so-called destiny of the world. He saw Islam making great strides in these tables, at least over the dangerous short run of the next few decades. Whereas world population from

1965 to 1990 grew at an annual rate of 1.85 percent, the rate in Muslim countries was never less than 2 and sometimes topped 3 percent. Of the world population of 6 billion, Muslims represent 1.18 billion, or nearly 20 percent, today and are expected to reach 30 percent in the year 2025.

The Muslim population surge has been disproportionately young, which has had significant political ramifications, Huntington wrote. "First, young people are the protagonists of protest, instability, reform and revolution." Youth "provide the recruits for Islamist organizations and political movements." The young population rose significantly in Iran before the 1978–1979 revolution and in Algeria as Islamist politicians were gaining strength. "In 1988 Crown Prince Abdullah of Saudi Arabia said that the greatest threat to his country was the rise of Islamic fundamentalism among its youth. According to these projections, that threat will persist well into the twenty-first century." Note that the Saudi youth "threat" occurred on the eve of U.S. troops arriving in Saudi Arabia for the Gulf War, a deployment that the wealthy Saudi Osama bin Laden used as an excuse for launching his campaign of terrorism against the United States.

Another phenomenon of expanding societies was witnessed in the seventh century as Muhammad's hungry followers launched their conquest of a huge chunk of the world. Dense or rapidly growing populations "tend to push outward, occupy territory and exert pressure on other less demographically dynamic peoples. Islamic population growth is thus a major contributing factor to the conflicts along the borders of the Islamic world between Muslims and other peoples."

Huntington saw the Islamic revival likely fading when "the demographic impulse powering it" weakens between 2010 and 2030. "At that time the ranks of militants, warriors and migrants will diminish, and the high levels of conflict within Islam and between Muslims and others . . . are likely to decline." But what might happen before then? Clearly, the next few decades will be a hazardous era in world politics. It is Western Europe that for the past several decades has faced the challenge of absorbing Muslim workers—into Germany from Turkey and Yugoslavia, into Italy from Morocco and Tunisia, and into France from North Africa. Of the thirteen million Muslims in Western Europe by the mid-1990s, four million, or nearly one-quarter, lived in France, where Islam has become the second-largest religion. Huntington turned up some interesting statistics. In the early 1990s, it was said, Arabs accounted for half the births in Brussels, migrants for 10 percent of all births in Western Europe.

In the mid- and late-1990s Western European countries took increasing steps to reduce immigration. It was clear their traditional majorities did not want to assimilate immigrants; what was not at all clear was whether the Muslim immigrants actually wanted to be assimilated. So the issue, Huntington proposed, was not whether Europe would be Islamized, but whether it would become a cleft society "encompassing two distinct and largely separate communities from two different civilizations." This notion of European Muslims as a separate community had been envisaged by a Frenchman, Jean Marie Domenach, who in 1991 said there was "a fear growing all across Europe . . . of a Muslim community that cuts across European lines, a sort of thirteenth nation of the European Community." By 2025, however, with the decline of the population rate in North Africa and the Middle East, Muslim emigration should recede, Huntington said, adding that "the threat to Europe of 'Islamization' will be succeeded by that of 'Africanization' " for similar demographic reasons. Huntington seemed to have permanently circled his wagons.

But many other scholars find both Huntington, with his graphs and tables, and Bernard Lewis too pat, leaning too heavily toward, as one said, "the inevitability of armed conflict waged by blindly religious ideologues." Lewis certainly did paint a grim threat, warning that "the suicide bomber may become a metaphor for the whole region, and there will be no escape from a downward spiral of hate and spite, rage and self-pity, poverty and oppression, culminating sooner or later in yet another alien domination." But if the peoples of the Middle East "can abandon grievance and victimhood . . . and join their talents, energies, and resources," they can make the region once again "a major center of civilization. For the time being, the choice is their own." [19] And what do Lewis's critics say? That's not fair.

If the future of the predominantly Islamic countries is up to the moderates and progressives within, how, Bruce Lawrence at Duke asks, "are these Muslim wannabe moderns going to succeed, especially against the grim odds painted by Bernard Lewis and Samuel Huntington?" Moreover, why should the future of those countries be up to Muslims alone? The post-World War II period of international aid and cooperation that reigned in the West is not quite dead yet, but in recent years it has been headquartered not in America but in Europe. "The U.S. remains the last of the great martial nation states, one that defines its sovereignty in absolute terms and defends it with force of arms," Michael Ignatieff, of Harvard's Kennedy School of Government, wrote recently. "European states think they are beyond this adolescent stage in the development of nations. They believe they represent the future: pooled sovereignty, reduced military budgets, foreign policy as a branch of humanitarian social work. Americans believe just as firmly that Europeans live in a dream world, made possible by American protection."[20]

To imply, as Lewis does, that when it comes to ensuring the future of the Middle Eastern peoples "the choice is theirs alone" almost suggests that only the Muslims are to blame for today's dangerous world, that they have no grievances even worth listening to, whether one agrees with them or not. "It is much easier to appreciate the evil of September 11," as Ignatieff wrote, "than it is to grasp that the U.S. and its civilisation are widely seen in the Middle East as the unique source of all the evils that beset the Islamic world—the existence of Israel, the dispossession of the Palestinians, the U.S. military presence in the holy lands. As the fount of all evils, the U.S. then becomes the only target that matters." As we have seen, though, Ignatieff guessed wrong about the terrorists' current goals. The Europeans, including the Russians, and the Australians are now also targets in the terrorists' new campaign against multinational economic targets. For a time, within six months of the attacks on New York and Washington, the West-versus-Islam scenario that Lewis and Huntington emphasized was pulled off center stage, to be replaced by an America-versus-Europe scenario, which only got hotter with the American destruction of the Saddam Hussein dictatorship. But whenever the terrorists broaden their jihad to include all the infidels, the West's solidarity is restored for a time.

Looking further ahead, the urgent, overarching concern is not how Europeans might adjust in the future to the challenges of divided, if not actually "cleft," societies, but how both the Muslim and the non-Muslim worlds respond to the danger of what has finally become "thinkable": World War III. This is why European governments blanched at the Bush administration's suggestion that was there was an "evil axis" among Iraq, Iran, and North Korea. *Axis* conjures *world war* to some, as in the Axis powers of Nazi Germany and Fascist Italy, just as the president's "crusade" remark, quickly withdrawn, sniffed of war. Perhaps the son merely inherited the father's unlucky taste for wartime words and phrases, such as the latter's plea for "a new world order," which unfortunately, and quite innocently, recalled Hitler's. Happily, he also inherited Ronald Reagan's handy talent of forgetting whatever it was he just said. If only he knew that other people do not forget.

For the moment, much hope does indeed rest within Islam, with those Muslims who know that Islam, like Judaism and Christianity, can still accommodate the ideals of freedom and civilization. They were, after all, the ideals of Islam's grandest days. But if the moderates do not act, hope within Islam is still not lost, at least according to Salman Rushdie. In that case, he wrote recently, it will lie with the courageous few who stand up and speak out and whom the terrorists threaten by labeling them "Rushdies":

> If the moderate voices of Islam cannot or will not insist on the modernization of their culture—and of their faith as well—then it may be these so-called "Rushdies" who have to do it for them. For every individual who is vilified and oppressed, two more, ten more, a thousand more will spring up. They will spring up because you can't keep people's minds, feelings and needs in jail forever. . . . The Islamic world today is being held prisoner, not by Western but by Islamic captors. . . . As long as the majority remains silent, this will be a tough war to win. But in the end, or so we must hope, someone will kick down that prison door.[21]

But isn't Rushdie asking too much of human beings? How many individual Americans in the Deep South sprang up against slavery during two centuries of American slavery? What it took to end it was a massive, almost unimaginably bloody civil war (it also took the other causes that helped bring on the war). How many individual Germans in Germany risked their lives by springing up against Hitler? What it took to stop him was an even bloodier world war. Rushdie himself exaggerated his own position a bit here, for he did not know beforehand that *The Satanic Verses* would bring him a formal death sentence, whereas Muslims who would openly defy their terrorist fellow Muslims today—as the Iranian Ali Tabatabai once did in Washington—would now know they could well be killed for it, as Tabatabai was. Of course, Rushdie at the same time has proved his own great courage once more because his continuing defiance clearly puts his life in jeopardy again.

But what about the many millions of the East? How will they make their future, and to a large extent ours? One must add to our opening list of illusions a final, and perhaps the most important, misunderstanding that has kept America and the West in the dark.

This is the illusion that by *Islam* and *Muslims* is meant the religion of Saudi Arabia, homeland of Islam, and the other Arab countries, whereas many millions of Muslims live far off in central and eastern Asia. Indeed, it is in that direction that hope is found by an American expert. Ralph Peters is a retired United States Army officer and author who recently traveled in India and Indonesia. On the eve of 2003, he personally had no illusions about the critical struggle going on within the Muslim community, but it was not going on in the Middle East, as so many think:

> This great battle—this war for the future of one of the world's great religions (and, certainly, its most restive and unfinished)—is not being fought in the Arab homelands, which insist upon our attention with the temper of spoiled children. It is time to recognize, belatedly, that Islam's center of gravity lies far from Riyadh or Cairo—that it has, in fact, several centers of gravity, each more hopeful than the Arab homelands. On these frontiers, from Delhi to Jakarta to Detroit, Islam is a dynamic, vibrant, effervescent religion of gorgeous potential. The U.S. government can never be a decisive factor in this struggle for Islam's future. That role is reserved for Muslims themselves. But we can play a more constructive role. Until now, we have not even bothered to participate.[22]

It is not only Islam that has a future in Asia, but also the local terrorists who regularly hijack it. And with the Islamic world changing so rapidly, America's participation has become inevitable.

As for massive American military responses to terrorism, John L. Esposito, a leading authority on Islam, writes: "While some forms of terrorism, like some forms of cancer, respond to radical surgery, this deadly disease can only be effectively countered first by understanding how it originates, grows stronger, and spreads, and then by taking action."[23]

Achieving this understanding has been one of the chief goals of this book, but the reader can decide when and whether it would be wise to take the next steps—political and economic initiatives—based on the argument, as Esposito puts it, that "the cancer of global terrorism will continue to afflict the international body until we address its political and economic causes." Many will say this is blackmail, that there is no acceptable link between terrorism and the political and economic travails of the Muslim countries. That there can be no such compromise with terrorism. That, in fact, the multimillionaire Bin Laden and many of his educated, upper-middle-class terrorist cohorts could clearly be counted among the world's greatest criminals, rich perpetrators of crimes against humanity, not victims of poverty or injustice. And, further, that political and economic assistance to the democratic forces in the predominantly Muslim countries is, simply and clearly, another conversation. There is, and must be, no link.

Still, as Islam's ancient and continuing appeal across the globe unfailingly reminds us, we are faced today with the question of not only Islam's future, but the world's. America, the West, and the rest of the non-Islamic world must still assume their share of the burden. Western governments and citizens cannot afford the luxury of saying, when faced with world catastrophe, that *all* hope rests with Islam, or with the predominantly Muslim countries, and that the choice belongs to Muslims alone. Hope rests with everyone. The choice of war or peace, of a reign of terror or an era of enlightenment, belongs to everyone. It demands of all of us, every individual, our best.

Notes

Bibliography

Index

Notes

1. What Would Muhammad Do?

1. Several Koran translations are used throughout the book, but unless otherwise indicated, the citations are from Abdullah Yusuf Ali, trans., *Holy Qur'an.*

2. On early Western responses to Islam, see Francis Robinson, *Atlas of the Islamic World since 1500*, 16–20; and Philip K. Hitti, *The Arabs: A Short History*, 34, 44, 191, 211.

3. The two Koran translations are A. Y. Ali, *Holy Qur'an;* and Dr. Muhammad Taqi-ud-Din Al-Hilali and Dr. Muhammad Muhsin Khan, *Noble Qur'an.*

4. See Fred McGraw Donner, *Narratives of Islamic Origins: Beginnings of Islamic Historical Writing*, for a thorough discussion of the revisionist critiques, the debate, and the views of Professor Donner, outgoing chair of the Department of Near Eastern Languages and Civilizations at the University of Chicago.

5. Anthony Nutting, *The Arabs*, 27.

6. Hitti, *The Arabs*, 31.

7. Alfred Guillaume, trans., *Life of Muhammad: A Translation of Ishaq's Sirat Rasul Allah*, 100.

8. Hitti, *The Arabs*, 31. As for Hitti's landmark work, *History of the Arabs*, I used the tenth, or thirty-third-anniversary, edition.

9. For this supremely important verse, I have chosen Albert Hourani's translation in *History of the Arab Peoples*, 16.

10. Ibid.

11. David E. Sanger, "Bin Laden Is Wanted in Attacks, 'Dead or Alive,' President Says."

12. Sir Richard F. Burton, *Personal Narrative of a Pilgrimage to Al-Madinah and Meccah*, 1:6.

2. Paradise and Islam's Four Core Beliefs

1. Rick Lyman, "*Chicago* Is Big Oscar Winner, but *Pianist* Surprises."

2. H. W. Crocker III, *Triumph: The Power and the Glory of the Catholic Church, a 2,000-Year History*, 46–47.

3. C. J. Chivers, "Veterans of Soviets' Old War Warn of Betrayal and Brutality."

4. Anthony J. Wilhelm, *Christ among Us: A Modern Presentation of the Catholic Faith*, 305.

5. Ibid., 306.

6. "Questions for V. S. Naipaul."

7. Maulana Muhammad Ali, trans., *Holy Qur'an*, 1137; Kenneth Cragg, trans., *Readings in the Qur'an;* Al-Hilali and Khan, *Noble Qur'an.*

8. See the translation by Capital Communications Group, of Washington, D.C., and its translator, Imad Musa, in "Notes Found after the Hijackings."

9. See Edward Fitzgerald, trans., *Rubaiyat of Omar Khayyam*, 5th ed., Electronic Literature Foundation, www.arabiannights.org/rubaiyat/Index2html; or Fitzgerald, trans., *Quatrains of Abolfat'h Ghia'th-e-din Ebrahim Khayam of Nishapur* (Teheran: Tahrir Iran, [ca. 1909]).

10. Lisa Miller, "Visions of Heaven: How Views of Paradise Inspire—and Inflame—Christians, Muslims, and Jews"; Kenneth L. Woodward, "The Bible and the Qur'an: Searching the Holy Books for Roots of Conflict and Seeds of Reconciliation."

11. Wilhelm, *Christ among Us*, 452–56.

12. H. G. Wells, *Outline of History*, 1:576–78.

3. The First Islamic State

1. Hourani, *History*, 20.

2. Quoted in Karen Armstrong, *Islam: A Short History*, 4.

3. A. Y. Ali, *Holy Qur'an*, 8. This quote is not from the Koran itself, but from the commentaries that Ali added.

4. For an intimate look back at the Israeli capture of the West Bank of the Jordan and travel in the area, see my "Little Truce of Bethlehem" and "What's Left of the Road in the Age of the Moon?" For a good history of the Six-Day War, see Michael B. Oren, *Six Days of War: June 1967 and the Making of the Modern Middle East.*

5. An excellent summary of the October 1973 Arab-Israeli conflict is Insight Team of the Sunday Times, *Insight on the Middle East War.*

6. William Safire, "On Language: Words of War."

4. The First Women of Islam

1. A. Y. Ali, *Holy Qur'an*, 1113.

2. For a recent treatment of Abraham, see Bruce Feiler, *Abraham.*

3. Wells, *Outline of History*, 1:575–76.

4. Alfred Guillaume, *Islam*, 194.

5. I resurrected Hilaire Belloc, *Great Heresies*, from the Web site www.ewtn.com/library/HOMELIBR/HERESY4.TXT, 2.

6. Quoted in Robinson, *Atlas of the Islamic World*, 20.

5. "General" Muhammad and the First Jihad

1. Blair quoted on Islam by John O'Sullivan in the *National Review:* www.nationalreview.com, Oct. 9. 2001, 1. Other Blair remarks in the same speech were quoted in Alan Cowell, "Blair Declares the Airstrikes Are an Act of Self-defense."

2. Andrew Sullivan, "This *Is* a Religious War," 44.

3. Alan Cooperman, "UNC Draws Fire, Lawsuit for Assigning Book on Islam."

4. Hitti, *The Arabs,* 15–16.

5. James Reston Jr., *Warriors of God: Richard the Lionheart and Saladin in the Third Crusade,* 11.

6. Kevin Sullivan, "A Body and Spirit Broken by the Taliban."

7. Wells, *Outline of History,* 1:575.

8. Yosef Bodansky, *Bin Laden: The Man Who Declared War on America,* 3.

9. Barton Gellman, "CIA Weighs 'Targeted Killing' Missions."

6. Separating from Judaism and Christianity

1. Armstrong, *Islam: A Short History,* 21–22.

2. Arieh Stav, *Peace: The Arabian Caricature—a Study of Anti-Semitic Imagery;* Hitti, *The Arabs,* 36.

3. Malcolm X (as told to Alex Haley), *The Autobiography of Malcolm X,* 344; M. Muhammad Ubaidul Akbar and Mumtaz-ul-Muhaddetheen Maulana, trans., *Orations of Muhammad, the Prophet of Islam,* 88.

4. Al-Hilali and Khan, *Noble Qur'an,* 39.

5. Hourani, *History,* 19.

6. Burton, *Personal Narrative,* 1:8.

7. Ibid., 14–15, 304.

7. One Worldwide Religion?

1. Robert Tomsho, "A Difficult Mission: Some Christians Try to Convert Muslims."

2. See, for example, A. Y. Ali, *Holy Qur'an,* 449; and Al-Hilali and Khan, *Noble Koran,* 758.

3. M. M. Ali, *Holy Qur'an,* 393. See chapter 8 for the version of Islamic triumphalism preached by Maulana Muhammad Ali's sect, the Ahmadis.

4. Hitti, *The Arabs,* 39; D. G. Hogarth, *Arabia,* 52.

5. *S* is not the correct initial for our manager.

6. Bernard Lewis, "The Roots of Muslim Rage."

7. On English translation, see Hitti, *The Arabs,* 43; Robinson, *Atlas,* 28.

8. Robinson, *Atlas,* 30.

9. Lewis, "Roots of Muslim Rage."

8. Conquering Half the World

1. Hitti, *The Arabs*, 69.

2. For detailed accounts of Islam's first civil war, see P. M. Holt, Ann K. S. Lambton, and Bernard Lewis, eds., *Cambridge History of Islam*, 1:69–73; and Hugh Kennedy, *The Prophet and the Age of the Caliphates*, 75–81.

3. For Lewis's perspective on the Dome of the Rock and some of the points that follow, see Bernard Lewis, *The Middle East: A Brief History of the Last 2,000 Years*, 67–71. For a delightful appreciation of the Damascene Old City today, see Siham Tergeman, *Daughter of Damascus*.

4. On reasons for the early Islamic military successes, see Hitti, *The Arabs*, 56–60; Lewis, *Middle East*, 56; and Milton Viorst, *In the Shadow of the Prophet: The Struggle for the Soul of Islam*, 106–7.

5. M. M. Ali, *Holy Qur'an*, 393. See also p. 693 for more on Ali's views.

6. Howard Schneider, "An Italian Envoy to Saudi Arabia, and to Islam."

7. On Islam's scientific contributions then and now, see Dennis Overbye, "How Islam Won and Lost the Lead in Science"; and Pervez Amir Ali Hoodbhoy, "How Islam Lost Its Way." King is quoted in Overbye.

8. Quoted in Hourani, *History*, 34.

9. Maria Rosa Menocal, in her lecture "Culture in the Time of Tolerance: Al-Andalus As a Model for Our Own Time," begins her discussion of Muslim Spain's three important features on p. 9. I am indebted to Washington attorney Douglas Rosenthal for pointing out her Istanbul lecture. See also Menocal's *Ornament of the World: How Muslims, Jews, and Christians Created a Culture of Tolerance in Medieval Spain*.

9. The Crusades: A Christian Jihad

1. Todd S. Purdum, "Bush Warns of a Wrathful, Shadowy, and Inventive War."

2. Crocker, *Triumph*, 133.

3. Quoted in ibid., 134.

4. Nicholas de Lange, *Atlas of the Jewish World*, 35.

5. On this and other developments mentioned here, see Amin Maalouf's valuable *The Crusades Through Arab Eyes*. The Radulph of Caen remark appears on p. 39.

6. Ibid., 51. On this event, and also for an excellent overview of the Temple Mount's main features, see Ghattas J. Jahshan and Maheeba Akra Jahshan, *Guide to the West Bank of Jordan*. Umar in discussed on pp. 16–18.

7. For a lively discussion of these and some other events in the Crusades, especially the Third, see Reston's remarkable *Warriors of God*.

8. Quoted in Maalouf, *Crusades*, 204–10.

9. Winston S. Churchill, *Second World War: The Hinge of Fate*, 100.

10. Quoted in Menocal, "Culture," 13, which is eloquent on the age of Al-Andalus.

11. The pope and the grand mufti are cited in Reston, *Warriors of God*, xix. Crocker, *Triumph*, 422.

12. Maalouf, *Crusades*, 262–66.

13. Quoted in ibid., 264.

14. Ibid. Maalouf sums up his conclusions in his excellent epilogue (261–66).

15. Robinson, *Atlas*, 72–87, 134–37.

16. Quoted in ibid., 79. For more on the Church of St. Sophia, see M. Hadi Altay, *Saint Sophia*.

17. Robinson, *Atlas*, 72.

18. Ibid., 136.

19. Lewis, *Middle East*, 387.

10. A (Personal) Persian Interlude

1. "Days of Captivity: The Hostages' Story."

2. Robinson, *Atlas*, 44. For a good discussion of Safavid Iran, see pp. 44–57, 110–15.

3. Ibid., 112.

4. George Lenczowski, ed., *Iran under the Pahlavis*, 17–24.

5. Ibid., 39.

6. Ibid., 97.

7. Smith is quoted in Ann Gerhard, "Air Force Flier in the Ointment."

8. Ed(ward) Hotaling, "Iranian Wrestling: Great Heritage Culminates in World Reputation."

9. Quoted in Viorst's brilliant *In the Shadow*, 187.

10. Edward Hotaling, "LBJ Makes Strong Plea for Progress."

11. Edward Hotaling, "Riots in Iran Stem from Religious Rite."

12. "Days of Captivity."

13. See, for example, John F. Burns, "Iranian's Career: From Hostage-Taker to Reformer."

14. Quoted in Viorst, *In the Shadow*, 176.

15. V. S. Naipaul, *Beyond Belief: Islamic Excursions among the Converted Peoples*, 146.

16. Quoted in Viorst, *In the Shadow*, 199.

17. Salman Rushdie, "No More Fanaticism As Usual"; Caryn James, "After the Fatwa: Playwriting and Partygoing."

18. Viorst, *In the Shadow*, 194–95.

19. A revealing account of the Salahuddin case is Ira Silverman, "An American Terrorist."

20. Quoted in Lewis, "The Revolt of Islam," 50.

11. The Terrorists' Handbook

1. Thomas L. Friedman, "World War III"; Rushdie, "No More Fanaticism."

2. Quoted in Gustav Niebuhr, "Injunctions to Pray and Orders to Kill."

3. "Captured Terrorist Manual Suggests Hijackers Did a Lot by the Book."

4. Peter L. Bergen, "Al Qaeda's New Tactics."

5. For texts of the letter, see translation by Capital Communications Group of Washington, D.C., and its translator, Imad Musa, in "Notes Found After the Hijackings"; and "Oh God, Open All Doors for Me." For news reports, see Niebuhr, "Injunctions to Pray"; and Bob Woodward, "In Hijacker's Bags, a Call to Planning, Prayer, and Death."

6. Quoted in B. Woodward, "Hijacker's Bags."

7. David Remnick, "Many Voices."

12. A "Clash of Civilizations"?

1. Lewis, "The Revolt of Islam," 50.

2. See Ezzedin Ibrahim and Denys Johnson-Davies, trans., *An-Nawawi's Forty Hadith*, available at the Islamic Center of Washington, D.C.; Abdul Hamid Siddique, *Selection from Hadith;* and Hoodbhoy, "How Islam Lost Its Way."

3. Friedman, "World War III" and "Defusing the Holy Bomb."

4. Hoodbhoy, "How Islam Lost Its Way."

5. Ibid.

6. See Kathleen Trigiani, "Societal Stockholm Syndrome."

7. D. T. Max, "The Making of the Speech."

8. Bernard Lewis, *What Went Wrong?* 151.

9. Ibid., 152.

10. I am indebted to Bruce B. Lawrence, professor of Islamic Studies and outgoing chair of the Duke University Department of Religion, for steering me to Clifford Geertz's "Conjuring with Islam."

11. Lawrence, letter to the author, Feb. 18, 2003.

12. Quoted in Robinson, *Atlas,* 181.

13. Rev. Msgr. Thomas M. Duffy, "From the Pastor." Quoted in V. S. Naipaul, *Among the Believers: An Islamic Journey*, 82.

14. Ibid.

15. Lewis, "Roots of Muslim Rage."

16. Samuel P. Huntington, *Clash of Civilizations and the Remaking of the World Order,* 13.

17. Elaine Sciolino, "Iran Chief Rejects Bin Laden Message."

18. Thomas L. Friedman, "Smoking or Non-Smoking?"

19. Lewis, *What Went Wrong?* 159.

20. I am again indebted to Bruce Lawrence at Duke, this time for directing me to Michael Ignatieff, "The Divided West." Ignatieff is director of the Carr Center for Human Rights at the Kennedy School of Government, Harvard University.

21. Rushdie, "No More Fanaticism."

22. Ralph Peters, "Turn East from Mecca," adapted from his article "Rolling Back Radical Islam."

23. John L. Esposito, *Unholy War: Terror in the Name of Islam,* 160.

Bibliography

Koran Translations

Al-Hilali, Dr. Muhammad Taqi-ud-Din, and Dr. Muhammad Muhsin Khan, trans. *Noble Qur'an*. Medina, Saudi Arabia: King Fahd Complex, 1996.

Ali, Abdullah Yusuf, trans. *Holy Qur'an*. Washington, D.C.: Islamic Center, 1978.

Ali, Maulana Muhammad, trans. *Holy Qur'an*. Lahore, Pakistan: Ahmadiyyah Anjuman Isha'at Islam, 1995.

Arberry, Arthur J., trans. *The Koran Interpreted*. London: George Allen and Unwin, 1955.

Cragg, Kenneth, trans. *Readings in the Qur'an*. London: Collins Flame, 1988.

Sells, Michael, trans. *Approaching the Qur'an*. Ashland, Oreg.: White Cloud Press, 1999.

Other Sources

Akbar, M. Muhammad Ubaidul, and Mumtaz-ul-Muhaddetheen Maulana, trans. *Orations of Muhammad, the Prophet of Islam*. New Delhi: Kitab Bhavan, 1994.

Altay, M. Hadi. *Saint Sophia*. Izmir, Turkey: Ticaret Matbaacilik, n.d.

Armstrong, Karen. *Islam: A Short History*. New York: Modern Library, 2000.

Atiyeh, George N., ed. *Arab and American Cultures*. Washington, D.C.: American Enterprise Institute for Public Policy Research, 1977.

Baraheni, Reza. *The Crowned Cannibals: Writings on Repression in Iran*. New York: Vintage, 1977.

Barber, Benjamin R. *Jihad vs. McWorld*. New York: Ballantine, 1995.

Belloc, Hilaire. *Great Heresies*. TAN Books, 1991. (On-line version: www.ewtn.com/library/HOMELIBR/HERESY4.TXT.)

Bergen, Peter L. "Al Qaeda's New Tactics." *New York Times*, Nov. 15, 2002, A27.

———. *Holy War, Inc.: Inside the Secret World of Osama bin Laden*. New York: Free Press, 2001.

Bodansky, Yossef. *Bin Laden: The Man Who Declared War on America.* New York: Random House, Prima, 1999.

Burns, John F. "Iranian's Career: From Hostage-Taker to Reformer." *New York Times,* Oct. 13, 1999, A3.

Burton, Sir Richard F. *Personal Narrative of a Pilgrimage to Al-Madinah and Meccah.* Vols. 1–2. New York: Dover, 1964.

"Captured Terrorist Manual Suggests Hijackers Did a Lot by the Book." *New York Times,* Oct. 28, 2001, B8.

Chivers, C. J. "Veterans of Soviets' Old War Warn of Betrayal and Brutality." *New York Times,* Oct. 22, 2001, B1.

Churchill, Winston S. *Second World War: The Hinge of Fate.* Boston: Houghton-Mifflin, 1950.

Cohen, Mark. *Under Crescent and Cross: The Jews in the Middle Ages.* Princeton: Princeton Univ. Press, 1994.

Cooperman, Alan. "UNC Draws Fire, Lawsuit for Assigning Book on Islam." *Washington Post,* Aug. 7, 2002, A1.

Cowell, Alan. "Blair Declares the Airstrikes Are an Act of Self-defense." *New York Times,* Oct. 9, 2001, B6.

Crocker, H. W., III. *Triumph: The Power and the Glory of the Catholic Church, a 2,000-Year History.* New York: Random House, Prima, 2001.

"Days of Captivity: The Hostages' Story." *New York Times,* Feb. 4, 1981, A9.

de Lange, Nicholas. *Atlas of the Jewish World.* Oxford: Facts on File, 1989.

Donner, Fred McGraw. *Narratives of Islamic Origins: Beginnings of Islamic Historical Writing.* Princeton: Darwin, 1998.

Duffy, Rev. Msgr. Thomas M. "From the Pastor." *Blessed Sacrament News* (Washington, D.C.), fall 2001, 1, 3.

Esposito, John L. *Unholy War: Terror in the Name of Islam.* Oxford: Oxford Univ. Press, 2002.

Feiler, Bruce. *Abraham.* New York: Morrow, 2002.

Friedman, Thomas L. "Defusing the Holy Bomb." *New York Times,* Nov. 27, 2002, A23.

———. "Smoking or Non-Smoking?" *New York Times,* Sept. 14, 2001, A27.

———. "World War III." *New York Times,* Sept. 13, 2001, A27.

Geertz, Clifford. "Conjuring with Islam." *New York Review of Books,* May 27, 1982, 25.

Gellman, Barton. "CIA Weighs 'Targeted Killing' Missions." *Washington Post,* Oct. 28, 2001, A1.

Gerhard, Ann. "Air Force Flier in the Ointment." *Washington Post,* Jan. 7, 2002, C12.

Gerson, Allan, and Jerry Adler. *Price of Terror: Lessons on Lockerbie for a World on the Brink.* New York: Harper Collins, 2001.

Glubb, John Bagot. *Soldier with the Arabs.* London: Hodder and Stoughton, 1957.

Guillaume, Alfred. *Islam.* New York: Penguin, 1979.

————, trans. *Life of Muhammad: A Translation of Ishaq's Sirat Rasul Allah.* London: Oxford Univ. Press, 1955.

Haddad, Yvone Yazbeck, and Adair T. Lummis. *Islamic Values in the United States.* Oxford: Oxford Univ. Press, 1997.

Hanson, Victor Davis. *Carnage and Culture: Landmark Battles in the Rise of Western Power.* New York: Doubleday, 2001.

Hasan, Asma Gull. *American Muslims: The New Generation.* New York: Continuum, 2001.

Hitti, Philip K. *The Arabs: A Short History.* Washington, D.C.: Regnery Gateway, 1996.

————. *History of the Arabs.* 10th ed. New York: St. Martin's Press, 1970.

————. *Islam: A Way of Life.* Washington, D.C.: Regnery Gateway, 1987.

Hogarth, D. G. *Arabia.* Oxford: Clarendon Press, 1922.

Holt, P. M., Ann K. S. Lambton, and Bernard Lewis, eds. *Cambridge History of Islam.* 2 vols. Cambridge: Cambridge Univ. Press, 1970.

Hoodbhoy, Pervez Amir Ali. "How Islam Lost Its Way." *Washington Post,* Dec. 30, 2001, B4.

Hotaling, Edward. *The Arab Blacklist Unveiled: A Research Report on the Arab Boycott, Its History, Rules and Regulations, and Effects on World Trade. The American Antiboycott Movement in 1977.* Los Angeles: Landia, 1977.

————. "Iranian Wrestling: Great Heritage Culminates in World Reputation." *Tehran Journal,* June 3, 1962, 7.

————. "Israeli Spy's Tale of Sabotage and Death." *Business Week,* Aug. 16, 1976, 10.

————. "LBJ Makes Strong Plea for Progress." *Tehran Journal,* [1961].

————. "Letter from Beirut: Toughing It Out During the Shooting." *Business Week,* Nov. 3, 1975, 18.

————. "Little Truce of Bethlehem." *Village Voice,* Dec. 24, 1970, 22.

————. "Riots in Iran Stem from Religious Rite." *New York Herald-Tribune,* June 6, 1963, n.p., Paris ed.

————. "What's Left of the Road in the Age of the Moon?" *Village Voice,* Aug. 14, 1969, 5.

Hourani, Albert. *History of the Arab Peoples.* New York: Warner, 1992.

Huband, Mark. *Warriors of the Prophet: The Struggle for Islam.* Boulder: Westview, 1999.

Huntington, Samuel P. *Clash of Civilizations and the Remaking of the World Order.* New York: Touchstone, 1997.

Ibrahim, Ezzedin, and Denys Johnson-Davies, trans. *An-Nawawi's Forty Hadith.* 1979. Available at the Islamic Center of Washington, D.C.

Ignatieff, Michael. "The Divided West." *Financial Times,* Aug. 31, 2002, 8, London ed.

Insight Team of the Sunday Times. *Insight on the Middle East War.* London: Deutsch, 1974.

Jahshan, Ghattas J., and Maheeba Akra Jahshan. *Guide to the West Bank of Jordan.* 4th ed. Jerusalem: Franciscan Press, 1965.

James, Caryn. "After the Fatwa: Playwriting and Partygoing." *New York Times,* Mar. 9, 2003, sec. 2, p. 23.

Kennedy, Hugh. *The Prophet and the Age of the Caliphates.* London: Longman, 1986.

Lawrence, Bruce B., ed. *The Rose and the Rock: Mystical and Rational Elements in the Intellectual History of South Asian Islam.* Durham: Duke Univ. Press, 1979.

———. *Shattering the Myth: Islam Beyond Violence.* Princeton: Princeton Univ. Press, 1998.

Lenczowski, George, ed. *Iran under the Pahlavis.* Stanford: Hoover, 1978.

Lewis, Bernard. *The Middle East: A Brief History of the Last 2,000 Years.* New York: Touchstone, 1997.

———. "The Revolt of Islam." *New Yorker,* Nov. 19, 2001, 50–63.

———. "The Roots of Muslim Rage." *Atlantic,* Sept. 1990. (On-line version: www.theatlantic.com/issues/90sep/rage.htm.)

———. *What Went Wrong?* Advance copy. Oxford: Oxford Univ. Press, 2002.

Lewis, B[ernard], Ch. Pellat, and J. Schacht, eds. *Encyclopedia of Islam.* Leiden, Netherlands: E. J. Brill, 1965.

Lyman, Rick. "*Chicago* Is Big Oscar Winner, but *Pianist* Surprises." *New York Times,* Mar. 24, 2003, E1.

Maalouf, Amin. *The Crusades Through Arab Eyes.* Translated by Jon Rothschild. New York: Schocken, 1984.

Mackay, Sandra. *The Reckoning: Iraq and the Legacy of Saddam Hussein.* New York: W. W. Norton, 2002.

Malcolm X (as told to Alex Haley). *The Autobiography of Malcolm X.* New York: Ballantine, 1992.

Max, D. T. "The Making of the Speech." *New York Times Magazine,* Oct. 7, 2001, 34.

Menocal, Maria Rosa. "Culture in the Time of Tolerance: Al-Andalus As a Model for Our Own Time." Yale Law School Occasional Papers, 2d ser., no. 6. New Haven: Yale Law School, 2001.

———. *Ornament of the World: How Muslims, Jews, and Christians Created a Culture of Tolerance in Medieval Spain.* Boston: Little, Brown, 2002.

Miller, Judith, Stephen Engelberg, and William Broad. *Germs: Biological Weapons and America's Secret War.* New York: Simon and Schuster, 2001.

Miller, Lisa. "Visions of Heaven: How Views of Paradise Inspire—and Inflame—Christians, Muslims, and Jews." *Newsweek,* Aug. 12, 2002, 44–52.

Monteil, Vincent. *Iran.* Paris: Editions du Seuil, 1957.

Naipaul, V. S. *Among the Believers: An Islamic Journey.* New York: Vintage, 1982.

———. *Beyond Belief: Islamic Excursions among the Converted Peoples.* New York: Vintage, 1999.

Niebuhr, Gustav. "Injunctions to Pray and Orders to Kill." *New York Times*, Sept. 29, 2001, B3.

"Notes Found after the Hijackings." *New York Times*, Sept. 29, B3.

Nutting, Anthony. *The Arabs*. New York: Mentor, 1964.

Nye, Joseph S., Jr. *Paradox of Power: Why the World's Only Superpower Can't Go It Alone*. Oxford: Oxford Univ. Press, 2002.

"Oh God, Open All Doors for Me." *Washington Post*, Sept. 28, 2001, A18.

Oren, Michael B. *Six Days of War: June 1967 and the Making of the Modern Middle East*. Oxford: Oxford Univ. Press, 2002.

Overbye, Dennis. "How Islam Won and Lost the Lead in Science." *New York Times*, Oct. 30, 2001, D1.

Peters, Ralph. *Beyond Terror*. Mechanicsburg, Pa.: Stackpole, 2002.

———. "Rolling Back Radical Islam." *Parameters: U.S. Army War College Quarterly*, autumn 2002.

———. "Turn East from Mecca." *Washington Post*, Dec. 1, 2002, B1.

Pipes, Daniel. "Fighting Militant Islam, Without Bias." *City Journal*, Aug. 2001, n.p. (On-line version: www.city-journal.org.)

———. *Militant Islam Reaches America*. New York: W. W. Norton, 2002.

Purdum, Todd S. "Bush Warns of a Wrathful, Shadowy, and Inventive War." *New York Times*, Sept. 17, 2001, A2.

"Questions for V. S. Naipaul." *New York Times Magazine*, Oct. 28, 2001, 19.

Rashid, Ahmed. *Taliban: Militant Islam, Oil, and Fundamentalism in Central Asia*. New Haven: Yale Univ. Press, 2001.

Reeve, Simon. *The New Jackals: Ramzi Yousef, Osama Bin Laden, and the Future of Terrorism*. Boston: Northeastern Univ. Press, 1999.

Remnick, David. "Many Voices." *New Yorker*, Oct. 15, 2001, 53.

Reston, James, Jr. *Warriors of God: Richard the Lionheart and Saladin in the Third Crusade*. New York: Doubleday, 2001.

Robinson, Francis. *Atlas of the Islamic World since 1500*. New York: Facts on File, 1982.

Rushdie, Salman. "No More Fanaticism As Usual." *New York Times*, Nov. 27, 2002, A23.

Safire, William. "On Language: Words of War." *New York Times Magazine*, Sept. 30, 2001, 26.

Sakr, Ahmad H. *A Course on Islamic Shari'ah*. Lombard, Ill.: Foundation for Islamic Knowledge, 1999.

———. *Themes of the Qur'an*. Lombard, Ill.: Foundation for Islamic Knowledge, 2000.

———. *Understanding the Qur'an*. Lombard, Ill.: Foundation for Islamic Knowledge, 2000.

Sampson, Anthony. *Arms Bazaar: From Lebanon to Lockheed*. New York: Viking, 1977.

Sanger, David E. "Bin Laden Is Wanted in Attacks, 'Dead or Alive,' President Says." *New York Times*, Sept. 18, 2001, A1.

Schneider, Howard. "An Italian Envoy to Saudi Arabia, and to Islam." *Washington Post,* Dec. 17, 2001, A12.

Sciolino, Elaine. "Iran Chief Rejects Bin Laden Message." *New York Times,* Nov. 10, 2001, A1.

Siddique, Abdul Hamid. *Selection from Hadith.* Safat, Kuwait: Islamic Book Publishers, 1983.

Silverman, Ira. "An American Terrorist." *New Yorker,* Aug. 5, 2002, 26.

Stav, Arieh. *Peace: The Arabian Caricature—a Study of Anti-Semitic Imagery.* Jerusalem: Gefen, 1999.

Sullivan, Andrew. "This *Is* a Religious War." *New York Times Magazine,* Oct. 7, 2001, 44–47, 52–53.

Sullivan, Kevin. "A Body and Spirit Broken by the Taliban." *Washington Post,* Jan. 5, 2002, A1.

Tergeman, Siham. *Daughter of Damascus.* Austin: Univ. of Texas, Center of Middle Eastern Studies, 1994.

Tomsho, Robert. "A Difficult Mission: Some Christians Try to Convert Muslims." *Wall Street Journal,* Nov. 26, 2001, A1.

Trigiani, Kathleen. "Societal Stockholm Syndrome." In *Out of the Caves: Exploring "Gray's Anatomy."* (On-line version: www.web2.iadfw.net/ktrig246/out_of_cave/sss.html.)

Viorst, Milton. *In the Shadow of the Prophet: The Struggle for the Soul of Islam.* New York: Anchor, 1998.

Viswanathan, Gauri, ed. *Power, Politics, and Culture: Interviews with Edward Said.* New York: Pantheon, 2001.

Wells, H. G. *Outline of History.* 2 vols. New York: Macmillan, 1921.

Wilhelm, Anthony J. *Christ among Us: A Modern Presentation of the Catholic Faith.* New York: Paulist Press, 1981.

Woodward, Bob. "In Hijacker's Bags, a Call to Planning, Prayer, and Death." *Washington Post,* Sept. 28, 2001, A1.

Woodward, Kenneth L. "The Bible and the Qur'an: Searching the Holy Books for Roots of Conflict and Seeds of Reconciliation." *Newsweek,* Feb. 11, 2002, 50–57.

Yergin, Daniel. *The Prize: The Epic Quest for Oil, Money, and Power.* New York: Touchstone, 1992.

Index